THE CLINTON
CHARISMA

THE
CLINTON
CHARISMA

A Legacy
of Leadership

Donald T. Phillips

palgrave
macmillan

THE CLINTON CHARISMA

First published in 2007 by
PALGRAVE MACMILLAN™
175 Fifth Avenue, New York, N.Y. 10010 and
Houndmills, Basingstoke, Hampshire, England RG21 6XS.
Companies and representatives throughout the world.

PALGRAVE MACMILLAN is the global academic imprint of the Palgrave
Macmillan division of St. Martin's Press, LLC and of Palgrave Macmillan Ltd.
Macmillan® is a registered trademark in the United States, United Kingdom and
other countries. Palgrave is a registered trademark in the European Union and
other countries.

ISBN-13: 978–1–4039–7816–5
ISBN-10: 1–4039–7816–6

Library of Congress Cataloging-in-Publication Data

Phillips, Donald T. (Donald Thomas), 1952-
    The Clinton charisma : a legacy of leadership / by Donald T. Phillips.
        p.   cm.
    Includes bibliographical references and index.
    ISBN 1–4039–7816–6
    1. Clinton, Bill, 1946–   2. Political leadership—United States.   3. United
States—Politics and government—1993–2001.   I. Title.
E886.2.P45   2007
973.929'092—dc22

                                                                    2007013465

A catalogue record of the book is available from the British Library.

Design by Letra Libre

First edition: November 2007

10 9 8 7 6 5 4 3 2 1

Printed in the United States of America.

CONTENTS

"This is our time. Let us embrace it."

—Bill Clinton
Inaugural Address
January 20, 1993

INTRODUCTION

Not since the days of the Great Depression had a person assumed the American presidency in more difficult and challenging times than Bill Clinton. It was a time of worldwide change. A time of economic struggles and global recession. With the near complete collapse of communism, many nations suddenly had allies who had formerly been enemies. Maps and globes rapidly became outdated, with large countries endlessly partitioning into smaller separate pieces. New nations were fighting to break into emerging international markets, and established nations were fighting to stay on top economically. The global business community was struggling to advance worldwide free trade agreements such as the North American Free Trade Agreement (NAFTA) and the Global Agreement on Tariffs and Trade, while large numbers of people fought to remain isolationist.

It seemed as though everybody was fighting—fighting with themselves, their neighbors, the world. Age-old ethnic hatreds resurged after more than half a century of suppression by force. The end of the cold war left America with no perceptible enemy around which to rally the masses. And the lack of a well-defined enemy made it impossible to justify inordinately high spending in defense of the country.

In the United States, as around the world, distrust of government was high. The American people demanded solutions to economic problems such as health care, welfare reform, and job creation. Yet, they wanted it done without taxes being raised. The American people wanted change, but when proposed change hit a little too close to home, it was met with resistance. With special interest groups covering every issue, no one could come to a consensus on how to change anything. Skeptics and pessimists lurked around every corner—ready to pounce on any new initiative.

In the middle of all this chaos, a startling and unlikely development took place. Emerging to take the leadership reins of the free world was William Jefferson Clinton, a relatively unknown governor of the small southern state of Arkansas, the entire population of which was less than a good-sized American city. The circumstances of his election were highly unusual. It was as if the waters parted and barriers fell in order to let him through.

In the early stages of the campaign process, big-name Democrats decided to stay out of the presidential race, fearing political suicide if they challenged incumbent President George H. W. Bush, who was riding high in the polls (near 90 percent approval) after a decisive victory in a war with Iraq. Then, as the formal primary season started and Bush's popularity began to decline, the Democrats who had entered the race seemed unsure of themselves and were viewed by the electorate as less than compelling.

As the economic cloud hanging over the nation grew darker, the emergence of a viable third party candidate further served to hurt the incumbent and help the Democratic Party. Billionaire Texan Ross Perot created a platform that focused on out-of-control big government and the ineffective leadership of President Bush. "Send me to Washington," he told Americans, "and I'll clean out the barn." Later, Clinton would benefit tremendously as Perot dropped out of the race and stated his opinion that Democrats had gotten their act together. Many Perot backers became Democratic supporters, largely because they wanted change. Even when Perot reentered the race later in the fall, he had lost too much credibility with most of his constituency to harm Clinton's campaign.

And then, remarkably, the Republican Party, taken over by extreme elements of the religious right, seemed to self-destruct. Many Americans were put off when the Republican National Convention in Houston, Texas, deteriorated into a name-calling, hate-filled, almost racist event. President Bush further compounded things when, against his better judgment, he followed the advice of his campaign advisers and compared Clinton and vice presidential candidate Al Gore to his dog Millie, and distastefully referred to them as "Bozos."

Not since 1860, when Abraham Lincoln won election with only 39 percent of the vote over a divided Democratic Party, has fate seemed to so drastically intervene and alter the outcome of a presidential election. July 1992 found Bill Clinton easily winning the Democratic presidential nomination. And in November, he was elected with a mere 43 percent of the popular vote—the smallest winning percentage in nearly a century.

During the campaign, Clinton appeared to be a political genius, an inspiring candidate who moved the American electorate away from a party that had been in control of the White House for more than a decade, ultimately unseating a relatively popular incumbent president who seemed to have lost his way. Yet after three months in office, Clinton was himself being roundly dismissed as incompetent and inept. After four months, his national approval rating stood at 36 percent, the lowest of any president since World War II. And six months into his presidency, anti-Clinton paraphernalia such as buttons, bumper stickers, and T-shirts that read "Don't Blame Me—I Voted for Bush," were being sold at the rate of 10,000 per day. "President" Clinton had become a joke—a national laughingstock.

The American public wondered if this president was destined to go the same route as the previous incumbent—voted out of office after one term. At the same time, many rational people had to ponder whether or not Clinton's early faltering was due less to a lack of ability and more to the chaotic, intolerant, and politically unforgiving environment that the changing times had wrought.

Despite his early stumbles, Clinton did not back away from taking action, but instead continued introducing bold initiatives that forced public discussion and debate. "We simply cannot say this is a complicated time and we're unequal to the challenge," he asserted. "We are determined to stop avoiding our problems and start facing them, to embrace them as challenges, to turn them into opportunities, to seize the future."

As President of the United States, Bill Clinton's achievements have been well documented. Not only did he secure the passage of a remarkable amount of new legislation, he also balanced the budget, eliminated the federal deficit, created millions of new jobs, and presided over the longest sustained economic boom in United States history. And he is one of only a dozen U.S. presidents who served two full four-year terms.

Paradoxically, Bill Clinton is also one of the most reviled presidents in American history. A lightning rod for hate, ridicule, and opposition, he was the target of an endless series of attacks perpetrated by a well-organized and well-funded group of political enemies. While nearly all of the charges leveled against him were ill-founded, Clinton ended up feeding the frenzy by engaging in an adulterous affair with a young White House intern, and then lying about it to his family, his friends, the court, and the American people. As a result, he became only the second United States president to be impeached by the House of Representatives. Even though he was acquitted in the Senate, the damage to his reputation was extensive. Ultimately, the questions regarding his leadership while president were left to historians and pundits to filter and figure out.

Nearly every month for the eight years of his presidency, there was some sort of orchestrated attack on Bill Clinton's personal character (as documented between chapters of this book). Despite that fact, and despite his personal flaws, Clinton left office in 2001 with a 67 percent public approval rating—the highest for a departing president in the history of poll-taking.

How in the world did that happen? Many analysts have pointed to Clinton's personal magnetism as the reason for his being both loathed and loved to extremes. They point to his uncanny ability to charm people, his superb communication skills, especially in public speaking, and an undeniable talent in connecting with others—physically, intellectually, and emotionally. "It's all part of the Clinton charisma," some have suggested.

Whether it was charisma or not, many questions regarding Bill Clinton's presidency remain. Was he a good leader? How will he be judged by historians? Are there lessons to be learned from his time in office—from his damage-control strategies, from his ability to implement diversity, or from his decision-making process? By studying Bill Clinton's personal leadership style, can modern leaders around the world pick up some useful tips to apply in rapidly changing times?

In his first inaugural address, President Clinton recognized the significance of the changing world in which he lived. He spoke about the "profound and powerful forces . . . . shaking and remaking our world." He noted the power of technology in creating a new global economy. And he urged all Americans to step to the forefront of change—to be bold in renewing America. "This is *our* time," he asserted. "Let us embrace it!"

"It is becoming clear that Mr. Clinton's complexities may be
well suited for these times."

—*New York Times* op. ed.
July 31, 1994

*Governor Bill Clinton declared his candidacy for the presidency in **October 1991**. Shortly thereafter, a handful of Arkansas right-wing conservatives, all of whom had their own reasons for disliking Clinton, organized against his campaign. They included: Larry Nichols, fired in 1990 by Clinton from his job as marketing consultant for the Arkansas Development Finance Authority (the state bonding agency); Larry Case, a private detective from Little Rock; Sheffield Nelson, former oil and gas executive who ran unsuccessfully for governor against Clinton in 1990; and Cliff Jackson, a Republican lawyer, Christian fundamentalist, and lifelong personal rival of Bill Clinton.*

Nichols and Case cultivated relationships with tabloid newspapers and television shows that were willing to pay for scandal stories about Clinton. Nelson prepared to utilize the Arkansas Republican Party's established ties with national newspapers and media outlets. And Jackson formed an organization called Alliance for Rebirth of an Independent America (ARIAS), to fight Clinton's candidacy.

⤜⤛

*In the weeks leading up to the New Hampshire Democratic primary on February 18, 1992, political attacks were launched against Clinton, who had emerged as the favorite. On **January 28, 1992**, Star magazine ran a derisive expose titled, "Ex-Aide Charges in Court Dem's Front-Runner Bill Clinton Cheated With Miss America And Four Other Beauties." In the article, Larry Nichols named and supplied photographs of five women he claimed had affairs with Clinton. It was further charged that the governor had used state funds to wine and dine them and take "love trips" to New York. One of the women denied the charges and the magazine printed a retraction, three did not comment, and the fifth (Gennifer Flowers) was preparing her own series of accusations for publication. Nichols reportedly received $50,000 for the story.*

*Two weeks later, the **February 11, 1992**, issue of Star featured Flowers (a forty-two-year-old singer, former state employee, and personal friend of Larry Nichols), who claimed to have been "Bill Clinton's lover for twelve years." The story had been swirling around for weeks after having been leaked to the mainstream media and picked up by major television networks and newspapers across the country. In response, Clinton appeared with his wife on CBS's 60 Minutes. He refuted the claim of a twelve-year affair, but admitted "wrongdoing" and "causing pain in my marriage."* Bill Clinton later admitted under oath that he'd had a one-night stand with Flowers in 1977. *The Star reportedly paid Flowers $150,000 for the story, and she later received $250,000 for doing a nude photo layout in Penthouse* *magazine. Flowers' total revenue from her story (including two "tell-all" books) is believed to have exceeded $500,000.*

Cliff Jackson's group, ARIAS, paid for advertisements labeling Clinton a draft-dodger. The Wall Street Journal *researched the story and published an article stating that, during the Vietnam War, Clinton manipulated the system to avoid being drafted. Specifically, it was charged that, while studying as a Rhodes Scholar at Oxford, the twenty-two-year-old young man was granted a draft deferment by promising to join the ROTC upon his return to Arkansas the next year.*

After a week of answering questions, Clinton's campaign released a December 3, 1969, letter written by Clinton to ROTC Colonel Eugene J. Holmes in which he expressed thanks for "saving me from the draft . . . last summer," and explained his "opposition to the Vietnam War," his turmoil about what to do, and his wish to "maintain my political viability within the system." Bill Clinton then appeared on ABC's Nightline *and explained to Ted Koppel that he had decided not to join the ROTC, but to let his deferment lapse and take his chances with the draft lottery. Ultimately, Clinton received a high number and was not called.*

On **February 18, 1992,** *the day of the New Hampshire primary,* The Globe, *a supermarket tabloid, published a four-page layout titled, "Bill Clinton's Four In A Bed Sex Orgies With Black Hookers." The article claimed that an African American Little Rock prostitute, Bobbie Ann Williams, had been impregnated by the Arkansas governor during an orgy at the home of Virginia Kelley, Clinton's mother. Photos of a young boy were printed under the heading, "Clinton's Love Child." After the primary, Bobbie Ann Williams came forward and publicly stated that she had never met Clinton, nor was she a prostitute.*

Despite all the negative criticism, Bill Clinton finished a strong second to Massachusetts senator Paul Tsongas (Tsongas 33.2 percent; Clinton 24.8 percent; Bob Kerrey 11.1 percent). Labeled "The Comeback Kid" by the national media, Clinton emerged as the Democratic front-runner.

PART I
PEOPLE

"I try to bring people together."

—Bill Clinton,
To Tom Brokaw of NBC News
January 26, 1995

"I will give you an administration that looks like America."

—Clinton Campaign Promise
May 11, 1992

"Unless we can find strength in our diversity, our diversity of race, our diversity of income, our diversity of region, our diversity of religious conviction, we cannot possibly meet the challenges before us."

—Bill Clinton,
At a White House Interfaith Breakfast
August 30, 1993

CHAPTER ONE

DIVERSITY

The Oval Office was redecorated in August 1993 during the two weeks that President Clinton and his family were vacationing on Martha's Vineyard. Prior to his departure, Clinton voiced only one request about the new look. He said he wanted his office to somehow reflect diversity.

When he returned, the president found not only gold drapes and a deep blue carpet, but also a new statue to go along with Rodin's "The Thinker." It was the likeness of a Native American on horseback entitled "Appeal to the Great Spirit," and was chosen from the permanent White House art collection to "celebrate the stoicism and dignity of Native Americans." The sculpture stood alone on a small table and was intended to symbolize the diversity of people that made America great, and the diversity that Bill Clinton intended to champion during his administration.

A more appropriate table for viewing the diversity reflected in the Clinton administration, however, was located a few doors down the hall in a major conference room. It was the table at which the president's cabinet sat. Never before had there been more African Americans, Hispanic Americans, or women directing and guiding the United States Government. As a matter of fact, within a few months after Bill Clinton took office, the United States cabinet, for the first time in the history of the nation, was not composed of a majority of white males.

As president, Clinton did more than simply recognize and tolerate individuals from various cultures, he actively sought out and surrounded himself with people who represented America's multitudes, with people who had a wide range of experiences, and with people who could offer a perspective different than his own.

CASTING THE NET WIDE

"I will give you an administration that looks like America," stated Clinton during his run for president. At the time, that promise seemed implausible to implement and simply campaign rhetoric. However, within a few months of taking office, Clinton had set in motion a process that eventually resulted in an administration that reflected the demographics of the nation. And after one year in office, a full 14 percent of Clinton's appointees were African American compared to 12 percent of the total U.S. population; 46 percent were female compared to a roughly 50–50 split nationwide between men and women; and while 75 percent of the population was Caucasian, Clinton's appointments tallied 76 percent. Moreover, his administration's appointments of Hispanics, Native Americans, and other minorities were remarkably consistent with nationwide demographic statistics.

In Clinton's original cabinet alone, five members were African American: Ron Brown (Commerce), Jesse Brown (Veterans Affairs), Lee Brown (Drug Czar), Mike Espy (Agriculture), and Hazel O'Leary (Energy); two were Hispanic: Henry Cisneros (Housing and Urban Development) and Federico Pena (Transportation); and six were women, including: Madeleine Albright (U.N. Ambassador), Carol Browner (EPA), Janet Reno (Attorney General), Donna Shalala (Health and Human Services), and Laura D'Andrea Tyson (Council of Economic Advisers).

Only eight members of the original cabinet were white males: Bruce Babbitt (Interior), Lloyd Bentsen (Treasury), Warren Christopher (State), Mickey Kantor (U.S. Trade Representative), Leon Panetta (Office of Management and Budget), Les Aspin (Defense), Robert Reich (Labor), and Richard Riley (Education).

During the appointments process, President Clinton was criticized by members of the press and the Republican Party for being slow with his nominations. Seven months into his presidency he was behind the nomination paces set by Presidents Carter and Reagan—but ahead of George H. W. Bush's. He was also chastised early on by impatient women's rights groups for not appointing enough females to positions of authority.

The entire process was slowed, in part, by Clinton's own demand for a combination of diversity and competence in all his prospective appointees. Another reason for the delay was the scarcity of qualified minority and female candidates. Women and minorities in the workforce between the ages of thirty and sixty-four were few in number, which made the searches significantly more difficult. Furthermore, once qualified candidates were identified, they had to be talked into coming to work for the federal government, which, at the time, was not an appealing thought to most successful business people.

Clinton, however, consistently ignored the criticism and continued to focus on the long-term view of his administration. He would not be rushed into his appointments—and he would personally involve himself throughout the review and selections process. Frequently, the president handed back lists of potential appointees with the admonition that he wanted "more diversity." Eventually, Clinton's White House staff leveled out at 45 percent women and 20 percent minorities, with significant diversity in age—from "elders" like Lloyd Bentsen and Leon Panetta, to the so-called Youth Brigade headed by thirty-two-year-old George Stephanopoulos and Dee Dee Myers, the first female White House Press Secretary in American history.

In addition to his own staff at the White House, the new president made tremendous strides in diversifying the federal judiciary. As a matter of fact, 61 percent of his appointments were either women or minorities, the most notable selection being that of Supreme Court Justice Ruth Bader Ginsburg. Eleven percent were Latinos, and Clinton even appointed the first blind federal judge, David Tatel, to fill Ginsburg's vacated seat.

Nearly all branches of the federal government saw increases in the numbers of females within their ranks. President Clinton nominated women to head the Federal Deposit Insurance Corporation (Ricki Tigert), the Air Force (Sheila Widnall), and the National Endowment for the Arts (Jane Alexander). He also made Joycelyn Elders the nation's first African American surgeon general, Mary Ellen Withrow Treasurer of the United States and, in 1997, Madeleine Albright the first female secretary of state.

Overall, Clinton's attitude toward women as equals was decidedly different from previous presidents. He not only reached out to them, but his pace at appointing women to leadership roles was unprecedented in American history. By doing so, he took a bold step forward in changing the status quo, challenging to embrace true equality in government service, and helped set the stage for a more equal distribution of talent in future administrations.

In order to assure that he received a broad range of advice, Clinton surrounded himself with liberals and conservatives, often from both the Republican and Democratic parties. On issues dealing with communications or foreign affairs, he relied, in part, on David Gergen, who had served Republican presidents Nixon, Ford, and Reagan. For legal advice, he consulted with, among others, Lloyd Cutler, who was Democratic President Jimmy Carter's White House counsel. And several years into his administration, Clinton appointed Republican senator William Cohen secretary of defense.

Clinton frequently took advantage of the skills and talents of members of his own and the opposing party. For instance, he was able to persuade William Frenzel, a Republican member of the House of Representatives for twenty years, to join the White House team attempting to secure passage of the North American Free Trade Agreement (NAFTA). He dispatched Robert Oakley (who served under George H. W. Bush) to Somalia to negotiate with General Mohammed Farah Aideed for a resolution to the festering problem in that country. And in a last-ditch effort to avoid an invasion of Haiti, Clinton asked the triumvirate of Jimmy Carter, retired General Colin Powell, and Senator Sam Nunn to travel to Port-Au-Prince to persuade the military dictators to leave the country of their own accord.

When confronting controversial or difficult situations, as in the Haiti situation, Clinton often consulted with members of Congress from both parties. "Every time I have consulted the Congress," he said in May 1993, "they say to me in private: 'You're the only president that ever took us into counsel beforehand. Instead of telling us what you were going to do, you actually ask us our opinion.'"

Many people interpreted this practice of asking for advice as an inherent weakness in his leadership style. But Clinton demurred. "I want the best and most creative advice I can get across the broad range of areas with which we must deal," he said. Most leaders intuitively realize that diversity is a plus in both decision making and in effectively representing a mixture of people in a democratic society. That's because they know that diversity is very much a part of the American dream. But more important, it is part of democracy's continuing success. Clinton commented on this belief at a town hall meeting in Moscow in January 1994: "Many leaders . . . have come from basically quite humble circumstances," he said. "That's a great thing for a nation, to make it possible to cast the net for talent very wide so that anybody has a chance to rise to the top if he or she has the ability and the good fortune to do so."

A HISTORY WITH DIVERSITY

Clinton's promotion of diverse people did not begin when he assumed the presidency. As governor of Arkansas, he was known for his interest in the issues of race and gender. At each of his four inaugurations, he saw to it that the festivities reflected the diversity of religion, race, and gender evident in the state. In his first inaugural address, he mentioned the issue outright. "For as long as I can remember," said Clinton, "I have believed passionately in the cause of equal opportunity, and I will do what I can to advance it."

And advance it he did. Fully 15 percent of his appointments to Arkansas public offices and government jobs were African Americans. Clinton also appointed more minorities to state positions than all the prior governors of Arkansas combined. Part of Clinton's passion on this issue can be traced back to his childhood. When he was very young, his mother left him for several years in the care of his grandparents, who lived in Hope and ran a grocery store in a poor section of town heavily populated by African Americans. Clinton's grandfather relied on good relations in the community for a meager livelihood. And as a boy, Clinton could not understand why he wasn't allowed to go to school with the youngsters he played with at home. Apparently, it was an experience he never forgot.

When Clinton left Arkansas for college, he became known for his "color blindness." His former roommate at Georgetown University called Bill "the most unprejudiced person I have ever met," and said further that "any manifestation of bigotry distresses him." Later, at Yale Law School, Clinton once brashly plopped himself down at the school cafeteria's "black" table. The young African American law students were at first offended by such audacity, but eventually grew to be his friends.

In part, Bill Clinton's interest in diversity stemmed from his innate desire to care for people, to reach out and give others a hand up the ladder, and to help others realize their maximum potential. "All my life," he once said, "I've wanted to be involved with people and help them with their problems. I've been interested in all kinds of people. Politics has just given me a way to pursue my interest and my concern on a large scale. I've given it all the energy and spirit I can muster; I've tried to bring out the best in people through politics; and I've really been very happy doing it."

SPEAKING THEIR MINDS—ACTING ON THEIR OWN INITIATIVE

Among his cabinet members and aides, President Clinton encouraged freedom of thought and expression through frank and open discussions. Because he encouraged such openness, most of his cabinet officers and advisers did not feel they were walking on eggshells when they were around him. They could state their cases whether or not he liked what they had to say. People would not be punished for speaking their minds. In late April 1993, for example, when Budget Director Leon Panetta received criticism for publicly stating that the president would have trouble getting things passed in Congress unless he did "a better job of picking and choosing the battles he wants to go through," Clinton remarked at a press conference that Panetta "had a bad day, because he got his spirits down." When a reporter inferred that Panetta might be disciplined, Clinton responded: "I want to buck him up. I don't want to take him to the woodshed." A little more than a year later, Panetta was appointed White House Chief of Staff. The president then appointed Panetta's deputy, Alice Rivlin, the first woman to head the Office of Management and Budget.

Labor Secretary Robert Reich once commented that Clinton, in assembling his cabinet, looked for "people who could work together . . . not loose cannons or prima donnas." Yet the new president appointed some very strong-willed people to high positions in the administration. People like Reno, Reich, Bentsen, Cisneros, Pena, Shalala, and Elders all had strong personalities combined with a vision of what they wanted to accomplish in the administration.

Clinton knew that choosing such results-oriented people would allow him to achieve more. Almost immediately, that strategy began to pay off. It was no coincidence, for example, that the five government agencies with the highest percentages of minority employees (Agriculture, Commerce, Housing and Urban Development, Transportation, and Veterans Affairs) were also those that were led by minorities. In each case, diversity gave rise to more diversity. Like Clinton, the president's minority choices appointed people reflecting their own experiences—in effect, turning the president's ideas and thoughts into actions far beyond what he could have accomplished on his own.

By choosing people who were action-oriented, and then empowering them to act, Clinton took a risk that they would fight with him on many of his own initiatives. And for Clinton, that turned out to be the case in a number of instances. Attorney General Janet Reno, for instance, steadfastly refused to combine the Department of Alcohol, Tobacco, and Firearms with the FBI (as Clinton and Gore had recommended in their Reinventing Government initiative). In a meeting on welfare reform in late March of 1994, the entire cabinet balked at an idea proposed by the president's task force that called for financing the $15 billion program through major cuts in aide to disadvantaged families. And many of his cabinet members and senior staff advised against presenting to Congress a 1,342-page healthcare plan. They believed it was too detailed, too bureaucratic, and would not get through either house of Congress. In the end, after listening to all the advice, Clinton decided to submit the proposed legislation as it stood and then offer to compromise. But his dissenting advisers turned out to be right as the plan was eventually scrapped.

Moreover, most of Clinton's cabinet secretaries began forceful and dynamic initiatives of their own. Reich, for example, a friend of Clinton's for more than twenty-five years, pursued an ambitious agenda that included retraining laid-off workers, revitalizing the American workplace, and eliminating decades of hostility between labor unions and management in major corporations. In the year he was secretary of defense, Les Aspin moved boldly to open the American military to women by creating more than 15,000 positions aboard warships and combat aircraft. Henry Cisneros mobilized the Department of Housing and Urban Development with his "shared vision of hope," and created a movement toward more subsidized housing in suburbs and less in central urban areas. And Attorney General Janet Reno took swift action after the murder of a Pensacola doctor at an abortion clinic. She stormed Capitol Hill to urge Congress to move more quickly in making it a federal crime to threaten either abortion providers or women seeking abortions. In addition, Reno worked with Director Louis J. Freeh to add a woman, a Hispanic man, and an African American man to the top management of the FBI.

DIVERSITY IN THE MODERN ARENA

Building strength through diversity is something altogether different from the "politically correct" syndrome that engulfed the United States in the late twentieth century. In the early 1990s, nearly half of all major corporations had formal programs promoting cultural diversity within their ranks. Part of the reason for this trend can be attributed to the growing process of globalization. When expanding into new global markets, corporations were forced to employ people who mirrored their new and prospective customers. It became nothing less than a matter of survival during a time of intense competition and change.

Diversity in the workforce also fits in well with teamwork, in that a variety of opinions and perspectives result in greater productivity and problem solving. Increased diversity, coupled with working in teams, leads to better decision making. The best, most effective leaders realize that when they are making decisions that affect a diverse populace, it becomes critical to consult a variety of people. For instance, if Bill Clinton was confronted with a decision that could impact African Americans or

Hispanics, he could readily seek advice and counsel from members of his own cabinet like Hazel O'Leary or Federico Pena.

Where it was a common and even natural tendency for others to perceive differences as threats, Bill Clinton viewed differences as strengths. He had no qualms about sharing power with people who were unlike himself. Throughout his tenure in office, Clinton continually voiced his "commitment to make our diversity in this country a strength and not a weakness."

By greatly increasing the role of women in government, Clinton was following a rising trend that was unprecedented in world history. Many countries had already chosen women for a leading role in their governments. In addition to economic powers like Canada, France, Great Britain, Ireland, and Norway, lesser economically powered nations like Nicaragua, Iceland, Turkey, Pakistan, and Bangladesh had also placed women in prominent government roles. The year Clinton was elected president the U.S., Congress nearly doubled its number of female representatives. And as a result, 1992 was fittingly dubbed "The Year of the Woman" by the American media. It was the peak of a rising trend over two decades that saw the number of female city mayors and state representatives expand at spectacular rates. This trend was clearly recognized by Bill Clinton. And even though the nation had not elected a woman to the executive branch of government, he took it upon himself to follow public opinion and elevate a record number of women to leadership roles in the federal government.

Clinton also was well aware of the fact that, in business and industry, women had made tremendous gains in non-clerical jobs, accounting for nearly half of all white-collar positions. However, when he took office, the number of women in managerial positions lingered between only one-fourth and one-third of the total workforce. Leading women's groups voiced concern over such a male-dominated hierarchy. They maintained that it was next to impossible for women to make significant gains in managerial roles as long as a male-dominated culture existed at the highest levels of the federal government and corporate America.

As with a major corporation, the federal government can only achieve diversity if it is championed by the highest echelons of its leadership. If top leaders *appoint* women and minorities to high levels, there is a greater probability that future generations will *elect* them. Even though Bill Clinton did not garner much credit for it, he definitely assumed this bold stance. Clinton single-handedly changed the practical function of the United States government by making women and minorities an integral part of the institution, rather than leaving them on the outside looking in. In so doing, he endured harsh criticism for having the courage to change the status quo.

In appointing ethnically diverse people to high positions in the executive branch of government, Clinton was also fulfilling a long-overdue promise spelled out in both the Declaration of Independence and the Constitution of the United States. In the more than two centuries since the founding of the nation, neither the Congress nor the executive and judicial branches of government had ever consisted of people who truly reflected the ethnic demographics of the country. Clinton paved the way for future generations of Americans who had previously held no hope that their government would ever stop treating them as second-class citizens. Through his diverse appointments, Bill Clinton gave the American people due representation at the highest levels of government—for the very first time. In the long run, the country was made stronger and more effective because of it.

"Diversity is not an end in itself. It is simply the only way we can build a larger community to which everyone belongs, in which everyone has a common stake in the future, and in which everyone can have a decent life."

—Clinton, at the NAACP Legal Defense
and Educational Fund Dinner
May 16, 1994

"The faces in this crowd are willing to make America a model of what every society in the world ought to be in the 21st century, where diversity is strength, where diversity is richness and laughter and fullness and hope."

—Clinton, at Our Lady of Help Christian School
in Los Angeles, California
November 21, 1993

*On Sunday, **March 8, 1992**, a few weeks before major primaries in New York and California, and just two days before the "Super Tuesday" primaries in six Southern states,* The New York Times *ran a front-page story about Whitewater, a pseudo-scandal that would dog Bill and Hillary Clinton for the next eight and a half years. Under the banner, "The 1992 CAMPAIGN: Personal Finances; Clintons Joined S&L Operator In an Ozark Real Estate Venture,"* The Times *article began by stating: "Bill Clinton and his wife were business partners with the owner of a failing savings and loan association that was subject to state regulation early in his tenure as Governor of Arkansas, records show."*

Whitewater was a 200-acre development located in a remote part of the Arkansas Ozarks, in which the Clintons had invested with Jim and Susan McDougal in 1978. According to the Times, *the Clintons faced little financial risk, but might have cashed in big if their investment had done well. When the development became financially troubled, the governor used his powers to grant preferential treatment to Madison Guaranty, the McDougal-owned trust company that financed the Whitewater development. Eventually, the company became insolvent, cost taxpayers more than $49 million, and was taken over by federal regulators.*

Most of what appeared in this article was erroneous. The Clintons shared proportionate risk in the project. Madison Guaranty wasn't formed until five years after the Whitewater partnership began, by which time the development was an obvious failure. And the Clintons ended up losing money on their investment. It was later revealed that the reporter had spoken extensively with Sheffield Nelson, who claimed credit for putting The New York Times *onto Whitewater. And since the initial story had appeared on the front page of the most prestigious newspaper in the country, the accusations and innuendo against the Clintons would be repeated extensively in other media outlets. Whitewater would eventually become the one charge against Bill Clinton upon which all others would be built or attached. It mobilized Clinton's enemies, focused their efforts, and accelerated their actions to harm his presidency.*

*On **August 31, 1992** (six weeks after Clinton had gained the Democratic Party's nomination for president, and ten days after the Republican National Convention), federal fraud investigator L. Jean Lewis filed an unusual criminal referral with the FBI and the U.S. attorney in Little Rock. Lewis worked for the Resolution Trust Corporation, a temporary federal agency created to aid savings and loan depositors and liquidate assets of institutions seized by the government. Lewis's referral made serious allegations about Whitewater, and named Bill and Hillary Clinton as material*

witnesses. A Justice Department investigation quickly convened, immediately garnered media attention, and thus created another cloud of suspicion over Bill Clinton's personal character. Future FBI and Justice Department documents noted that "no facts can be identified to support the designation" of the Clintons as witnesses. FBI special agent Steven Irons later stated that Lewis's actions were an attempt to influence the election against Clinton.

∽

*Bill Clinton was elected President of the United States on **November 3, 1992*** (Clinton, 43 percent, 370 Electoral Votes; Bush, 37 percent, 168 Electoral Votes; Perot, 19 percent, 0 Electoral Votes). *In the wake of Clinton's victory and subsequent inauguration, conservative outrage was voiced from a variety of directions. The new president was denounced as "an enemy of the people"; his wife, Hillary, was called a "Marxist." Senate Minority Leader Bob Dole branded the Clinton presidency "illegitimate." Fundamentalist Christians said it was "a repudiation of our forefathers' covenant with God," and that "the nation deserves the hatred of God under Clinton." House Minority Whip Newt Gingrich, at a seminar for the Republican political action committee GOPAC, charged that "left wing Democrats represent the party of total hedonism, total exhibitionism, total bizarreness, total weirdness, and the total right to cripple innocent people in the name of letting hooligans loose." Gingrich further labeled Democrats sick, grotesque, loony, stupid, corrupt, anti-family, and traitors.*

Gingrich's vilification of all things associated with the Democratic Party signified the beginning of a long-term strategic plan to attack, smear, discredit, and possibly destroy Bill Clinton and his presidency. The entire effort was reportedly funded by several wealthy donors, among them Peter W. Smith (a successful Chicago investor) and Richard Mellon Scaife (a Pittsburgh-based heir to the Mellon family banking, oil, and steel fortune). Countless organizations were created or enlisted to take part in the effort, including: The Federalist Society, the Heritage Foundation, the Landmark Legal Foundation, the Bradley Foundation, the Institute for Justice, and the Free Congress Foundation, to mention just a few.

"Back east where I work, consensus is often turned into cave-in. People who try to work together and listen to one another ... are accused of being weak, not strong. And the process is 100 times more important than the product. Beats anything I ever saw."

—Clinton, to the National Governor's Association
Tulsa, Oklahoma
August 16, 1993

"We will make the White House a place of teamwork and free flow of ideas."

—Clinton, announcing selections for his White House staff. At a White House Interfaith Breakfast
January 14, 1993

CHAPTER TWO

CONSENSUS THROUGH TEAMWORK

During the summer of 1993, sustained torrential rains resulted in massive flooding throughout the Midwest—one of the worst natural disasters in American history. The damage was so severe that Vice President Al Gore, when comparing before and after satellite photographs of the area, remarked: "It's as if another Great Lake has been added to a map of the United States."

President Clinton cut short his planned three-day vacation return trip from the G–7 Summit in Tokyo and went directly to the scene of the flooding. He flew over the flood-ravaged areas in a helicopter, walked the streets of Des Moines, helped fill sandbags, and mingled with victims of the flooding.

When he was back in Washington, Clinton continuously monitored the situation. As the floods worsened, he made another trip to the

Midwest. Only this time he put "Team Clinton" into action. The president sequestered a high school gymnasium in Arnold, Missouri, just outside of St. Louis, and convened a "Flood Response Mobilization and Recovery" Summit. He brought most of his cabinet members with him, including: the Secretaries of Agriculture, Transportation, Commerce, Housing and Urban Development, Labor, Health and Human Services, the budget director, and the director of the Environmental Protection Agency. In addition, he dispatched to the scene the head of the Army Corps of Engineers, the Commandant of the Coast Guard, the head of the National Weather Service, the Head of the American Red Cross, the White House chief of staff, and the Vice President of the United States.

But Clinton didn't stop there. He also invited governors of the eight states most severely affected: Missouri, Iowa, Wisconsin, Illinois, Nebraska, North Dakota, South Dakota, and Minnesota. All of them showed up as did those members of Congress the president asked to attend (four senators and six representatives of the most devastated districts).

The conference lasted one day. Issues were discussed. Appropriate responsive actions were defined. Consensus was reached. Both federal and state governments were immediately mobilized in a joint effort to help victims of the flooding. And most importantly, talk turned quickly into action.

All the members of the rapidly convened task force congratulated the president for leading a quick and comprehensive federal response to the disaster. It was an unprecedented effort. It was also vintage Bill Clinton.

TEAMWORK IN EVERY DECISION

As President of the United States, Clinton emphasized teamwork in everything he did, in every decision he made. He wanted to tear down walls that hampered effective communication. He wanted to hear as many different ideas as he possibly could. And he worked especially hard at eliminating the interdepartmental fighting that had plagued federal governments of the past. "We're organizing the appropriate Federal agencies to ensure that they work together as a team," said Clinton in his weekly radio address of July 8, 1993.

This team approach was clearly evident from the very beginning of Clinton's tenure in office. For instance, in announcing his selections for the White House staff, he vowed to "make the White House a place of teamwork and free flow of ideas." And that's exactly what he did. Clinton's entire administration was quite a contrast to the rigidity and formality of prior administrations. His White House was a place that seemed to thrive on chaos and, as *Newsweek* noted, it was also "a very postmodern one, where management [was] more horizontal than hierarchical."

The new president set up a process to formulate policy that was similar to what many leading businesses were doing at the time. He did not allow White House staff or cabinet members to formulate policy in a vacuum. Rather, Clinton set up task forces, committees, or loosely structured groups of advisers. He even used this approach in selecting key members of his administration prior to taking office, making many of his decisions around a kitchen table in the governor's house in Little Rock. The three people that were fixtures at that table were Clinton, Al Gore, and Hillary Clinton. Other experts were brought in for advice at various intervals.

After assembling his team, Clinton held the cabinet's first strategy meeting at Camp David. It was intended to be an informal, get-acquainted session and, at the suggestion of Vice President Gore, a facilitator was brought in. She immediately encouraged everyone to be open and honest with each other—and not to feel threatened by President Clinton or any other member of the cabinet. As they began, everyone was asked to relate a story harkening back to their childhood. Clinton went first and talked about the fact that, as a child, he was teased and made fun of because he was fat. After the president set the tone, other members of the cabinet each took their turn in the barrel. Through this get-together, Clinton let members of his cabinet know that he considered them all equal parts of his team.

In order to focus on more specific issues and details, the president also formed sub-teams that included cabinet members and other key people in his administration. In his first term, Clinton considered his economic team to be composed of Lloyd Bentsen (Secretary of the Treasury), Leon Panetta (Director of the Office of Management and Budget), Robert Rubin (Coordinator of Economic Policy), Laura Tyson (Chair of the Council of Economic Advisers), and Ron Brown (Commerce Secretary). In Clinton's second term, his national security team was composed of: Madeleine Albright (Secretary of State), Bill Cohen (Secretary of Defense), Tony Lake (Director of the CIA), Bill Richardson (United Nations Ambassador), and Sandy Berger (National Security Advisor). With time, members of Clinton's teams changed, but the teams themselves stayed intact.

All the members of the administration's new team were believers in Clinton's teamwork style—and that's one reason they were chosen. Not only would they work together effectively in order to find solutions to complex problems, they would also employ the very team strategies that were being championed by the president. Henry Cisneros put teams together to aid the homeless and move subsidized housing out of the inner-cities. He also chaired a four-day flood summit meeting in Des Moines designed to aid people who had lost their homes. Robert Reich convened conferences on retraining laid-off American workers and creating new jobs. Other cabinet members followed suit.

As comfortable as they were working in teams, some of Clinton's top tier of leaders had some difficulty adjusting to the president's methods of operation, largely because those methods were not conventional by federal government standards. No longer did they have the ultimate say on all matters in their domains. No longer was there a president who barked out orders from above and then demanded that they be carried out. Rather, Bill Clinton was adamant that every issue be discussed and debated. All members of the team had input on all issues—and sometimes an individual's feelings were hurt. In 1993, during a Saturday meeting at the White House, for instance, Secretary of Transportation Federico Pena was forced to defend his plans for dealing with a proposed investment in USAir by British Airways. This team approach, involving dialogue and discussion, resulted in Pena's idea being rejected. It was a hard meeting for the Transportation Secretary, but it was typical of Clinton's leadership style, which was to achieve consensus on as many issues as possible. Everyone was to soon realize that Federico Pena would not be the only cabinet member to undergo the experience of needing to compromise.

After only a few months in office, the president's team approach garnered national interest and the press coined the phrase, "a Clinton-like consensus." It was frequently used in describing, for example, the president's approach to foreign affairs. Rather then deploying troops to war-torn Bosnia and other regions of the world by his authority alone—as Lyndon Johnson had done in Vietnam, Ronald Reagan in Grenada, and George H. W. Bush in Panama—Clinton chose to work through the United Nations Security Council.

In 1993, when Clinton recommended sending troops to Bosnia, the Council wouldn't go along. So U.S. troops were not deployed. But when the president recommended similar action in 1994 in regard to Haiti, the UN did go along and troops were sent in. And in December 1994, Clinton agreed to send up to 25,000 troops to Bosnia after NATO requested that the United States participate in a safe withdrawal. This was a relatively new approach to international affairs for the United States—and it was one for which Bill Clinton was criticized. But he always maintained that it was the right thing to do in a post–cold war world. Changing times demanded new methods, he believed.

Many old-line thinkers had serious doubts about Clinton's "consensus" approach, which was interpreted as a lack of leadership on the part of the United States that could result in a loss of credibility. When *The New York Times* columnist William Safire questioned the administration's policy regarding Bosnia, Clinton defended his decision by pointing out that the United States was one member of a larger team, the United Nations: "There is a Security Council," said the president, "and some people on it have a veto. And [those that do] have vetoed what I think is appropriate [action] in Bosnia." He went on to say that he had "yet to read a compelling case for why the United States on its own should either send a large number of troops or start a bombing mission all by ourselves."

Despite all the criticism, Clinton more or less maintained this consistent approach throughout his tenure in office. He worked through the United Nations in dealing with Somalia, Iraq, North Korea, Haiti, and other trouble spots around the world. Moreover, in mid-1993, when Congress strenuously objected to the president's actions in Bosnia, Clinton pledged to work as a team with the House and Senate. He even agreed *in writing* to consult with the Congress in any such decisions—the first time an American president had ever done so.

It was, however, a commitment that he nearly broke about a year later when United States troops were on the verge of invading Haiti. Clinton knew that he could not get a majority of Congress to support an invasion and subsequent occupation of the small Caribbean nation. But he was determined to end the murderous reign of the military dictator, General Raoul Cedras, and return to power the democratically elected leader, Jean Bertrand Aristide. As a matter of fact, President Clinton actually pushed up the date for an invasion by twenty-four hours in an effort to avoid impending votes in the Senate and House of Representatives. Only a last-minute agreement worked out by former President Jimmy Carter (at Clinton's direction) prevented a forced invasion. For all his rhetoric and demonstrated action involving teamwork, Bill Clinton was also prepared to act on his own regardless of what his advisers or other key individuals might have thought.

TASK FORCES AND CONFERENCES

As president, Bill Clinton created a variety of task forces on high-profile initiatives, such as health care reform, reinventing government, and welfare reform. But there were literally dozens of others that received less notoriety. There was the Interagency Climate Change Mitigation Group composed of nearly 300 people focused on reducing greenhouse gas

emissions. There was the task force on government entitlement programs—a group with thirty members headed by U.S. Senators John
Danforth and Bob Kerrey, who were charged with revamping entitlement programs to aid in deficit reduction. There was the Airline Task
Force Study that reviewed the regulations and safety of the airline industry. President Clinton also formed a task force devoted specifically to
helping solve the poor economy in California. He appointed the Secretary of Commerce, Ron Brown, to head the group, and also took a personal interest by traveling to Los Angeles for one session that included
U.S. senators and other leaders from the state. Since it was carried as a
live television event, California citizens were able to listen in as the team
discussed ways to increase jobs and spur economic recovery. "I held that
conference," Clinton said, "in an attempt to get the best ideas I could
from all kinds of people."

Clinton faithfully used this teamwork process on all his initiatives,
whether it was the yearly budget or the North American Free Trade
Agreement. According to *Time* magazine, he held "as many as thirty
meetings with key advisers on each subject," and "took copious notes in
those sessions, always asked the best question, sometimes taking an opposing view when his advisers had reached consensus."

If a full-blown task force wasn't appropriate, Clinton would convene
a conference that usually lasted one to three days. This process began
even before he took office when, as president-elect, Clinton held an economic conference in Little Rock in December 1992. Many of the 300
economic experts in attendance expressed divergent opinions. However,
the tone of the meeting, set at the outset by Clinton and Al Gore, was
one of amiability and a willingness to work together. A variety of views
was encouraged, and both the president and vice president spent most
of their time listening rather than speaking.

The purpose of the economic conference was three-fold. In Clinton's own words, it convened: (1) "So that all of us can hear and give an
assessment of where our economy is today and what has been happening to it over the last two decades"; (2) "So that we could bring together
a diverse and talented group of Americans who make this economy
work, and get your ideas and your input on how we should implement
our economic progress"; and (3) "To begin through this very public
process to reconnect the American people to their government, and to
ask for their help, too, in making economic progress."

Even though there was a great deal of conflicting advice on the details of how to proceed, the economic forum did yield two very clear
goals: (1) to spur growth in the short term; and (2) to reduce the deficit
over the long haul. These goals, although general in nature, provided a

clear focus for members of the administration as they took office. In fact, during Clinton's first year in office the federal deficit was reduced and action was taken to spur short-term growth.

This economic conference was crucial for a president who could not rely only on short-term problems to solve complex economic issues. By being on national television, and by including a relatively diverse group of clear and educated thinkers, Clinton actually parlayed the information forum into a major learning event for the American public. People were very interested in the new man who had just been elected—so they tuned in. And as they watched, viewers heard a great deal about the current state of the economy. Over the course of his tenure in office, Clinton consistently staged many other similar forums as learning events.

During his first few months in office, Clinton convened summit talks in the Pacific Northwest timber dispute—just as he had promised to do during the presidential campaign. The White House brought an enormous show of executive power to the issue; including Vice President Al Gore, administration environmental leaders, four cabinet members, and the governors of California, Oregon, and Washington. The conference produced a task force, which released results three months later, on July 1, 1993. When announcing what amounted to a compromise action plan, President Clinton mentioned the task force process in some detail: "We reached out to hundreds of people," he said, "from lumber workers and fishermen to environmentalists, scientists, business people, community leaders and Native American tribes. We've worked hard to balance all their interests and to understand their concerns. We know that our solutions will not make everybody happy. Indeed, they may not make anybody happy. But we do understand that we're all going to be better off if we can act on the plan and end the deadlock and divisiveness."

Like the group assembled to resolve the Pacific Northwest timber dispute, President Clinton strove to appoint competent people to his task forces. He charged them with solving a problem and making key recommendations. He also usually let the members set the date of completion. They met regularly over an extended period of time and drafted proposals, plans, or solutions pertinent to the issue at hand. The findings were then presented to the president, usually during a working session.

This sequence of events is exactly what occurred when the administration's task force on welfare reform presented its recommendations to Clinton in 1994. The president, however, chose to delay the presentation of the plan to Congress in favor of his health care legislation. In retrospect, critics cited that decision as a major error because no substantive action took place—health care reform did not pass, nor was welfare reform introduced. But in January 1995, President Clinton convened another bipartisan task force dedicated to welfare reform that included Democratic and Republican members of Congress, governors, and other officials from across the nation.

One reason Clinton's task forces worked is that they provided a high learning curve in a relatively short period of time. People from broad ranges and backgrounds coalesced and reached a consensus as to the best way to approach the problem. Moreover, bipartisan task forces did not represent any special interest group that might benefit from the final outcome. When the work was done, the task force disbanded, and members went back home to their normal jobs and lives.

Another benefit of Clinton's task force approach was the fact that it brought in fresh thinking to solve the nation's problems. Members of these groups were not caught up in a massive government bureaucracy that tended to strangle their own policy formulators. It was an example of *fresh* thinking—and *free* thinking—at its best. In general, Clinton's task forces bucked the traditional government bureaucracy. He offered a different approach by having a more amorphous or ad hoc organizational structure. Clinton's Reinventing Government initiative, for instance, did not emanate from the Office of Management and Budget. Rather, it was led by Vice President Al Gore. And health care reform wasn't led by Donna Shalala and the Health and Human Services Department. The acknowledged leader was First Lady Hillary Clinton, who was selected to chair the task force by the president himself. By appointing the vice president and the First Lady to lead these major reform efforts, Clinton gave instant credibility and a high profile to both initiatives. The message was clear that these were not to be "just more government committees" or "business as usual."

Much of the entrenched establishment, though, had problems with such an "ad hoc" organizational structure. Many members of Congress did not understand how such a system could work effectively. They simply weren't used to it. "We want our White House . . . to be organized and to have a distinct chain of command," objected Senator Larry Pressler, a Republican from South Dakota. And future vice president Dick Cheney remarked on CNN that Clinton's administration was "lacking [in] intellectual rigor and tight command and control."

Hillary Clinton, especially, brought a storm of controversy and energy to a task that faced some of the strongest opposition of an initiative ever brought before the American people. As *The New York Times* reported: "[She] presided over scores of closed meetings, huddled with hundreds of members of Congress and traveled to more than a dozen states to help create the President's ambitious health care plan."

Even the president marveled at the action of Hillary's task force: "They spoke with self-employed people," he said. "They talked with people who had insurance and people who didn't. They talked with union members and older Americans and advocates for our children. The First Lady also consulted extensively with governmental leaders in both parties, especially on Capitol Hill. They received and read over 700,000 letters."

Once that task force had come up with a plan, President Clinton named forty-seven doctors, nurses, and other medical experts to evaluate the proposal and make comments. He took this unusual step well before the initiative was submitted to Congress because it helped assuage criticism that members of the medical community had not been consulted adequately. It also provided more credibility to the plan once it was finalized. However, even more important than that—as both Clinton and the American public realized—was the fact that people who were going to have to implement it and live with it had been consulted and involved in the process.

Once the reform package was presented to Congress, the staff of the health care task force disbanded. Its more than 500 members returned to their jobs in the private sector and government agencies. Through their efforts, Clinton had pulled together a comprehensive plan—with broad, overarching goals and specific details—in a relatively brief period of time. His next step was to begin a campaign of persuasion.

"We're going to have an honest and open debate on this," said Clinton. "I want the American community to sit down and really visit about this health care thing and talk it through. This is not going to be some sort of a blitzkrieg deal. We're going to take some time and really discuss it and debate it."

TWELVE STEPS TO CREATING AN EFFECTIVE TASK FORCE

Even though President Clinton had the noble goal of providing affordable health care access to forty million uninsured Americans, the final task force proposal was one of the few major initiatives of his administration that failed. Republican leaders in the House and Senate vowed to block any health care legislation while, at the same time, presenting a number of alternative plans to confuse the public and dilute the issue.

In addition, special interest groups spent $300 million spreading disinformation as to what was really in the plan and labeling it big government run amok. The attacks so warped the public's view of the administration's proposal that Clinton's approval ratings dropped significantly. However, when focus groups were accurately presented with the major points of the plan, more than sixty percent supported it.

While meaningful health care legislation failed to be enacted, many more of Clinton's proposals succeeded. And the process he employed in creating task forces was remarkably consistent over the course of his presidency. In general, it involved about a dozen steps—from the initial formation to the eventual disbanding. These twelve steps can be applied for any task force in virtually any organization:

1. Define the problem and announce the formation of a task force to solve it.
2. Appoint a high profile, results-oriented person as chair.
3. Recruit competent and diverse people to the team.
4. Meet with members personally and charge them with solving the problem by coming up with a comprehensive plan.
5. Provide a general timeframe for completion. Encourage regular meetings over that period of time, but allow the team to set specific dates and goals.
6. Have the plan and recommendations presented to you during a working session in which you take detailed notes, ask questions, take an opposing viewpoint, and debate the findings.
7. Present a copy of the plan to experts other than those on the original team and ask them to review it and make comments.
8. Take some time to review and reflect on the recommended action.
9. Reconvene the task force one last time to review recommendations from outside experts. Finalize the plan accordingly.
10. Acknowledge and reward members of the team. Give them credit for a job well done.
11. Disband the task force.
12. Communicate the findings. Debate the impact. Implement the final recommendations.

THE VALUE OF TEAMWORK IN LEADERSHIP

It is a paradox of leadership that while leaders must relinquish responsibility, they can and should delegate authority. A leader's skill at effectively organizing a team or a task force is a way of dealing with this paradox. Leaders can flatten the management structure by forming a solid team, empowering it to get the job done, and then holding its members accountable for results.

As president, Bill Clinton strove to do all these things. By convening conferences and task forces, he involved people in both the formulation and implementation of policy. He listened to their concerns and, in doing so, was better able to act for the people's express wants and needs. His initiatives were broader, more flexible, and more detailed than any that could have been created by a single individual. And perhaps, most importantly, Clinton's team process led to more creative performance in the government, which is exactly what was needed in a rapidly changing global environment.

The fact that Clinton embraced teamwork to such an extent is not surprising given the nature of his personality, which, according to some analysts, had a strong feminine element to it. A variety of research has clearly shown that women are particularly suited to an involved team process that constantly searches for consensus. Deborah Tannen, in her book *You Just Don't Understand: Men and Women in Conversation,* noted that: "The role of peacemaker reflects the general tendency among women to seek agreement." This sounds strikingly familiar when one considers the phrase: "A Clinton-like consensus," and it begs some questions. Was Bill Clinton's approach decidedly more feminine in nature, and did he implement a process that went against the nature of most men? Could that be a reason he suffered severe negative criticism in a decidedly male-dominated hierarchy like the federal government? Is it possible that the trend toward teamwork in the 1990s also resulted in the ascendancy of more women in roles of leadership because they are innately better suited than men to a consensus approach to leadership?

It was clear that Clinton's tendency toward fashioning a consensus was viewed as weak leadership by elder members of the opposing Republican Party. Yet the president did not waver in this natural inclination, even in the aftermath of the 1994 midterm elections when Republicans gained majorities in both houses of Congress. As a matter of fact, Clinton called the new speaker of the house, Newt Gingrich, the morning after the election and invited both him and Senate Leader Bob Dole to the White House. And Clinton vowed publicly that he would try to seek common ground with Congress on as many issues as possible.

And that's exactly what Clinton did. He confounded and frustrated Gingrich and Dole by adopting a policy of triangulation, which simply involved a move to the center of the political spectrum. By occupying a middle position between conservative Republicans on the right and liberal Democrats on the left, Clinton kept his "community" together and interdependent on one another. In doing so, he was able to attract a diverse group of voters, gain popular support for his initiatives, and pass a remarkable amount of legislation.

Deborah Tannen could just as easily have been writing about Bill Clinton's first few years in office as about women in general when she stated: "Seeing people as interdependent, women expect their actions to be influenced by others, and they expect people to act in concert. Their struggle is to keep the ties strong, keep everyone in the community, and accommodate to others' needs while making what efforts they can at damage control with respect to their own needs and preferences. "

In his leadership role as the nation's chief executive, Bill Clinton constantly advocated consensus and community, especially when trying to forge new partnerships. On November 19, 1993, when he convened the APEC Conference in Seattle, Washington, Clinton opened the first session with fifteen Pacific Rim leaders with this statement:

> I believe that discussion can help to foster among us a sense of community, not a community of formal, legal, economic integration . . . but a community such as neighbors create when they sit down together over coffee or tea to talk about house repairs or their children's schools, the kind of community that families and friends create when they gather on holidays to rejoice in their common blessings.

Leaders do not divide and conquer. They *represent* people, bring them together, and work out their differences. Doing so often involves employing a team-oriented approach that encourages collaboration, builds consensus, and gains commitment. Leaders cannot effectively practice the art of leadership without it. Creating consensus and action through teamwork is part of a solid foundation for effective leadership.

"Nobody knows what kind of future you can build better than your own people."

Clinton, to citizens in Alameda, California
August 13, 1994

"Teamwork is the order of the day."

Clinton, to victims of Midwest flooding
July 8, 1993

On *May 19, 1993*, *seven long-serving employees of the White House Travel Office were fired. Prior to Clinton taking office, a whistleblower had prompted the FBI to investigate allegations of financial wrongdoing within the office. Once alerted to the problem, the new administration took swift action, but overreacted by dismissing too many individuals without cause. Only the Travel Office director was charged with a crime, of embezzling more than $50,000.* (He was later acquitted in court.) *Congressional Republicans immediately seized on the issue and charged that the firings had taken place so that friends of the president could get the business for themselves. After the story was picked up by the media, and played upon by conservatives, the entire affair became known as TravelGate. The House Government Reform and Oversight Committee eventually launched a three-year inquiry during which Republicans charged Clinton with obstructing their efforts. In the end, TravelGate produced no evidence of wrongdoing by Bill Clinton or any member of the White House staff.*

In the late afternoon of *July 20, 1993*, *Deputy White House Counsel Vince Foster was found dead at Fort Macy Park on the banks of the Potomac River in Virginia. Born in Hope, Arkansas, Foster was a childhood friend of Bill Clinton and a former partner of Hillary Clinton at the Rose Law Firm in Little Rock. In the weeks leading up to his death,* The Wall Street Journal *published two editorials targeting Foster, his work, and his relationship with the Clintons. It was subsequently revealed that Foster suffered from depression and had been prescribed antidepressant medication. A resignation letter found torn up in pieces at the bottom of Foster's briefcase stated, in part: "I was not meant for the job or the spotlight of public life in Washington. Here, ruining people is considered sport." The note also mentioned* "Wall Street Journal *editors who lie without conscience." About a month later, the Justice Department, the FBI, and the Park Police jointly announced that the results of their investigations concluded that Foster had committed suicide.*

In *October and November 1993*, *Arkansas businessman and part-time municipal judge David Hale made a series of stunning allegations against President Clinton. Hale, who ran a bank called Capital Management Services, was authorized to make federal loans to disadvantaged and minority businesses. Back in 1986, according to Hale, Governor Clinton had pressured him into giving a $300,000 loan to a firm controlled by Jim and Susan McDougal. The money would be used for two purposes, Hale claimed. Most of it would be spread among the Democratic "political family" in Little Rock,* *but $110,000 would be earmarked to help bail out the Clintons' investment in Whitewater. Hale further claimed that he had possessed documents proving the illegal transaction, but that they had been confiscated by federal investigators.*

With the help of Sheffield Nelson and Cliff Jackson in Arkansas, Hale's story was picked up by The New York Times, The Washington Post, The Los Angeles Times, NBC News, ABC News, *and other national media outlets. David Hale, however, did not mention that he was under investigation by the U.S. Attorney in Little Rock on fraud charges, specifically that he had stolen $3.4 million from the Federal Small Business Administration. In addition, Hale's lawyer was attempting to negotiate a plea deal that would prevent his client from going to jail. Subsequent investigation into this matter by the FBI found no evidence to incriminate Bill Clinton of any wrongdoing. The story, in fact, was later proven to be a total fabrication. However, because the FBI's search of David Hale's office occurred on the same day that Vince Foster committed suicide, and because it seemed related to L. Jean Lewis's allegations regarding the Resolution Trust Corporation, it provided grist for the political rumor mill and was used to justify an extended investigation of Whitewater.*

Not long after Hale's statement about Clinton was first made public, NBC Nightly News *explicitly linked his allegations to both Whitewater and Vince Foster. Subsequently,* The Washington Times *reported that White House counsel Bernard Nussbaum had spirited away the Clintons' personal legal files from Foster's office a few days after his death. According to the conservative newspaper's editorial page, this was a "cause for profound suspicion." These statements resulted in a media frenzy during the remaining months of 1993 as national newspapers like* The Washington Post, The New York Times, and The Los Angeles Times *tried to outdo each other by speculating such things as the theory that Foster killed himself because he was afraid about his own wrongdoing in the Whitewater scandal. The Clintons maintained that their personal legal papers were simply moved out of Foster's office along with everything else so that the office could be reassigned.*

"Our challenge is the challenge of all advanced nations. We will only act most effectively when we act together."

—Clinton, upon leaving for G–7 Summit
July 5, 1994

"I worked year-in and year-out to try to establish partnerships with the private sector."

—Clinton, to the National Federation
of Independent Business
June 29, 1993

CHAPTER THREE

RELATIONSHIPS AND ALLIANCES

On March 2, 1993, barely five weeks after he took office, Bill Clinton did something that few modern American presidents had ever attempted. He went to Capitol Hill specifically to confer with members of the opposing party—the Republican members of Congress. He held two separate meetings that were open, informal, and designed to be two-way communication. Those congressman and senators with whom he met praised him for his efforts. Senate Republicans served him a Big Mac and French fries and those in the House offered him cake.

Clinton told the lawmakers that his purpose in meeting with them was "to consult" and to get acquainted. "We're all in this together," he said. After a few opening remarks, he engaged them in dialogue on a variety of issues including health care and the general state of the economy. In a similar meeting with Democrats, Connecticut Senator Joseph Lieberman recalled that Clinton "struck a balance between being personable and standing his ground."

This first trip was one of dozens of "official" visits to Capital Hill during Clinton's presidency. Clinton also conducted hundreds of more informal meetings with members of Congress. In general, such personal exchanges were part of an overall strategy that involved becoming more familiar with legislators. "There is a mindset that these are our friends and that we need to recognize that," said Howard Paster, White House congressional liaison at the time.

STRATEGIC DOMESTIC ALLIANCES

Clinton went to Congress to establish relationships and build trust; to get to know the members, let them get to know him, and to forge personal bonds that might later come in handy during debates on controversial issues. In early 1993, *The New York Times* reported that Clinton had a "strategy of stroking Democratic and Republican lawmakers more intensely than any President in nearly three decades. His frequent excursions to Capitol Hill suggest almost a parliamentary-style government, where the President works in tandem with legislators."

Soon after taking office, Clinton was able to build strong alliances with key members of the Democratic leadership in Congress. For example, he forged a tight bond with Representative Dan Rostenkowski, chairman of the House Ways and Means Committee. And even though Rostenkowski was under investigation for misusing funds from the House post office, Clinton traveled to his district in Illinois in 1994 to help the congressman's struggling campaign for reelection. When Rostenkowski later was forced to step down from his leadership role, the president began building a tighter relationship with the new chairman, Florida's Sam Gibbons. In addition to inviting him to a special White House dinner, Clinton named Gibbons (a D-Day veteran) as a "special representative" for the fiftieth anniversary celebration at Normandy in June of 1994.

Clinton also allied himself with Senator Edward M. Kennedy, chairman of the Senate's Labor and Human Resources Committee, whose support would be crucial in winning passage of a comprehensive health care plan. While on vacation at Martha's Vineyard in August 1993, the Clintons and the Kennedys went sailing together. Just a month after that, the president was in Boston with Senator Kennedy, dedicating the new museum at the John F. Kennedy Presidential Library. And less than a year later, he attended and spoke at the funeral of Jacqueline Kennedy Onassis.

Clinton forged a bond with Senate Majority Leader George Mitchell— a potential ally in getting all legislation passed in the Senate. So close was their relationship that, in April 1994, when Justice Harry Blackmun announced his retirement, Clinton offered Mitchell an appointment to the Supreme Court. The senator, however, declined the nomination and later that year worked tirelessly in the futile effort to shepherd health care reform through Congress.

Building personal relationships with the likes of Mitchell, Rostenkowski, and Kennedy was important, because they were the leaders who could help the President get his legislative agenda to the floor for a vote. And Clinton also paid attention to individual senators and congressmen who would cast votes for or against his initiatives. Furthermore, he paid special attention to freshmen senators and congressmen, whom he invited to the White House for discussions, dinners, and casual conversations. He knew they had been elected to change things, just as he had been. As such, they provided a group of natural allies for him to help secure safe passage of his legislative agenda. Whether they were freshmen or seniors, Democrats or Republicans, Clinton called most members of Congress by their first names. He regularly asked them to go jogging or to travel with him on Air Force One. Often those travels were to their home districts, where the president would appear on stage and praise them in front of their constituents.

Congressmen and senators were not the only politicians Clinton courted. He attended national governor's meetings and met with mayors of the nation's largest cities every chance he got. In March 1993, Clinton hosted the U.S. Conference of Mayors at the White House. At that forum, more than forty of the mayors voiced their support publicly for the President's economic program. And in January 1994, Clinton brought to the White House more than 1,000 mayors from around the nation to help him lobby for his anti-crime bill. He asked them to "come back [to Washington] with your colleagues, your police chiefs, and work for the next sixty days walking the beat in the halls of Congress." "The main thing," Clinton advocated, "is [that] we do not need to fool around with this for six months."

It was Clinton's relentless quest for achievement that led him to bring so many people to the White House. In March 1994, *Business Week* noted that "you can hardly visit the White House these days without tripping over a CEO . . . . Corporate America loves the open-door policy." Hundreds of business leaders were invited to meet and dine with the president in the White House. A typical lunch might include: Robert Crandall of American Airlines, August Busch III of Anheuser-Busch, Jack Smith of General Motors, and Sanford Weill of Travelers. Other notable business leaders invited to build a relationship with President Clinton were: Norman Augustine of Martin Marietta, Robert J. Eaton of

Chrysler, Harold Poling of Ford, Warren Buffett of Berkshire Hathaway, Paul Allaire of Xerox, Frank Popoff of Dow Chemical, Michael Walsh of Tenneco, and Jack Welch of General Electric.

A *Wall Street Journal* article in late 1993 noted that at least eighty high-profile business leaders had spent some time with Clinton in Washington during his first ten months in office. The *Journal* further observed:

> The President's affinity for the business establishment continues a pattern from when he was governor of Arkansas. There, he formed a close working relationship with the group of top corporate executives, nicknamed the Good Suit Club. "He made a very strong commitment to job creation, and that's where jobs come from," says Betsey Wright, who was his chief of staff in Arkansas and now is a Washington lobbyist.

Clinton's strategy of building relationships with business leaders paid off in handsome dividends. Dozens supported and actively campaigned for passage of the North American Free Trade Agreement. More than sixty appeared on stage with the president to endorse the administration's 1993 deficit reduction plan. Even Michael Walsh of Tenneco and Lodwrick Cook of ARCO were there despite the plan's original call for higher energy taxes. Walsh was particularly emphatic in his ringing endorsement for action: "Quit fooling around," he said, echoing Clinton's earlier comments.

In order to help improve the American economy, Clinton strategically built a relationship with the chairman of the Federal Reserve Board. Clinton was well aware that, not only was Alan Greenspan appointed by a Republican, but his board operated independently from the executive and legislative branches of the government. As such, the president had no executive power over the board except through persuasion. Clinton further realized that the nation's economic recovery did not have much of a chance for success unless long-term interest rates (over which Greenspan had control) held steady or went down.

Immediately after winning the 1992 election, Clinton invited Greenspan to visit him in Arkansas. He asked the chairman to review his pending deficit reduction plan and to help select and approve the guest list for a December economic summit in Little Rock. As adviser George Stephanopoulos remarked at the time: "Clinton wanted to meet with Chairman Greenspan to establish a sound working relationship, to talk about the state of the economy and to lay the groundwork for a productive relationship in the future."

This alliance quickly paid dividends when, barely a month into Clinton's first term, Greenspan endorsed the administration's overall economic plan. That approval helped enable its passage only ten weeks after Clinton took office. And when Greenspan pushed interest rates to record lows, the nation's economic recovery had left the launching pad.

In other shows of support, Alan Greenspan joined Apple Computer's former CEO, John Sculley, and sat next to the First Lady during Clinton's speech to a joint session of Congress regarding deficit reduction. In the 1994 State of the Union Address, it was Jack Smith of General Motors and Lane Kirkland of the AFL-CIO who flanked Hillary. And during Clinton's health care address, C. Everett Koop, former Surgeon General during the Reagan administration, was there.

The administration's early recruitment of Koop, Greenspan, and others was part of Clinton's strategy to court high-profile individuals to back his initiatives. For the North American Free Trade Agreement, Clinton enlisted the help of former Chrysler chairman Lee Iacocca; he also gained commitment from former presidents Ford, Carter, and Bush. And for his health care reform bill, Clinton managed to secure the endorsement of Kirkland, which was a notable achievement in itself when one takes into account that Lane Kirkland and his organization, the AFL-CIO, all but threatened to unseat Clinton from the presidency for pushing NAFTA.

TURNING ENEMIES INTO FRIENDS

After NAFTA's passage, Clinton actively sought a face-to-face meeting with Kirkland in hopes of reconciling their strained and adversarial relationship. For weeks, Kirkland put the president off. But jut ten days before Christmas, 1993, Clinton finally coaxed him into the Oval Office for a meeting, after which the two leaders mutually agreed to end their feud and work together on a comprehensive health care plan. This strategic move on Clinton's part, making up with organized labor, was crucial to the future success of his administration.

As he did with Lane Kirkland, Clinton made a habit of meeting with people who disagreed with him, and then trying to resolve issues of contention. In April 1994, for instance, when Native Americans criticized his health care plan, along with the administration's proposal to cut 13 percent out of the Indian Health Service's 1995 budget, Clinton invited to the White House leaders from all 547 tribes in the United States. It was the first time in American history that a president had done so. At the gathering, the Native American leaders were treated like heads of state, and Clinton saw to it that nearly every member of the cabinet and the vice president were present to honor them. He then dispatched

Bruce Babbitt and Janet Reno to meet with the leaders in Albuquerque the following month for a more in-depth working session.

It was also in April 1994 that Clinton ventured to Topeka, Kansas, where he pushed his health care plan. This was Senate Republican Leader Bob Dole's home territory, where Clinton was neither popular nor welcome by many people. But as *The New York Times* reported:

> Mr. Clinton got a warm greeting today even from those who disagree with him. After leaving the foundry here, he shook hands with a friendly crowd that included a group of anti-abortion protesters. "I voted against him," said Jeannie Kennedy, one of those who shook Mr. Clinton's hand. "But I'm thrilled to see him here. I don't agree with his policies, but I respect him because he's our President."

Whether patching things up with labor leaders or assuaging Native American leaders, it was all part of Clinton's ongoing efforts to make his enemies his friends. Even when things were going well, he worked hard at building relationships with supposed adversaries. Less than a month after taking office, the president phoned a Republican senator to thank him for voting in favor of the Family Leave Bill. Clinton tracked him down in Damascus, Syria. "It was unbelievable," said Senator James Jeffords of Vermont. "No one would believe that the President would call me in Damascus. No matter how long we've been around the Hill, there's nothing more exciting than a call from the President."

But personal phone calls and presidential appearances would not easily overcome the harsh negative feelings of the one group that seemed to distrust Clinton the most—the American military. Aside from the fact that the new president had no military experience, the core of the problem seemed to be a young Bill Clinton's 1969 letter to a University of Arkansas ROTC commander. In that letter, Clinton wrote that he and his friends found themselves "loving their country but loathing the military." He further exacerbated the problem when, during his first few months in office, he proposed allowing gays to serve in the armed forces.

When that political situation threatened to destroy his presidency before it began, Clinton quickly backtracked and agreed to a compromise that leaned more toward what the military wanted than what he was advocating. He also embarked on a crusade to win back their support and respect. In March of 1993, he visited the USS *Theodore Roosevelt*, anchored off the Virginia coast. In April, he dropped in unexpectedly at the Pentagon and mingled with soldiers. And amid shouts from some angry veterans, Clinton took part in 1993 Memorial Day ceremonies by delivering a moving speech at the Vietnam Veterans Memorial. He also nominated a retired admiral, Bobby Ray Inman, to replace Les Aspin as Secretary of Defense. And when Inman bowed out, Clinton offered the job to Senator Sam Nunn, the chairman of the Senate's Armed Services Committee who had spearheaded resistance to the proposal of allowing gays in the military. After Nunn declined, the job went to Aspin's second in command, William Perry.

Clinton also made continual attempts to extend a compromising hand to people who might tend to oppose him. He worked hard, for example, at building a personal relationship with General Colin L. Powell, then chairman of the Joint Chiefs of Staff. In response, Powell offered Clinton such good advice as dropping in at the Pentagon from time to time to get to know people. Powell also stood on the platform and introduced the president when he spoke at the Vietnam Memorial. Such support from Powell helped Clinton build much-needed credibility as the nation's new commander in chief of the armed forces.

In April 1993, *The Washington Post* analyzed Clinton's situation with the military by stating, in part:

> Behind the scenes, close bonds are forming between senior uniformed leaders and the Clinton national security team. General Colin L. Powell, chairman of the Joint Chiefs of Staff, tells associates privately that he is impressed with the new president and says Clinton's political skills will be critical to the nation's armed forces. In general, the officers who have the most contact with Clinton and his top echelons are likeliest to praise the new team.

Whether it was with members of the American military or members of the Senate and House, Clinton's ability to turn enemies into friends was an effective political strategy. It was similar to a move employed in many of the martial arts, especially Judo, for instance, where a person's adversary is drawn in so as to render him harmless. By standing in close, an opponent's ability to maneuver and inflict harm is limited because he can no longer extend his arms and legs to land effective blows. By reaching out to conservative Republicans, and moving in close, Clinton put them in the awkward position of being viewed as gridlock experts and partisan politicians if they were to oppose his reforms outright. Their other choice was to become involved with the president, and have a real chance to shape the new legislation. On some key issues like NAFTA, the Anti-Crime Bill, and GATT, that's exactly what happened.

ALLIANCE-BUILDING WITH WORLD LEADERS

As governor of Arkansas for twelve years, Bill Clinton's strong suit had been, necessarily, in domestic issues. He established successful relationships

with other governors, mayors, senators, congressmen, and business leaders. But in 1992, his weakness as a presidential candidate was clear: he
lacked experience in foreign affairs. This deficiency was readily seized
upon by George H. W. Bush and the Republican Party during the campaign. In the end, however, Clinton's lack of experience in the world arena
could not be overridden by Bush's failure to lead on domestic issues,
which was of paramount importance to voters in 1992. The American
people also sensed that the end of the cold war called for a new approach
to foreign relations and, frankly, that foreign affairs would be less vital.

From the moment he took office, Bill Clinton strove to overcome
his general lack of experience in foreign affairs. He immediately in-
structed aides to fill his schedule at the White House with meetings between himself and other world leaders. The reason for doing so, in part,
was aimed at creating new economic markets in order to pull the United
States out of the economic doldrums. During his first three months in
office, Clinton was visited by leaders of the nations of Japan, Germany,
Canada, Great Britain, France, Israel, Egypt, Italy, Spain, and dozens
more. The administration also invited United Nations Secretary General
Boutros Boutros-Ghali, NATO President Manfred Woerner, and Jacques
DeLors, head of the European Community, to meet with Clinton. In
April 1993 alone, no less than seventeen leaders paraded through the
White House. It was a striking display of stamina on Clinton's part when
one considers that also in April, the new president spent thirteen days
away from Washington visiting eleven cities in eight states, and also vis-
ited Canada for a few days, where he met with Russian President Boris
Yeltsin at the Vancouver Summit.

Clinton's seemingly frenetic pace in building new relationships
never really did subside. Over his first two years in office (January 1993
to January 1995), for instance, he averaged ten meetings per month in
pursuit of building international alliances. He met with leaders of some
of the world's religious organizations, including Desmond Tutu, the
Dalai Lama, and Pope John Paul II. He hosted the signing of the Israel-
PLO Peace Accord on the White House lawn (September 1993) and that
same month met with fifteen additional world leaders. Clinton also met
with heads of state in the Caribbean, Africa, and South America. And in
December 1994, he convened the Summit of the Americas in Miami,
with all thirty-four leaders in the Western Hemisphere (with the exception of Fidel Castro of Cuba) in attendance. "If we can continue to bring
down hemispheric trade barriers," said Clinton, in announcing the conference, "we can create a million new jobs by the turn of the century. At
the same time, the rising tide of democracy in this hemisphere helps
make us more secure."

Clinton also spent considerable time pursuing new markets in Asia. In November 1993, he convened the first APEC (Asia-Pacific Economic Cooperation) meeting in Seattle with leaders of the seventeen major economic nations of Asia and the Pacific Rim. At that conference, Clinton pressed hard for global economic reform that would lead to the creation of new markets and new jobs. In closing out the event, he summarized the meeting by saying, in part: "We have agreed that the Asia-Pacific region should be a united one, not divided. We have agreed that our economic policies should be open, not closed."

Earlier that same year, Clinton had attended the Group of Seven Summit in Tokyo. And while in Japan, he took the opportunity to focus on U.S.-Japanese relations. In a news conference with Prime Minister Kiichi Miyazawa, the president stated: "The focus of our relationship [is] strengthening the economic relationship between our two nations. We are moving away, I hope, from continued tension toward greater shared benefits." Even though Clinton courted Miyazawa, he also was politically astute enough to meet with members of the opposition party just a week before Japan's national election, which resulted in a new prime minister (Morihiro Hosokawa).

In addition to seeking out alliances in Asia and the Americas, Clinton's focus on Europe during his first two years in office was virtually unparalleled in presidential history. In January 1994 alone, he flew to Europe, attended a NATO conference, visited six countries, and met with twenty-six European leaders, including those of emerging Eastern European nations and the Baltic states. After that initial visit, Clinton flew back three more times. He was in Normandy for the fiftieth anniversary of the D-Day landing, in Budapest for the fifty-two-nation Conference on Security and Cooperation in Europe, and in Naples for his second G–7 Summit. During these trips to Europe, Clinton advocated economic reform and the opening of additional free markets. He also proposed a bold new initiative called the "Partnership for Peace," which allowed previously communist-dominated nations the opportunity to gain a toehold into the North Atlantic Treaty Organization. Clinton later explained his purpose:

The whole idea behind the Partnership for Peace was to develop a post–Cold War mechanism in which countries that shared the same commitments, in this case, the commitment to respect the territorial borders of their neighbors, a commitment to civilian control over the military, a commitment to joint planning and training and military exercises, that these countries could work together and could work toward eventual NATO membership if they wish it and if that is the direction that seems best for security in the post–Cold war world.

Part of Clinton's personal strategy for global security was to forge an especially close bond with the leader of the second most powerful nation on earth—President Boris Yeltsin of Russia. Clinton first met with Yeltsin at the Vancouver Summit in April 1993. They met again in Tokyo just three months later, when Yeltsin showed up as the "eighth man out" at the G–7 Conference. Immediately following that conference, they held individual talks. The two met a third time in Moscow when Yeltsin played host to Clinton after the NATO Summit in January 1994. And in September of that year, Clinton hosted Yeltsin for a few days at the White House.

Yeltsin seemed to take a shine to the younger Clinton, frequently referred to him as "my friend, Bill," and even coaxed him into playing the saxophone while in Russia. If theirs was a relationship built on bear hugs and talk, it quickly turned into one of action and support. Clinton, among other things, proposed and won approval for an economic aid package for Russia. He supported Yeltsin when force was used to quell an uprising in the Russian parliament. And together, they agreed to have a Russian cosmonaut travel aboard the U.S. space shuttle in February 1994—a largely ceremonial venture intended to signify a new partnership for cooperation in space.

But the ceremonial gestures quickly turned into substantive action as Clinton used his relationship with the Russian president to secure a number of concessions. Clinton persuaded Yeltsin, for instance, to withdraw all Russian troops from the Baltic nations in the summer of 1994. The deal was finally clinched at the G–7 Summit in Naples (July 1994) when Clinton handed Yeltsin a letter from President Lenart Meri of Estonia requesting a personal meeting. At that time, Bill pressed Boris into action by citing the continued presence of troops in the Baltics as a burden to the Russian-American relationship. That initiative ultimately resulted in the Bosnia-Croatia Peace Accord, which was signed at Wright-Patterson Air Force Base in Dayton, Ohio (November 21, 1995). Overall, President Clinton's personal relationship with Boris Yeltsin resulted in a friendly strategic alliance with Russia and, thereby, created a world safer from the threat of global nuclear catastrophe.

ALLIANCE-BUILDING PAYS OFF

Bill Clinton's strategy of building relationships and alliances began to pay off in the very first year of his administration. He managed to pull all the Democrats in Congress together to pass his initial budget proposal. Ways and Means Committee chairman Dan Rostenkowski muscled the program through the House while, at the same time, extolling the virtues of President Clinton. "We've got a President in the White House [who's] leading, and we've got a Congress that's following," said Rostenkowski. In the end, not a single member of the Republican Party voted in favor of the plan, which was passed by the slimmest of all possible margins in both the House and the Senate.

On the other hand, it was Clinton's strategic courting of the Republicans that paid off when the North American Free Trade Agreement passed in Congress. While many Democrats voted against the proposal, more than 100 Republicans lobbied furiously in favor of it. Passage of the trade agreement was in doubt in the House of Representatives until the final few days before the vote, but it passed by a comfortable margin in the Senate. Again, Clinton achieved passage of his legislation, only this time it was with support from the opposition party. Had he been left to rely on only members of his own party, NAFTA might never have been enacted into law.

In addition to political successes, Clinton was also able to utilize his relationships to mobilize help when natural disasters occurred. During summer flooding in the Midwest in 1993, for instance, the president was simply able to pick up the phone and call governors of the impacted states. Because he had forged personal relationships while governor of Arkansas and knew them all by their first names, Clinton was able to organize quickly, coordinate rapid federal, state, and local responses, and provide effective recovery efforts across the entire region.

Clinton's being on a first-name basis with many world leaders also paid off on a variety of fronts. For instance, just before U.S. planes bombed Iraq on June 26, 1993 (in response to an assassination attempt on former President George H. W. Bush), Clinton made personal telephone calls to more than a dozen leaders to tell them what was going to happen, and he received their unequivocal support. In April 1994, he fashioned support from NATO to aid the embattled cities of Sarajevo in Bosnia—and then later Goradze, Srebrenica, Ruzla, Zepa, and Bihac—through increased military air strikes against the Serbs. What's more, Boris Yeltsin endorsed Clinton's NATO plan, even though Russia had traditionally been an ally of the Serbs. Clinton also received support from the United Nations on Bosnian air strikes, sanctions against North Korea, withdrawal plans from Somalia, and an invasion of Haiti.

In the Haitian operation of September 1994, Clinton's initial meeting the prior year with Caribbean leaders helped pave the way for securing support from a multinational force. Less than one month before the United States sent in troops, the administration secured backing from all thirteen members of the Caribbean Community and Common Market. Furthermore, leaders from three of the four countries that

contributed armed troops to the operation (Jamaica, Trinidad and To-
bago, and Barbados) had met personally with Clinton at the White
House in August of 1993.

Perhaps the most dramatic and far-reaching results of Clinton's
early alliance-building came from his ability to create new markets for
American goods and services. The North American Free Trade Agreement opened new markets in Mexico and continued trade with Canada.
The Global Agreement on Tariffs and Trade (GATT) forged inroads to
the lucrative Western Europe markets, while Clinton's Partnership for
Peace did the same for those emerging in Eastern Europe. And Clinton's
early leadership with APEC set the stage for the organization's 1994 Indonesia meeting at which the members agreed to a "commitment to
achieve free and open trade and investment." That multi lateral commitment, in turn, resulted in a goal of establishing the world's largest free
trade market (including China) by the year 2020.

During the Clinton administration's eight years, there was a growing trend in business to create joint ventures and forge strategic alliances. As a global leader during those changing times, Bill Clinton
embraced that very trend. He understood that relationships and alliances are important in leadership because they both leverage resources
and lead to results. From experience, Clinton also understood that relationships and alliances are built on trust, and that trust has to be
earned—steadily, consistently, and over a period of time. "No public enterprise can flourish unless there's trust," said Bill Clinton.

> *"The future is for you to write and for you to make. But I come
> to say, from the bottom of my heart, the people of the United
> States and the President of the United States wish to be your
> partners and your friends."*
>
> Clinton, to the Russian people
> January 13, 1994

> *"Oh, I think it's like all other human relations, the more we're
> together the more natural it is. It got better as it went along—
> like life."*
>
> Clinton, to reporters about the APEC meeting in Seattle
> November 20, 1993

*By **November 1993,** planning was underway by people associated with American Spectator, a leading conservative magazine, to launch the "Arkansas Project." This clandestine enterprise became a four-year effort to dig up, make up, and publicize information designed to damage Bill Clinton and his presidency. Writers and some of their sources were paid for stories that alleged such things as drug-running, sex orgies, and murder. The Arkansas Project was reportedly subsidized by Richard Mellon Scaife, who, according to some estimates, had given American Spectator nearly $6 million since 1970. Several Scaife-owned organizations, including the Sarah Scaife Foundation and the Carthage Foundation, were believed to have contributed an estimated $2.4 million over the life of the Arkansas Project, which became a profitable business for right-wing publishers and radio talk show hosts. Once the project got underway, it not only gained a direct pipeline to Republican members of Congress, but the circulation of* American Spectator *jumped to more than 250,000.*

*In a story timed for release the week before Christmas, on **December 18, 1993**, the* American Spectator *published a 12,000-word article titled "His Cheatin' Heart." The story detailed the accusations of four Arkansas state troopers, who said they had witnessed Clinton engage in affairs with dozens of women in such varied places as hotel rooms, apartments, a school parking lot, a pickup truck, and the basement of the governor's residence. The troopers further charged that the governor had abused his power and misused state resources by ordering them to "act as intermediaries to arrange and conceal his extramarital encounters." Hillary Clinton was described in the article as a man-hating feminist who had an affair of her own with Vince Foster, and who ordered that visitors' logs confirming her husband's encounters be destroyed. The article also alleged that Bill Clinton had sexually harassed a woman named "Paula" in a room at the Excelsior Hotel in Little Rock.*

*On Sunday, **December 20, 1993**, copies of the* American Spectator *issue were sent out to national media contacts. The very next day,* The Los Angeles Times *released its own major article on the troopers' allegations, and CNN's prime time newscast led with the story and featured interviews with two of the officers. After that, the rest of the national media were relating the lurid allegations, as was the nationwide network of right-wing and Christian radio talk shows.*

*It was later revealed that the trooper story had been engineered by Cliff Jackson who, had related it to Peter Smith in mid-**August 1993**. When the officers expressed fear they'd lose their jobs by saying such things about Clinton, Smith reportedly guaranteed them employment outside Arkansas* *for seven years at $100,000 per year should they be fired. Although two of the troopers (Danny Ferguson and Ronnie Anderson) dropped out of the deal, the other two (Larry Patterson and Roger Perry) remained and were later paid approximately $6,700 each. Cliff Jackson also told the officers they might be able to make in excess of $2 million by writing a "tell-all" book.*

President Clinton termed the charges "outrageous" and, even though many of the facts and details were proven false, the damage was extensive. TrooperGate, as the pseudo-scandal came to be known, would bedevil Bill Clinton for the next seven years, in part because it led to "Paula" filing a sexual harassment lawsuit against him.

"I want the services you need to be delivered responsibly, efficiently and without delay. And most of all, I want you to be treated the way every American would ask to be treated if they were on the receiving end of this disaster—with compassion and effectiveness as neighbors and friends."

—Clinton, to flood victims of the Midwest
July 8, 1993

"Try to develop a genuine interest in the real problems and hopes of ordinary people, because in a democracy, the only way you can really keep going throughout all the ups and downs, is if you really care what happens to other people."

—Clinton, at a town meeting
January 14, 1994

CHAPTER FOUR

COMPASSION AND CARING

On March 1, 1993, Bill Clinton visited an adult learning center in New Brunswick, New Jersey, where the topic of discussion was the president's National Service Plan. When young Danyelle Marshall began weeping while telling of her struggle to better her life, Clinton immediately walked over to her, held her in his arms, and offered words of sympathy and encouragement.

During the height of flooding in the Midwest in the summer of 1993, Clinton was touring a water distribution site in Des Moines, Iowa, when twenty-four-year-old Christina Hein came up to him, shook his hand, and said, "Mr. President, we need help." At that moment, unable to control her emotions any longer, she burst into tears, saying, "I can't take it anymore." Clinton hugged her. "Hang in there," he said. "We're going to help you."

On August 3, 1994, Clinton welcomed to the South Lawn of the White House bus caravans that had been traveling cross-country in support of health care reform. One of the passengers, John Cox, of Athens, Texas, told the crowds that his wife, Jan, had died of stomach cancer while participating in the event. They had both thought it was the recurrence of an old ulcer, he said, and delayed seeing a doctor because his new job did not provide health insurance for her. Mr. Cox told the audience that his wife's dying wish was that he travel to Washington to "tell them that unless every person, no matter what color—unless they have affordable, guaranteed, universal health coverage—every other American is at risk."

Upon conclusion of these remarks, the audience erupted in applause and Clinton gave Mr. Cox a long sustained hug whereupon the man buried his face in the president's chest. *The New York Times* called it "an eye-dabbing scene evocative of a Frank Capra film." But Clinton's emotion appeared genuine. He wiped tears from his face, paused for a very long time at the podium, and then in a broken voice told the crowd that "Congress has to decide whether it's going to listen to the insurance companies, or to Jan Cox's last wish."

Were incidents like these merely a politician acting before the ever-present television cameras? Or were they indicative of something more, of a national leader who really cared about people? In studying Bill Clinton's record as President of the United States, it becomes clear that he was a leader who not only cared about people, but who also *acted* on that compassion.

INNATE CARING

When Clinton took office, he had the lowest net worth of any president in modern history. Growing up in a lower-middle-class family in Arkansas, he just never seemed to care much about acquiring wealth. What he did care about, however, was people—and that innate trait was reflected in his actions as a college student, as governor of Arkansas, and as President of the United States.

Clinton was at Georgetown University in April 1968 when riots erupted in Washington, D.C., in the aftermath of the murder of Dr. Martin Luther King, Jr. Unable to sit around and do nothing, he "put a big red cross on my car, and [drove] down to the burning areas of town to deliver supplies to people who had lost a lot of hope." As governor, Clinton championed such people-oriented issues as education reform, welfare reform, and job creation. And during the 1992 presidential campaign, Americans, in general, took note of an interesting response he gave to a representative of an AIDS action organization. When ACT UP member Bob Rafsky stated, "We're not dying of AIDS as much as we are dying of eleven years of government neglect," Clinton replied, "I feel your pain." The national media played up this response, and the candidate was roundly mocked and criticized as being insincere.

Clinton's caring nature, however, was genuine, and it manifested itself in a variety of ways after he was elected president. Noticing his tendency to physically embrace people, for instance, newspapers around the country labeled him the "huggingest President in U.S. history." Television cameras recorded Clinton and Boris Yeltsin wrapped in bear hugs at the Vancouver Summit; Clinton walking on the South Lawn of the White House with his arm draped over Les Aspin; and with his arm around Pope John Paul II when they met in Denver in August 1993. And of Clinton's trip to Europe in January 1994, *Newsweek* observed that "wherever you looked, the presidential arm was draped over someone's shoulder—a teenager asking him about the famous meeting with JFK [or] a politician lobbying for NATO membership."

Clinton reached out to colleagues or acquaintances when they were ill. He placed a phone call to Michael Walsh when it was disclosed that the CEO was suffering from brain cancer. He also called NBC White House correspondent Andrea Mitchell when she was in the hospital recuperating from surgery. "Don't hurry back," the president told her. "I'll still be screwing up when you get back."

Clinton never sidestepped an occasion of speaking at a funeral or memorial service, whether it was for Richard Nixon, Jacqueline Kennedy Onassis, fallen sailors at Norfolk, Virginia, the casualties of TWA Flight 800 in Jamaica, New York, or the victims of the terrorist bombing in Oklahoma City. One of Clinton's most moving displays of affection came in the wake of the suicide of his childhood friend and White House lawyer, Vince Foster. Immediately after being told of Foster's death, Clinton cut short an interview on *Larry King Live* at the White House. "The President ordered an unmarked van to take him to Georgetown to visit Foster's wife, Lisa," wrote *Newsweek*. "He stayed there for several hours, then returned for a vigil with friends at the White House, where he said 'we did a lot of crying and a little bit of laughing' remembering the man Clinton called his Rock of Gibraltar."

The day after Foster's death, the president called a meeting and offered some consoling words for the White House staff:

> For all of you who are younger, you will find the longer you live, the more you mark the shape of your life by the people you have truly loved who, for whatever reason, aren't around anymore. Remember that we're all people, and that we have to pay maybe a little more attention to our

friends and our families and our coworkers. And try to remember that work can never be the only thing in life.

Last night, when I was told what happened, I just kept thinking in my mind of when we were so young sitting on the ground in the backyard, throwing knives into the ground and seeing if we were adroit enough to make them stick.

At Foster's funeral, Clinton poignantly remarked: "The knives didn't stick, but the friendship did."

TURNING COMPASSION INTO ACTION

Clinton's comment to Andrea Mitchell about "screwing up" was more than just a kind and witty remark to the recuperating veteran newscaster. It was telling. Early in his presidency, Clinton had made many mistakes upon which the press quickly leaped. Whether it was a failed nomination, charges of extramarital affairs, the seemingly unending saga of Whitewater, or policies in Haiti, North Korea, or Bosnia—the public seemed to get a constant dose of Clinton's "screw-ups." Curiously, though, after a tumultuous fifteen months in office, a May 1994 *Time* poll revealed that 69 percent of the American people characterized President Clinton's handling of foreign policy as "compassionate." That percentage topped all other one-word characterizations in the survey, such as: intelligent, inconsistent, indecisive, confused, effective, and bold. And there was strong evidence to indicate that the public felt the same way regarding his handling of domestic policy.

What accounted for this odd poll? Part of the answer is clear. Many Americans had heard excerpts of his passionate speech in Memphis where he expressed concern for children in inner-city neighborhoods and said that he "could no longer justify going to bed at night thinking about these children killing other children—thinking about these kids planning their own funerals—and not doing something about it." Americans had seen pictures of him in newspapers and magazines hugging others. They had both seen and heard him on national television telling emotional stories about people having troubles with health care, economic misfortune, and crime. As such, Clinton's compassionate and caring nature became imbedded in the American stream of consciousness.

By occupying the office of President of the United States, Clinton was able to transform his concern for others into concrete action. He rapidly deployed himself to the area of natural disasters, such as flooding in the Midwest in the summer of 1993 and to flood-ravaged Grand Forks, North Dakota, in the spring of 1997. Clinton even visited the site of Hurricane Andrew in 1992 as a presidential candidate, and was surprised to hear complaints from both Florida officials and residents about the response of the Federal Emergency Management Agency (FEMA). Realizing that Republicans viewed the head of FEMA as a plum position for political supporters without experience in managing emergencies, Clinton made a mental note not to make that same mistake.

When devastating fires swept through Southern California in the fall of 1993, Clinton spoke by telephone with Governor Pete Wilson, dispatched to the scene Secretaries of the Interior (Bruce Babbitt) and Agriculture (Mike Espy), and sent twenty U.S. Forest Service air tankers along with many additional federal firefighters. In the aftermath of the Northridge earthquake in January 1994, however, the president did not wait for Governor Wilson to make a formal request for federal assistance. He immediately sent Federico Pena and Henry Cisneros (Secretaries of Transportation and HUD) to the site to coordinate efforts with James Lee Witt, director of FEMA. Pena at once made $45 million available for emergency assistance; and President Clinton asked Congress to appropriate more than $6 billion in federal aid. He also moved swiftly to involve the Department of Agriculture in setting up food kitchens and mobilized the Department of Defense and the U.S. Forest Service for manpower assistance in helping to clear away debris. And he persuaded the Small Business Administration to supply loans of up to $120,000 for people who had lost their businesses. A few days after the earthquake struck, Clinton was standing on the ground over its epicenter. "When I was out at the place where the highway broke down," Clinton said at the time, "I asked how long it would take to fix it. The highway engineer said, 'Oh, probably about a year.' And I said: 'Well, what do you have to do to fix it in less time?'" The Santa Monica Freeway opened less than six months later.

Much of the legislation pushed by Clinton was, in some way, linked to caring for citizens. One of his first official acts was to sign the Family and Medical Leave Act, which allowed people to take leave from work to spend time with a sick child without fear of losing their jobs. Prior to 1993, this bill was passed in both the House and Senate, but was vetoed by President George H. W. Bush. Passage of the Brady Bill (1994), requiring a background check for handgun purchasers, eventually prevented over 600,000 criminals from purchasing handguns, and helped lower the crime rate involving guns by forty percent. Also in 1994, Clinton pushed through a Middle Class Bill of Rights, which included a $500 child tax credit for families with incomes of $75,000 or less, tax deductibility for college tuition, and expanded IRAs.

Clinton, moreover, introduced a National Service Plan that included training and tuition aid for young Americans seeking college educations. He signed a bill that provided compensation for veterans of the Persian Gulf War who became ill as a result of the conflict. And he proposed a $20 billion plan to help industries hit hard by defense cutbacks and released more than $500 million to directly aid displaced workers. "We will not leave the men and women who helped to win the Cold War out in the cold," Clinton declared aboard an aircraft carrier in the Atlantic.

It wasn't only displaced workers in the defense industry that President Clinton tried to help. He increased the minimum wage, signed a $5.8 billion bill extending jobless benefits to all long-term unemployed workers, and, in a largely symbolic gesture, allowed for the reapplication of air traffic controllers fired by President Reagan in 1981. Through the Labor Department, the Clinton administration also called for a complete overhaul of the welfare and unemployment compensation systems. Secretary of Labor Robert Reich constantly advocated creating a new process that would include fresh career training and job searches for all displaced workers in the American economy. Welfare reform included a proposal to allow unwed fathers as well as mothers into the system, and then to provide job training so that they could better care for their children. During his campaign to pass NAFTA, Clinton remarked: "The profound sense of alienation so many people feel in our country has got to be healed, because we've got to do a lot of things to get America into the 21st century, to restore a sense of opportunity, to be able to create jobs and to be able to support incomes again that justify the hard work people do."

Four months after NAFTA passed Congress, in February 1994, Clinton enacted additional policies that went right to the heart of helping people. In a shift from past government policies, his administration directed every federal agency to guarantee protection against environmental hazards and eliminate their impact on minorities and poor families. It proposed a ban on smoking in all public buildings, and increases in spending for drug treatment and for programs that prevented drug abuse. And the administration's program for ending homelessness, which concentrated on health care, federally subsidized housing, and tax credits, was the first concrete action to aid the homeless in more than a dozen years.

In addition, Clinton's push for health care reform represented a major focus on giving people a lift out of poverty. Even though it failed, Clinton would later propose other health initiatives, such as the 1996 Ryan White CARE Act (which funded medical support services for HIV and AID victims) and the 1998 Patient's Bill of Rights. He also issued executive orders overturning restrictions on international family planning grants, allocating federal funds to counsel low-income women on abortion options, advocating stem cell research, and allowing the importation of the new birth control pill, RU–486.

In his second term, Clinton pursued a more global agenda that included support for the Kyoto global warming agreement, which concentrated on a long-term reduction of greenhouse gases. He also introduced a new, particularly compassionate global concept called "The Third Way," which stressed better education and health care, the alleviation of poverty, a more equal distribution of digital technology, environmental protection, and human rights. Nations involved in the program included members of the European Union, Sweden, The Netherlands, Argentina, Canada, Greece, New Zealand, Portugal, Chile, and South Africa.

CLINTON AND KIDS

While president, Bill Clinton demonstrated an unusually caring and open attitude toward children. When he was around young people, which was often, it was obvious that he enjoyed them. He sought out kids, walked into their schools, and provided specialized forums so they could ask questions. He held many "Kids Town Meetings" around the country, one of which (in April 1994) included a young girl, Zlata Filipovic, from Bosnia who had published her diary of life during the war there.

It's not surprising, then, that much of the president's proposed legislation dealt with the future of young people. Clinton's 1994 budget package focused on providing benefits for the youth of America. After the bill passed in August 1993, the president went to Charleston, West Virginia, and spoke of the program:

> I was attacked during the course of this budget debate because there was some new spending in this program. And I plead guilty. We spend some more money on the Head Start program to get poor children off to a good start in school . . . to immunize our children against serious childhood diseases . . . [for] apprenticeship training programs for young people who don't go on to college but need a skill so they can earn a decent income . . . [to make it] much easier for young people from working families to finance a college education through lower interest college loans, better repayment terms, etc.

Through his health care reform package, Clinton advocated full dental care for the young and free vaccinations for poor and uninsured children. Upon signing a proclamation for National Infant Immunization Week, he quoted from James Agee's book about the Great Depression, *Let Us Now Praise Famous Men:* "'In every child who is born,' [wrote Agee], 'no matter what circumstances and no matter what parents, the potentiality of the whole human race is born again.' That is what we are here about today," concluded the president. "And we are bound to do a better job."

Clinton also proposed a variety of legislation related directly to young people, including Megan's Law, the Child Support Performance and Incentive Act (a national program to fight teenage pregnancy), and a new public schools lunch program that improved nutrition for millions of children by calling for more fruits and vegetables and for appropriate limits on cholesterol, fat, and sodium.

On Thursday, June 24, 1993, Clinton wanted to visit a Washington, D.C. public swimming pool where several young children had been wounded by a gunman. The Secret Service, however, talked him out of it. But they couldn't talk him out of making a phone call from Air Force One to a young boy to thank him for the $1,000 check he mailed in to help pay off the national debt. Nor would they prevent him from writing a private letter to University of Michigan basketball star Chris Webber, who made a last-second blunder that cost his team the 1993 NCAA national championship. Clinton wrote that "what matters most is the intensity, integrity, and courage you bring to the effort."

"As we look into the eyes of our children filled with life and laughter and promise," said Clinton on Christmas Day, 1993, "we're reminded of our most sacred obligation: nurturing the next generation." Clinton may have had that thought in mind when, barely three weeks later, he engaged in a dialogue at a Russian town hall meeting. His extemporaneous response to a question posed by a young boy revealed the president's unusually compassionate nature.

"I'm thirteen years old," said Aleksandr Fyodorov. "I saw your picture shaking hands with President Kennedy, and I'd like to ask you how old you were when you got your idea to become a President of the United States."

Almost instinctively, Clinton replied: "Come here. Come up here. Come shake hands with me, and maybe you'll be President of Russia some day."

COMPASSION AND CARING IN LEADERSHIP

Sometimes, a leader who cares too much can experience difficulty in making tough decisions. Bill Clinton may have suffered from this particular pitfall. In December 1993, he was uneasy in moving Les Aspin out of his position as Secretary of Defense, largely because he didn't want to hurt Aspin's feelings. And in October 1994, when it came time to remove Agriculture Secretary Mike Espy for ethics violations, the president asked his Chief of Staff Leon Panetta to perform the difficult task. Also, Clinton sometimes appeared indecisive when it came to foreign affairs with the potential for combat. For instance, in the first planed phase of restoring democracy to Haiti in October 1993, he ordered the return of a U.S. ship when it was met with light armed resistance at the dock. He backpedaled several times on the issue of Bosnian air strikes to aid besieged cities under attack by the Serbs. And he refused to send American troops to Bosnia or Haiti unless it was part of a larger United Nations force. In these instances, it may have been, at least in part, that Clinton's compassion overrode his desire to act forcibly and utilize the full extent of his power as Commander-in-Chief of the Armed Forces.

Overwhelmingly, a leader's capacity to care about others should far outweigh any negative consequences it may cause. Bill Clinton's compassion actually kept him going when times got tough. Because he cared so much about people, it gave him a reason to get up when he was knocked down. It gave him a purpose, a mission. In short, Clinton's compassion motivated him to achieve. "Try to develop a genuine interest in the real problems and hopes of ordinary people," he advised at a town hall meeting, "because in a democracy, the only way you can really keep going throughout all the ups and downs, is if you really care what happens to other people."

When Clinton demonstrated that he wanted to help people; when he hugged someone, when he said or implied, "I feel your pain," he was *involving* himself with others. This is not only a recognized character trait of strong leadership, it is more often associated with women than men.

Author Deborah Tannen discussed this subject at length. "Offering sympathy and offering to do something," she wrote, "can be different ways of achieving the same goal: involvement with others." Of the difference between women and men, she went on to note: "Having information, expertise, or skill at manipulating objects is not the primary measure of power for most women. Rather, they feel their power enhanced if they can be of help. Even more, if they are focusing on connection rather than independence and self reliance, they feel stronger when the community is strong."

It is quite possible, then, even probable, that President Clinton felt stronger when he was attempting to push through health care reform than he did when he was ordering jets to bomb Baghdad. It may also explain why, in a male-dominated political system, his "I feel your pain" message was perceived as a weakness.

∝❧

From the time he was a little boy, Clinton had been very affectionate. There's a photograph in his family album that shows a group of youngsters in Miss Mary's 1951 kindergarten class in Hope, Arkansas. In it, one can view five-year-old Billy Blythe (Clinton) with his left arm affectionately draped over the shoulder of his little buddy, George Wright, and his right arm around pal Joe Purvis. He's the only one in the picture with an arm wrapped around anybody. It's not something a boy in kindergarten would do unless it came naturally.

More than forty years later, President Bill Clinton was still hugging people and encouraging others to do the same. During the Israel-PLO peace accord ceremony on September 13, 1993, *The New York Times* reported that "moments after the documents were signed, President Clinton took Yasir Arafat in his left arm and Yitzhak Rabin in his right arm and gently coaxed them together for their historic moment."

As Clinton later explained this gesture: "It sort of came naturally. I wanted to be supportive of them and of the importance of going through with their handshake, which they had agreed to do in advance, but which I think both of them thought would be a difficult moment. I thought I was making it easier for them."

> "All my life, I have seen people mistreated, disadvantaged—
> and then I have seen them inflamed with anger and enraged
> and taken advantage of. So I'm telling you, forget about us. We
> owe it to them to let them know we heard, and we're fighting
> for them—and we're going to deliver."
>
> —Clinton, to the Democratic Leadership Council
> December 6, 1994

> "Compassion is part of my philosophy."
>
> —Clinton, at a town meeting In Minneapolis, Minnesota
> April 8, 1994

On *January 6, 1994*, Bill Clinton's mother died after a long battle with cancer. Congressional Republicans, however, did not respectfully pause in their onslaught of criticism against the president. Senators Lauch Faircloth and Bob Dole led a chorus for the establishment of an independent counsel to investigate Whitewater and other charges. Editors from The New York Times *and* The Washington Post *echoed the call. Weary of all the negativism, and confident that he had done nothing wrong, President Clinton asked Attorney General Janet Reno to appoint a special prosecutor. He hoped to bring the issue to "a speedy and credible resolution," he said. Announcing her decision on *January 20, 1994*, Janet Reno selected Robert B. Fiske, a U.S. attorney from the Southern District of New York. The sixty-three-year-old Fiske was also a member of the Republican Party.*

As the new year rolled in, the media frenzy over Whitewater and TrooperGate escalated. In an interview with NBC News in Ukraine, where Clinton was building relationships with leaders of Central Europe, the president was asked only about Whitewater. Back in the States, editors of The New York Times, *sensing a potential Watergate-type scandal, called their investigative reporters together to organize and deploy. Six weeks later, the newspaper also held a reception for the Washington, D.C. press corps to discuss the merits of an all-out inquiry into Whitewater. By* **February 11, 1994**, *a crescendo of sorts was reached when Cliff Jackson held a press conference at the Omni Hotel in Washington, site of the annual conference of the Conservative Political Action Committee. Present to further discuss their accusations against the president were Arkansas state troopers, Larry Patterson and Roger Perry. And making her public debut was Paula Jones, the woman mentioned in the* American Spectator *article who had accused Clinton of sexual harassment.*

Specifically, Jones's allegation revolved around a state-sponsored conference held at Little Rock's Excelsior Hotel on May 8, 1991. As a clerical employee of the Arkansas Industrial Development Commission, she had been asked to be part of the staff for the conference. While there, according to Jones, she was approached by Arkansas trooper Danny Ferguson who told her that the governor wanted to see her in his hotel room. After riding the elevator upstairs with Ferguson, Jones met privately with Clinton, who, she claimed, subsequently made several "unsolicited and unwanted sexual advances," including exposing himself and propositioning her. After remaining silent for several years, she had finally decided to come forward with her story.

Through a spokesman, President Clinton vehemently denied the allegation. It was later revealed that Jones's sister and brother-in-law had

*stated that she was "suing over a stupid lie," and was in it for "the money."
With time, Jones would provide several versions of her encounter with the
Clintons, and details would change. Her work supervisor also later stated
that Jones had told him shortly after returning from the conference that she
"had met Governor Clinton and had shaken his hand."*

PART II

COMMUNICATION

"Some look at the evidence and believe that if their conclusions are logical, others should accept them automatically. That's not good enough. You have to communicate—constantly, emotionally, and directly."

—Bill Clinton,
November 1992

"We've worked out accommodations so that I can at least run every day. I try to get out and see the people when I can. If you don't spend some time with just ordinary people who tell you what they think, hey, you almost forget how to hear and how to listen and how to speak and the way that most people live."

—Clinton, in an interview with Larry King
July 20, 1993

"I walked the crowds today. I saw workers who hadn't slept, countless numbers of people who had lost their homes, children asking us to help get their schools fixed. [The damage is] amazing. There's a difference in seeing this, in actually standing here and looking at it."

—Clinton, viewing damage after an earthquake
struck parts of Los Angeles, California
January 18, 1994

CHAPTER FIVE

RUNNING WITH THE PEOPLE

Willard Scott, the colorful weatherman of NBC's *Today Show*, was broadcasting live from Washington's tidal basin one spring morning in 1993 when he noticed a familiar figure in the distance: A big man wearing a baseball cap, dressed in a sweatshirt and gym shorts that exposed large, pale legs. He was running with a group of men who were trailing slightly behind but spread out in equal distances around him. It was Bill Clinton out on his regular morning jog.

Willard waved, caught the president's attention, and motioned him over. Without hesitation, Clinton obliged by shifting his running route toward the tidal basin and Scott's eager television camera crew. The beaming weatherman then proceeded to have an amiable chat with a sweating, smiling, and cordial President of the United States.

While nothing of national importance was said during the interview, it was a memorable moment because it symbolized the arrival in Washington of a new president with a new style. Here was Bill Clinton, casual as they come, open and at ease on live television in what some would say was a remarkably vulnerable moment. It was a definite contrast to more recent presidents who had been careful to stage most appearances and script every remark. Even more striking was the realization that this was not an unusual or one-time happening for the new leader. He was, in fact, one of the few American presidents to schedule a daily event designed specifically to interact outside of the White House with average people. There were not many things that he would allow to interfere with his regular morning jogs.

BILL CLINTON'S PERSONAL SIGNATURE

By the end of his first two years in office, Clinton's running routine was quite familiar to the American public. In May 1993, he traveled to San Diego to conduct a town hall meeting on his economic plan. The next day local and national newspapers carried pictures on their front pages of the president jogging with a group of Navy servicemen on a Pacific beach. In September, Clinton journeyed to Houston to promote his reinventing government initiative. The next morning, there was a picture on the front page of *The Houston Post* showing the president running with a group of children. The same scene was replayed wherever he went domestically—whether it was in Central Park on a visit to New York, in a suburb of Cleveland, or in Minneapolis while campaigning for Democratic candidates prior to the 1994 midterm elections.

And Clinton did not let travels abroad interfere with his routine. He jogged on the streets of Vancouver the morning of his summit with Russian President Boris Yeltsin; he ran in South Korea with President Kim Young Sam; and he took an early morning jog in Prague prior to meeting with Vaclav Havel.

Clinton, in fact, spent so much time jogging that he frequently made announcements or learned of new world events during his runs. For example, while still dressed in sweats, the president confirmed in Houston that both Yitzhak Rabin and Yasir Arafat would be present for the signing of the Middle East peace accord in September 1993. And it was immediately after running three miles in San Francisco that he heard for the first time of the tragic deaths of eighteen servicemen in Somalia.

Bill Clinton said more than once that running early each morning helped him to "shake awake." It also provided much needed aerobic exercise to relieve stress and keep him in good physical condition, which was necessary to handle the pressures and demands of the job. Clinton used several different jogging routes in and around Washington. He took a three-mile path around the public golf course at Haines Point, and also used the oval route on the grounds of the National Defense University at Fort McNair. But the president's favorite jog, by far, was to run out the Southwest Gate of the White House, up to the Lincoln Memorial, over to the Capitol building, and back down the other side of Pennsylvania Avenue to the White House. It was on this route that NBC's Willard Scott spotted him.

In the early 1990s, jogging with President Clinton became something of a political opportunity for a picture with the nation's chief executive doing something other than posing in a business suit and tie. But Clinton also used jogging as a method for building personal relationships. He spent quite a bit of time running with Nebraska Senator Bob Kerrey, who later cast the final needed vote in the Senate to pass the administration's economic program. The president also ran with Oklahoma Congressmen Dave McCurdy and Mike Synar, both of whom came to the president's rescue in the House vote on the budget plan.

Unfortunately, such familiarity with the president came back to haunt some members of Congress who subsequently lost their 1994 midterm reelections, because conservative voters did not approve of their closeness to Clinton. While Kerrey survived, McCurdy lost a bid for the Senate and Synar was voted out of office in a primary election. Many people, however, kept right on running with Clinton even after Republicans took control of both the House and Senate.

In addition to congressmen and senators, the president jogged with average citizens, celebrities, businessmen, and children. His pace was usually slow enough so that he could still carry on a conversation or, more importantly, just listen to what others had to say. Going out to the field and running with the people became a signature of Bill Clinton's personal leadership style. "I met a lot of interesting people on those runs," Clinton wrote in his memoirs. "They were a way to keep in touch with the world beyond the White House."

GETTING OUT OF THE IVORY TOWER

Bill Clinton often made it clear that he did not like being cooped up in the White House. "It's a very isolating place," he said on NBC's *Meet the Press.* "I don't know whether it's the finest public housing in America or the crown jewel of the prison system. It's almost impossible to avoid getting out of touch."

In order to "stay in touch," Clinton tried to maintain as little distance as possible between himself and the people. He made it a point to get out of the White House frequently to spend time with members of his administration and other American citizens. "I get very homesick for the ability to communicate directly with people," he said just prior to his thirtieth high school reunion in the summer of 1994. This was a fact that did not escape the national media. *The New York Times* labeled him "the President who cannot get enough human contact."

To the delight of the people, and to the chagrin of the Secret Service agents guarding him, Clinton frequently plunged into crowds on the spur of the moment. He went out of his way to cross a street and shake hands with supporters cheering behind barricades in New York City after a speech at Cooper Union. And he did the same thing both in Moscow and in the streets of Tokyo, where throngs of children had come out to see him.

At times, it seemed as if any fear he might have had of being assaulted was overwhelmed by his inbred desire to interact with others. George Wright, Jr. of Hope, Arkansas, a personal friend of Clinton's, once referred to the kindergarten picture in which the future president had his arms draped over two of his classmates. "He *still* has that sensitivity," said Wright. "It is what made him, even at five years old, a national politician."

When governor of Arkansas, Clinton once remarked that he owed people "respect and some of my time. If I can solve their problem without creating a greater problem for others," he said, "it's my duty to try." This natural desire to care for people fed Clinton's perpetual circulation among the masses, which, in turn, helped make him a strong leader. Many people in Arkansas realized a special bond with Bill Clinton that they had never before felt with other politicians. One of the reasons, according to former associate Bobby Roberts, was that Clinton loved to drop in at out-of-the-way places. "He would stop at a remote crossroads store and visit at length with whomever he found," said Roberts. "Every three or four days, his travel aides tired out and were recycled back to Little Rock. But Clinton drew strength from the crowds and continued the relentless schedule seven days a week."

Clinton's personal presence also helped him repair faltering relationships, such as those with the U.S. military early in his first term as president. In April 1993, Clinton ventured across the Potomac River and dropped in unexpectedly at the Pentagon. He walked the halls, shook hands with military personnel, and mingled with crowds that had gathered. And more than once, Clinton boarded Naval vessels such as the USS *Theodore Roosevelt* and the USS *Eisenhower,* anchored off the coast of Virginia. Such visits were praised in the press as acts of courage for venturing into "enemy territory." More appropriately, however, they were acts of communication—ways for the president to build some alliances and bonds; a way for him to get to know people better.

In July 1993, though, Clinton actually did venture perilously close to "enemy territory" when he walked out on the "Bridge of No Return" in the demilitarized zone separating North and South Korea. He stopped only a few yards short of the border, where his every move was watched by North Korean sentries. While in the vicinity, Clinton made it a point to address the American troops at Camp Casey. He praised them for serving on "the frontier of freedom." He spoke to the soldiers informally, shaking hands, slapping backs, giving high fives, and listening to their concerns and ideas. The servicemen enjoyed the president immensely and even coaxed Clinton to play a tune on a saxophone borrowed from a member of the Army band.

During times when disaster struck the nation, rather than simply sitting in the White House and issuing orders, President Clinton responded by going on site. In the summer of 1993, he made four trips to the Midwest to view the ravaging effects of flooding, and immediately declared Iowa, Missouri, Illinois, Minnesota, and Wisconsin federal disaster areas. In an interview with WHO Radio in Des Moines, Clinton described what he had seen:

> I spent about a half an hour flying over the [flooded] area, and then I stopped in a supermarket lot where water was being distributed. I talked to people who had lost everything—they've lost their businesses, [they've] had their farms flooded out. It was a very moving thing. I talked to parents who were worried about their children and whether they could get adequate water and how they were going to do that safely. Some of them had been able to send their children to relatives in other communities; others had not.

In September 1993, one year after Hurricane Andrew came ashore, Clinton, Henry Cisneros, and Robert Reich ventured down to Homestead, Florida to follow up on the government's efforts to help people get back on their feet. They toured areas that had been hit the hardest, including abandoned apartment buildings and homes without roofs. In November, the president traveled to Pasadena and met with people who had been displaced by devastating California brush fires. In January 1994, he was in Los Angeles walking along the cracked freeways damaged by the most expensive natural disaster in United States history (up to that time), the Northridge earthquake. And one year later, in January 1995, Clinton flew back to view the government's rebuilding progress. During that trip, he also took the opportunity to tour Placer County,

California, and view effects of the state's disastrous flooding along the Sacramento River.

Everywhere he traveled, all during his two terms in office, Bill Clinton refused to maintain an arrogant, above-the-crowd demeanor. During his January 1994 trip to Europe, he stopped in a small café in Brussels to have a cup of Belgian coffee; he drank a beer at a jazz club in Prague and played saxophone while Vaclav Havel banged spoons on the table; and he waded into a large crowd in Red Square, put on a traditional Russian hat, and bought a loaf of bread from a Moscow bakery.

In his domestic travels, Clinton visited a jail in Ohio, attended the NCAA basketball tournament in Dallas and Charlotte, and signed a bill to improve America's schools at a high school in Massachusetts because, as he said, its diversity "really looks like America." Once he even ordered his motorcade to pull over at a Shell gas station just so he could shake hands with the people inside.

With all these excursions, one could easily get the impression that Bill Clinton was rarely ever *in* the White House, that he was chaotically gallivanting around the countryside. However, careful tracking of his travels reveals that Clinton strategically devoted, on average, at least one-third of his time toward getting out of the White House and mingling with the people. During his first year in office, for instance, Clinton made 118 trips and spent a full 35 percent of his time out of Washington, D.C., an average of 10.67 days per month. And there was no letting up during the second year of his presidency, when he began delivering weekly radio addresses from places like Los Angeles, Anchorage, and Kuwait. As a matter of fact, Clinton actually stepped up his pace of travel in 1994 as he visited *more* nations and spent 37 percent of his time out of Washington, D.C. (an average of eleven days per month). Halfway through his first term, Clinton had visited twenty-five countries, forty of the fifty states, and a staggering 170 cities.

Bill Clinton's travels during his two terms in office were precedent-setting. It is not an exaggeration to state that he spent more time *out* of the White House than any other president in American history. Moreover, he was extraordinarily diverse in his travels: from shooting baskets with Hispanic children on a school playground in East Los Angeles to a summit in Indonesia with leaders from eighteen Asian nations; from duck hunting on Maryland's eastern shore to visiting American troops in Kuwait; from a casual town hall meeting at the Future Diner in Queens, New York, to a formal peace signing ceremony on the border between Israel and Jordan. Clinton's travels out of the White House set a new standard of public outreach for the modern American presidency.

OPEN DOOR—REVOLVING DOOR

While Bill Clinton believed strongly that the best way for a leader to assess a situation was to be out in the field to personally collect information, there were times when he simply couldn't find the time to get away. So he let people come to him.

Clinton's accessibility and fondness for mixing with others was obvious on the very first full day of his presidency. On January 21, 1993, he opened up the White House to the public. All day there was a steady stream of visitors (some 3,000 in all) who shook hands with the new president and Mrs. Clinton and the new vice president and Mrs. Gore. Afterward, many people wandered around the grounds of the executive mansion taking pictures and peering in windows.

During his eight years as president, Clinton tried hard to maintain an openness at the White House that extended far beyond the normal presidential routine of meetings, receptions, and visiting delegations. Frequently, there were so many people around that the Secret Service became concerned about security. As a matter of fact, they ran out of security passes on September 21, 1993, when several hundred college students came to the White House to join the president for the signing of his National Service Program. Later that same day, Clinton hosted 250 national radio talk show hosts, 60 of whom set up tables to broadcast live from the South Lawn. All day long, citizens and reporters lined the walls of the White House and filled conference rooms. When someone asked Clinton how things were going, he quipped: "Place is buzzing like a beehive."

Bill Clinton was invigorated by meeting with people. But early in his first term, there were so many people visiting the White House that he began having problems getting things done. And it became a leadership paradox for the new president. A balance had to be struck between his innate desire to interact with people and his compelling desire to achieve results. So Clinton bit the bullet and became more selective on whom he met with during normal office hours.

IMPORTANCE OF INTERACTING WITH PEOPLE

Achieving results is directly proportional to a leader's willingness and ability to interact with people. The more frequent the human contact, the more results achieved. It's that simple. In general, there are four main reasons why Bill Clinton got out and ran with the people so often.

1. Obtain Key Information
    Clinton personally sought and required access to reliable, up-to-date information unfiltered by newspapers, television, or

polls. "You've got to go find the facts for yourself," he said, "and many of the good ones come from outside your inner circle." Such broad human contact gives leaders the firsthand knowledge needed to make informed, accurate, and timely decisions without having to rely solely on the word of others.

2.   Understand What People Think and Feel
On April 6, 1994, in his weekly presidential radio address, Clinton noted that he had previously visited the Rockwell Gardens in Chicago's housing projects. "Dozens of children rushed out to greet me, eager to have someone to tell their stories to," he said. "They talked of gunshots and drug dealers, of late-night knocks at their doors and hallways where they dared not to stray."

3.   Keep People Informed
Clinton was adept at letting people know exactly what he was up to. It was no accident, for instance, that many average Americans knew details of NAFTA, or of the administration's budget proposals, or of proposed changes in Welfare and Education programs. In many instances over the course of Clinton's presidency, the American people got this kind of information directly from their president. "This past week," Clinton said in April 1994, "I traveled across our country because I wanted the American people to hear directly from me about the progress we're making on their behalf and what we still have to do."

4.   Obtain Feedback
Clinton wanted to keep on track with the desires of the people he represented. So he used his forays out of the White House to ask people what they thought about how he was doing, about his new initiatives, and about their own personal needs. In January 1994, a reporter asked Clinton why he was waiting a few days before visiting the site of California's Northridge earthquake. "[I'd] basically like to take a firsthand view of things, but I don't want to be in the way," he responded. "When I go, I want to be a constructive presence. I'm going to get some feedback from the folks on the ground there."

Human contact is the most important form of communication for a leader, because it is the chief form of communication used when developing personal relationships and strengthening emotional bonds. And Bill Clinton was clearly great at that. Rather than being distant and disengaged, he was open and approachable. Clinton looked people in the eye, easily joined in one-on-one personal conversations, and enjoyed interacting in a crowd. This was a significant contrast from his immediate predecessors. Nixon, Ford, Carter, Reagan, and Bush were all far less approachable—and none of them devised ways to interact on a daily basis with their constituents as did Bill Clinton with his daily runs.

Anyone who had an opportunity to jog with the President would testify that he had deceptive strength and endurance. When Congresswoman Cynthia McKinney of Georgia did so, she had assumed Clinton would "chug along like a caboose." But she quickly discovered that he was "kicking up dust and leaving me in the wind." Bernadine Portensiki, a runner from New Zealand who had competed in the Boston Marathon, struggled to keep up with Clinton on a three-mile run in 1993. She reported that she felt the president ran the third mile in only six and one-half minutes—a full two minutes faster than he had run his first mile. Professional athletes call this phenomenon "running negative splits"—where the jogger continually builds strength, speed, and confidence throughout the run.

And that's the way it seemed to be when Bill Clinton ran with the people. He perpetually had more energy at the end of a day spent interacting with Americans than he did when he began in the morning.

> "The key to being an effective leader is getting around. You've got to go find the facts for yourself, and many of the good ones come from outside your inner circle. There's too much you miss if you don't forage around yourself."

> —Clinton,
> February 1992

> "I've been in the hills and hollows of Kentucky. I have walked up and down the poorest communities in America in the Mississippi Delta. I have been all over South Texas. I know those places. They have good people. And their children deserve a future."

> —Clinton, discussing Empowerment Zones
> and Enterprise Communities
> December 21, 1994

In the months of (**February, March, April, 1994**), national media outlets fanned the flames of Clinton accusations, and were especially focused on parlaying a link between Whitewater and Vince Foster's death. The Washington Times published a front-page story citing anonymous sources that claimed Whitewater files had been shredded at the Rose law firm. The New York Times ran a front-page article on the same subject, but added that one of the boxes of shredded documents had Vince Foster's initials on it. In that same issue was an editorial entitled, "White House Ethics Meltdown." Less than a week later, The New York Times ran another story stating that a "Courier at Little Rock Firm Recalls Shredding After the Inquiry Began."

Conservative talk show radio programs also promoted a plethora of wild and unsubstantiated theories. Foster killed himself, because he was involved in Clinton crimes and was about to be exposed. He was a closeted homosexual. He had an affair with Hillary and was subsequently rejected by her. Foster was involved with the Clintons in Whitewater-related crimes and then obstructed justice by covering them up. Foster had been murdered in an apartment owned by Hillary Clinton, and that the suicide scene at Fort Macy Park had been fabricated. It was further claimed that "journalists and others working on or involved in Whitewatergate have been mysteriously beaten and harassed in Little Rock. . . . [and] some have died."

Negative carping about President Clinton and Whitewater reached the floor of the House of Representatives on **March 24, 1994**, when Rep. Jim Leach of Iowa (ranking Republican on the House Banking Committee) delivered an unusually pointed speech. "Whitewater is about the arrogance of power—Machiavellian machinations of single-party Government," he began. Leach went on to suggest that "infusions of cash" had been "diverted . . . from a program designed for socially and economically disadvantaged people" to Whitewater; that funds were "used to pay off personal and campaign liabilities of the Governor:" and that "a review of the president's tax records" had raised questions about tax deductions and declared income.

Subsequent to Leach's oration, additional charges and innuendo were leveled by members of Congress, including: referring to Vince Foster's death as an "alleged suicide"; the Clinton's had made money on Whitewater, not lost it; David Hale's criminal transgressions were committed at Bill Clinton's request; the president had "hide and shred" standards and was guilty of "obstruction of justice." The national media also continued its barrage, with articles and/or editorials in Newsweek, The Washington Post, The New York Post, the New Republic, and The Wall Street Journal. Time magazine ran a cover story titled: "Deep Water: How the President's Men Tried to Hinder the Whitewater Investigation," while the Pittsburgh Tribune-Review published a series of articles charging fraud and cover-up in *the death of Vince Foster. And Pat Robertson's 700 Club on the Christian Broadcasting Network dedicated an entire broadcast to answering the question "Suicide or Murder?," suggesting that Foster was murdered and that President Clinton had covered it up.*

By the **spring and summer of 1994**, *more Christian Fundamentalist organizations became involved in the campaign against Bill Clinton's presidency. In April, for example, Randall Terry (founder of Operation Rescue, an anti-abortion group), set out on a seven-city tour through the Midwest on a large black bus with the words "Wake Up America! Should Clinton Be Impeached?" written on its side in large red letters. Also on this tour was Rev. Patrick Mahoney, executive director of the Christian Defense Coalition. The tour started in a parking lot across the street from the Rose Law Firm in Little Rock, and ended outside Bill Clinton's church (Foundry United Methodist) in Washington, D.C. Messages espoused on the tour included: "This is the single most un-Christian administration in the history of this country," and "This is not a Christian president."*

The Reverend Jerry Falwell's organization was also involved in the production and marketing of several anti-Clinton videos during the **1994 summer** *months. The first video, entitled* Circle of Power, *was a half hour in length, and alleged that thirty-four people linked to the Clintons had mysteriously died under suspicious circumstances.* The Clinton Chronicles, *a second and more ambitious project, charged that the "Clinton machine" in Arkansas had wielded "absolute control" and abused its power. Among the many untrue allegations in this video included the following: Bill Clinton had issued a pardon to a political supporter who had been convicted of dispensing cocaine; the financial records of Clinton's gubernatorial campaigns had mysteriously disappeared; the chairman of Tyson Foods had donated $700,000 to Clinton's campaign in return for a $10 million state loan that went unpaid; the Arkansas Development Finance Authority (ADFA) had been designed to help Clinton and his friends steal and launder state money (as well as millions of dollars in illegal drug money). A third video,* The New Clinton Chronicles, *was produced and distributed just few months before the 1994 midterm congressional elections.*

According to reports, Jerry Falwell produced his videos through "Citizens for Honest Government," a California-based, nonprofit organization with a 501C3 designation, which allowed it to solicit tax-deductible charitable contributions. Most of the individuals making accusations against Clinton were paid, and Larry Nichols, the former marketing consultant for ADFA, is also reported to have made money through a royalty arrangement for each video. The Clinton Chronicles *was promoted on the nationally syndicated television program* The Old Time Gospel Hour *as "Jerry Falwell Presents Bill Clinton's Circle of Power." It is believed that more than*

150,000 copies were sent out to people who made charitable donations of $40 each (plus $3 shipping and handling). Copies were sent to all 435 members of Congress, to members of the Washington, D.C. press corps, and were shown to members of evangelical churches during services across the country. Conservative and Christian radio and television programs also broadcast the charges leveled in these videos to millions of Americans.

"He had earned their respect because he went to places most leaders never visit, and listened to people most leaders never hear, and spoke simple truth most leaders never speak."

—Clinton, at a memorial Mass for Robert F. Kennedy
June 6, 1993

"We have to learn to talk to each other and to listen to each other, not to talk past each other and to scream at one another."

—Clinton, speaking at UCLA
May 20, 1994

CHAPTER SIX

LISTENING AND PUBLIC SPEAKING

Paul Newman and his wife, Joanne Woodward, enjoyed a long, leisurely dinner with Bill Clinton at a trendy restaurant one winter evening in Washington, D.C. As the two actors were departing, a reporter asked them how the conversation went. Newman thought for a moment and then replied: "It's nice to have a president adept at the fine art of listening."

Jack Nicklaus and Bill Clinton played a round of golf together one summer's day in Vail, Colorado. As they were standing on the first tee waiting to drive, Nicklaus politely inquired about the administration's economic program that had barely squeaked by the House and Senate just a few days earlier. Clinton finally finished his answer as they were walking off the third green.

"He just kept [talking]," remembered Nicklaus, who then diplomatically added: "But I really appreciate that. I thought it was very nice."

Which was the real Bill Clinton? The one who talked too much or the one who listened patiently? The answer is both. And even though the American people more often heard him talking, the fact is that Clinton listened just as much as he spoke.

THE GREAT LISTENER

Listening carefully to the people he represented became a part of Bill Clinton's leadership style in the wake of a very hard lesson learned. During his first term as governor of Arkansas, Clinton had pushed through an increase in motor vehicle license fees. Even though the increase was slight, voters were outraged. After returning from reelection campaign visit to a tire factory, Clinton complained to his campaign manager: "They're killing me out there! I go into these factories where people have always been kind to me, and they tell me I kicked them in the teeth." When asked if it was the amount of the fees people were complaining about, Clinton responded that it was not the fees themselves, but "the fact that the economy was bad, that working families were having a hard time making ends meet, and that we had needlessly raised their taxes. They said I kicked them when they were down."

In November 1980, after only one two-year term, Bill Clinton was kicked out of office by Arkansas voters. And when he won reelection on the next go-around, a more seasoned thirty-six-year-old never stopped listening to his constituents. As a matter of fact, his aides began using the terms "Clinton Standard Time" or "The Clinton Factor," which meant that the governor would be late to any scheduled event by at least thirty minutes. As Woody Bassett, a former assistant, explained: "I spent countless hours waiting for him to arrive—and then waiting for him to finish talking to the last person he could find. He lingered at every event, finding out what was on people's minds, and then hearing them out until he was finally pulled away, literally, by an aide who was charged with getting him to the next appointment."

The same pattern became obvious within six months of Clinton becoming president. Footage of his forays out of Washington conversing with constituents became commonplace viewing on evening news programs. He was dubbed "The Great Listener" by some members of the press and, in other circles, he was mocked for his, "I hear you, I understand you, I feel your pain" message as being too touchy-feely and too feminine. But Clinton rarely wavered in his determination to hear the voices of the people—what they thought of his ideas, what their concerns were, what they would like him to do. As a result, he was often late to scheduled engagements. Whether it was a two-day public forum on the economy or a stroll through a shopping mall, Clinton was out there listening. Beyond merely listening, however, he often changed his mind when it became apparent that his constituents didn't like what he was doing.

Many of Bill Clinton's detractors argued that he was too quick to change his mind on important issues. During his first hundred days in office, he offered a liberal policy on gays in the military and proposed raising taxes on a rather grand scale. These two major issues, combined with others that seemed to portray a left-wing, liberal politician rather than the middle-of-the-road "New Democrat" he touted himself as during the presidential campaign, resulted in the lowest presidential approval ratings in the history of poll-taking. In direct response to the polls, Clinton dumped most of the new taxes, cut government spending, and accepted a much more conservative policy regarding gays in the armed forces.

While there was some justification to the criticism that Clinton changed his mind too quickly, it seems clear that he also strategically presented new ideas before the American people, and then searched for their reactions. December 10, 1993, for example, was a typical day of news media coverage for the Clinton administration. On the front page of *The New York Times*, there were three stories about pending administration proposals. The first headline read: "Administration Floats Proposal for Licensing All Gun Owners: Despite Public Mood, Idea Raises Political Perils." This proposal came just days after a crazed gunman killed five people on a New York subway train.

A second headline read: "Clinton Panel Urges Expansion of Welfare for 2-Parent Homes." This article discussed a proposal by the Clinton administration's task force on welfare reform to "correct the welfare system's much criticized tendency to divide families by cutting off benefits when the father lives in the house."

The third story summarized the ongoing battle between the Pentagon and the Clinton administration regarding a "post–Cold War" strategy. Should President Clinton, the final authority, grant the military its request for an additional $50 billion, or should he honor his promises to cut the federal budget deficit and shift spending to domestic issues?

All three articles had the same thing in common: They were not articles about the President of the United States "proclaiming," "ordering," or "announcing" decisions he had made. They were articles about ideas his administration was considering. In essence, Clinton was "floating" them to the American public to see if they would fly. This strategy also served a more pragmatic purpose in that, when and if one of his floated initiatives was officially introduced, the people would have already been exposed to the idea. In this way, the natural human impediment of resistance to change was somewhat softened. The Clinton administration employed this strategy so frequently that its broader implications were often not noticed.

In April 1993, the administration floated the idea of a national tax (also referred to as a "value-added" tax) as a means of financing the president's new health care plan. When that idea didn't go over well, Hillary Clinton traveled to Williamsburg, Virginia, to speak to a group of business executives, where she proposed possibly financing the plan through payroll deductions. And in September, Clinton suggested the idea of so-called sin taxes, which focused on alcohol and tobacco sales and consumption. Over a period of approximately six months, the Clinton administration proposed several methods of financing a national health care policy. Because so many ideas were proposed, the national news media interpreted the president as being "undecided" on the issue. In reality, however, Clinton was trying to gauge what method would generate the most public support.

Past presidents had frequently relied on national poll-taking to help them make political decisions on policy, and Bill Clinton was no exception. He regularly scanned the newspapers, devouring any poll that gave him new information. White House aides were astounded at his ability to recall facts from a poll taken six months previously and then compare those numbers to the most recent findings. He also remembered who sponsored the poll, how many people were surveyed, and how it was conducted. And at any point in time, he could recite his own latest popularity ratings. This ongoing interest in his public approval rating was sparked more by a desire to lead effectively than by his need to analyze a current political position—although, certainly, political perceptions were a main reason he kept close tabs on the polls. Basically, though, Clinton realized that if his ratings were moving up at any given point in time, then he was probably doing a good job of acting on the public's desires. Conversely, if they were going down, he needed to change things.

The Clinton administration also set up a massive communications effort at the White House and then invited anyone and everyone to write to the president—and the American people responded to his invitation by sending him more mail than any president had ever received. During his first year in office, for instance, Clinton received more than twice as much mail as did George H. W. Bush. The sheer amount of correspondence seemed to indicate that Americans perceived this president to be very approachable and accessible, that they felt something of a personal connection with him. And that's exactly the way Clinton wanted it.

On an average day, the White House received 25,000 letters, 50,000 phone calls, and 250 telegrams. While these were standard ways of receiving information for past presidents, Bill Clinton created an entirely new category for incoming correspondence. On any given day, he received thousands of email messages. The White House, under the president's direction, moved into the Information Age by hooking into fledgling electronic computer highways such as CompuServe, Prodigy, and American Online. With these computer services, Americans could not only correspond with the president and Vice President, they could instantly download complete texts from recently delivered speeches or catch a glimpse of the President's daily schedule of events.

Bill Clinton was the first President of the United States to embrace and effectively apply the tools of the Information Age. Doing so was consistent with his general communications strategy of taking his message directly to the people whenever and wherever possible. By allowing citizens greater access to the White House, by making the texts of his daily remarks instantly available to any person who wanted them, Clinton, in effect, stepped into a new age where no person had to receive information filtered by conventional sources.

PERSUADING FROM THE PODIUM

Before President Clinton addressed the nation about a crisis in Haiti on September 16, 1994, a full two-thirds of the American public was opposed to a U.S.-led invasion of the tiny Caribbean island. After the speech, however, 56 percent approved of his plans to invade. In addition, the president's overall approval rating jumped by four points. Usually when Clinton spoke to a national television audience, there were noticeable rises in his popularity ratings. But it wasn't always that way.

At the 1988 Democratic National Convention, Bill Clinton gave a disastrous nomination speech for presidential candidate Michael Dukakis, which led to the widespread perception that he was a terrible public speaker. Clinton went over his allotted time, droning on for more than forty-five minutes as the rowdy delegates called for Dukakis to come out. Clinton talked so long that several of the networks shifted coverage away from him, and the only time he received applause was near the end when he remarked: "In closing. . . ." Criticism of Clinton lasted for weeks. NBC's John Chancellor remarked that the young governor had "put a blot on his record." And Johnny Carson made Clinton a national joke when he quipped that "The Surgeon General has just approved Bill Clinton as an over-the-counter sleep aid."

At first, Clinton was devastated. "I fell on my sword," he lamented. But after accepting an invitation from Carson to appear on *The Tonight Show*, Clinton made fun of himself by saying that Dukakis had just asked him to give the same nominating speech for his opponent, George

H. W. Bush. Carson not only told him that his saving grace was that he had a good sense of humor, but invited Clinton to play the saxophone with Doc Severinson's band. In recalling the ill-fated speech years later, Clinton would remark: "It wasn't my finest hour. It wasn't even my finest hour and a half."

Few people in 1988 would have dreamed that Bill Clinton would return four years later as the Democratic Party's presidential nominee. Fewer still would have expected to see a presidential candidate so in command, so knowledgeable, and so at ease in front of an audience. As an extemporaneous speaker, Clinton was fluid, smooth, and casual. He was also able to retain detailed facts about his initiatives and then, in a lucid and organized manner, adeptly communicate them to any group or individual. As a matter of fact, some members of the press viewed him as a "policy wonk" or a guy with a "CD-ROM" mind filled with minute details of complex, uninteresting, and boring data.

Clinton was also adept at tailoring remarks specifically to his audience. In an interview at the White House with members of the Louisiana media, Clinton was asked how the lives of people in Shreveport would be better if his economic plan passed in Congress. "I can tell you three or four specific reasons," he responded instantly. After mentioning how a reduced deficit would lead to lower interest rates, Clinton referred specifically to Louisiana: "More than ninety percent [of small business people] in Louisiana are eligible for significant and retroactive tax reductions if they invest in their business," he said. "Over a quarter of the working families of Louisiana will be eligible for relief under the earned income tax credit, because they earn less then $30,000 a year. So there will be more cash in Louisiana, in Shreveport and more economic incentives to invest in the economy. And a lower deficit helps everybody." At this event, Clinton's comments were personalized and made without the benefit of notes or prompting.

Modern national politicians rely heavily on a cadre of speechwriters to script every word and phrase. Clinton also had speechwriters, but he didn't seem to rely on them as much as past presidents. And when speeches were prepared for him, he made frequent changes, scratched out entire sections and rewrote them. Often, Clinton would think out loud what he wanted to say and then either he or an aide would write it down and place it in the text. His speechwriters complained that the president was always drifting away from their formal script. And on many occasions, he completely ignored the speechwriters and crafted his own remarks. For instance, in preparation for his address to the nation announcing a "Middle Class Bill of Rights," in December 1994, *Time* reported that "Speechwriters Bruce Reed and Don Baer produced countless drafts before Clinton finally dictated the speech into a tape recorder. 'He was intent,' said counselor Mack McLarty, 'on this being his speech.'"

During his two terms as president, Clinton frequently garnered wide-ranging praise for his eloquence and effectiveness when it came to making speeches. His formal remarks at the Israel-PLO signing ceremony were hailed by *The New York Times* columnist William Safire as "the best speech of his life." After Clinton's passionate and rousing address introducing NAFTA, George H. W. Bush, who was also on the podium, remarked that he now knew why Clinton was "on the inside looking out, and I'm on the outside looking in." And *Newsweek* labeled the president's passionate remarks to 5,000 ministers at a church in Memphis, Tennessee, as "the one truly great speech of his presidency."

The Memphis speech was delivered on November 13, 1993, at the same church that the Rev. Dr. Martin Luther King, Jr. gave his final sermon in 1968. There, Clinton evoked the memory of King and asserted that, "if he were to reappear by my side today and give us a report card on the last twenty-five years," he would applaud the many advancements in civil rights. Clinton then continued with an eloquent and passionate plea for the ministers in the audience to help end violence in America:

> But [Dr. King] would say, I did not live and die to see the American family destroyed. I did not live and die to see thirteen-year-old boys get automatic weapons and gun down nine-year-olds just for the kick of it. I did not live and die to see young people destroy their own lives with drugs and then build fortunes destroying the lives of others. That is not what I came here to do. I fought for freedom, he would say, but not for the freedom of people to kill each other with reckless abandon, not for the freedom of children to have children and the fathers of the children walk away from them and abandon them as if they don't amount to anything. I fought for people to have the right to work but not to have whole communities and people abandoned. This is not what I lived and died for.
>
> My fellow Americans, he would say, I fought to stop white people from being so filled with hate that they would wreak violence on black people. I did not fight for the right of black people to murder other black people with reckless abandon.

The president's speech was interrupted many times by shouts of "Right!" and "Amen!" and, in the end, he received sustained applause. He was passionate, articulate, eloquent, and animated in his delivery. He rose above the occasion of a normal speech by interacting with his audience, by touching on their personal concerns, by responding to their needs, and by truly engaging them.

Another part of Bill Clinton's success as a speaker was that he spoke in simple and familiar language that everyone could understand. Henry Cisneros, the administration's first Secretary of Housing and Urban development, remarked that the "particular genius of President Clinton was his ability to find the language that bridges."

A detailed inspection of his speeches, both extemporaneous and scripted, finds that the president used plain language, common metaphors, and stories and anecdotes with a simplicity and directness to which every person can relate. "The Government is broken, and we intend to fix it," he said upon introducing the Administration's initiative to reinvent government. He began his health care address the same way: "This health care system of ours is badly broken, and it is time to fix it," he stated to Congress and a national television audience. In early September 1993, as his administration was about to tackle all at once the North American Free Trade Agreement, the Reinventing Government initiative, and comprehensive health care, Clinton explained in plain English how they were all linked together:

> In our lives, we understand that we often have to do several things to reach one goal. Think about the talk at your kitchen table, when you discuss the challenges facing your own families. You might be talking about whether you can afford to buy a home or send your youngest child to college, or whether to build a new business of your own or go to night school to learn a new skill. Of course, these are separate questions, but they all add up to one challenge—building a better life for you and your family.
>
> It's the same with building our country's future. These pieces must all fit together. To control the deficit we have to reform health care and give families more security. To create new jobs for our workers, we have to open new markets for our companies and our products. And for government to be a help and not a hindrance in economic growth, we must make it less bureaucratic and more productive.

By linking health care, NAFTA, and Reinventing Government, Clinton not only gave a higher level of meaning to each initiative, he also provided an ongoing format for constant, repetitive communications. Scarcely could one be discussed without mentioning the other two.

LISTENING AND PUBLIC SPEAKING IN LEADERSHIP

Many times, Bill Clinton said that he viewed the presidency as his "job," the White House as his office, and that his duty was to get up and go to work every day for the American people. Clinton also believed in using the tools of the trade to do his job. Since the United States presidency is one of the world's ultimate leadership positions, and since leadership, itself, involves acting for the wants and needs of people in the organization, the tools of leadership must include both listening and public speaking.

Listening is important in leadership for three primary reasons:

1. It allows leaders to understand what people in the organization think, feel, and expect.
2. It is an important means of gathering specific information with which to make strategic decisions.
3. It shows interest and caring; it is a way to build trust, relationships, and to connect with people.

Bill Clinton clearly understood the value of listening in leadership, and said as much on several occasions. During his remarks in nominating Ruth Bader Ginsburg to the Supreme Court, for instance, he noted: "The greatest figures of the American judiciary have been . . . willing to listen and to learn." And at a memorial mass for Robert F. Kennedy, Clinton noted that Kennedy had earned the people's respect, in part, because he "listened to people most leaders never hear."

The importance of public speaking as a leadership tool is both self-evident and undeniable. It is used to communicate information, to persuade people, and to inspire others to take action. In addition, Bill Clinton utilized his extraordinary speaking ability to bring people together. Nowhere is that more apparent than in his nomination acceptance speech at the 1992 Democratic National Convention:

> Tonight every one of you knows deep in your heart that we are too divided. It is time to heal America. We must say to every American: Look beyond the stereotypes that blind us. We need each other. All of us, we need each other.
>
> For too long politicians have told most of us that are doing all right, that what's really wrong with America is the rest of us. Them. Them, the minorities. Them, the liberals. Them, the poor, them, the homeless, them, the people with disabilities. Them, the gays. We've gotten to where we've nearly "them'ed" ourselves to death. Them and them and them.
>
> This is America. There is no them; there is only us. One nation, under God, indivisible, with liberty and justice for all.

"I came here today to listen, to learn, and to try to explain what we're trying to do."

> —Clinton, during a question And answer session in
> Bernalillo, Mexico
> December 3, 1993

"Thanks for listening."

> —Clinton, ending all his weekly radio addresses

On May 4, 1994, The Washington Post *ran an article detailing the accusations of Paula Jones against the president. One of the authors was Michael Isikoff, who had been introduced to Jones by Cliff Jackson at his February press conference.* The Post's *article was timed to coincide with the filing of a lawsuit by Jones against Clinton. That occurred two days later, on May 6, 1994, the last possible date to avoid expiration of the three-year statute of limitations. With help from the Landmark Legal Foundation, Jones's lawyers listed four counts against President Clinton: (1) Clinton denied Jones "equal protection of the laws" under the United States Constitution by "sexually harassing and assaulting" her on May 8, 1991, and by creating "a hostile work environment"; (2) Clinton conspired to deprive Jones of her constitutional rights; (3) Clinton was accused of "odious, perverse, and outrageous" conduct; (4) Clinton defamed Jones. Late on the afternoon of the filing, Jones issued a statement through her lawyers that "any proceeds from this litigation, above the costs of the case, will be donated by my husband and me to a Little Rock charity."*

The Jones lawsuit ultimately became a vehicle to probe Bill Clinton's personal life through the legal system. As British journalist Ambrose Evans-Prichard put it: "The ticking time bomb of the lawsuit lies in the testimony of other witnesses . . . . The political purpose of [it] is to use the legal power of discovery." With time, a clandestine group of powerful lawyers (who called themselves "the elves") would organize to make the most of the Jones legal effort against President Clinton.

❦

By the summer of 1994, constant clamoring by Republican congressional leaders resulted in enough Democrats voting for investigative hearings. In July, the Senate Banking Committee, led by the ranking Republican, New York Senator Alfonse D'Amato, began hearings on Whitewater and the death of Vince Foster. Jim Leach took the lead as the House of Representatives Banking Committee began similar hearings. These congressional inquiries were implemented despite the objections of Independent Counsel Robert B. Fiske, who claimed they would "pose a severe risk to the integrity" of his own investigation.

Fiske had already indicted Webster Hubbell, a former associate of Hillary Clinton at the Rose Law Firm, on charges that he had overbilled his clients and defrauded his partners. Hubbell immediately resigned his position as associate U.S. attorney general, but later pled guilty to related charges of mail fraud and tax evasion. He subsequently served eighteen months in prison. On June 30, 1994, Fiske released two reports, one regarding the death of Vince Foster, the other concerning Whitewater. Foster, he concluded, had "committed suicide by firing a bullet from a .38-caliber revolver into his mouth," and "there is no evidence to the contrary." With regard to Whitewater, the independent counsel determined that "the evidence is insufficient to establish that anyone within the White House . . . acted with the intent to corruptly influence a RTC investigation." Therefore, Fiske stated, he would issue no indictments in either matter.

The conservative press immediately launched a public attack on Fiske and his entire investigation. The Wall Street Journal *editorial page accused Fiske of participating in a White House "cover up." The New York Times columnist William Safire wrote: "What's with this non-independent counsel who helps Democrats avoid oversight? Find a way to get rid of him." As right-wing media outlets joined the fray, a mid-July meeting took place between North Carolina Republican senators Lauch Faircloth and Jesse Helms—and Judge David B. Sentelle, who served on the special three-judge panel responsible for appointing the independent counsel. Like Faircloth and Helms, Sentelle was from North Carolina and a conservative who did not like Bill Clinton. Sentelle admitted later that the subject of a new independent counsel may have come up during the meeting. When August rolled around, Attorney General Janet Reno routinely sent Fiske's renomination as independent counsel before the three-judge special panel. The next day, Lauch Faircloth took the floor of the Senate and lambasted Fiske for having a conflict of interest. His law firm, Faircloth charged, had once represented a company that sold land to Jim and Susan McDougal. Subsequently, on **August 5, 1994,** the three-judge panel announced the removal of Fiske and the appointment of Kenneth W. Starr. "It is not our intent to impugn the integrity of the Attorney General's appointee," noted the panel in a written statement, "but rather to reflect the intent of the [Independent Counsel] Act, that the Act be protected against perceptions of conflict [of interest]."

Kenneth Starr was a committed conservative, a member of the Federalist Society, and a former solicitor general in the Bush administration who had been on George H. W. Bush's short list to be nominated for the U.S. Supreme Court, but was passed over in favor of Clarence Thomas. In addition, Starr had several apparent conflicts of interest much more egregious than did Robert B. Fiske. As senior partner in the Washington office of Kirkland & Ellis, he and some of his associates had worked to support Paula Jones. Starr also quickly announced that he intended to continue as a partner at his law firm, which meant that he would be drawing a seven-figure annual salary from a company that not only routinely litigated against the federal government, and was actively working against the president.

"I was beginning to tell a story. You know, the first job I ever had was working in a grocery store. I was thirteen years old."

—Clinton, to a group of employees At
a Pathmark Grocery Store in New York
May 9, 1994

"You've got to continue to bring this level of intensity, of energy, of passion to this battle. You have the most powerful weapon of all—the power of personal stories."

—Clinton, to the National Breast Cancer Coalition
October 8, 1993

CHAPTER SEVEN

CONVERSATION AND STORYTELLING

In late May 1993, just as new opinion polls put his overall job performance rating at the lowest percentage in presidential poll-taking history, Bill Clinton placed a call to Democratic representative Ike Skelton of Missouri in an attempt to solicit his vote for the administration's budget plan. Later that day, the plan would be voted on in the House of Representatives. When the sixty-two-year-old veteran congressman was informed that Clinton was on the line and wanted to speak to him, Skelton "sprinted out of the Democratic cloakroom" rather than take the president's call. He did not want to explain why he was going to vote against the plan, nor did he want to give Clinton the opportunity to talk him out of his decision.

Skelton wasn't alone in his desire to avoid a conversation with the president. Florida congressman Harry Johnston, who voted in favor of the budget plan, reported that "I went down to the gym and there were people hiding there from the President of the United States." One of those congressmen in hiding was Colin C. Peterson of Minnesota. He, too, had decided to vote against the budget proposal and frantically tried to avoid speaking to Clinton, who persistently attempted to get a hold of him all afternoon. Just minutes before the vote, Clinton tried once more, and this time Peterson relented and took the call. Among other things, the president told him that "I'm new on the job, and I need your help. Give me a chance and I'll try to help you out with your problems." When Clinton agreed to reduce proposed taxes on energy, Peterson consented to vote for the plan. According to *The New York Times*, "Mr. Peterson's decision was one of a handful of last-minute switches that helped Mr. Clinton eke out his victory."

EMPLOYING PERSUASIVE SKILLS

Bill Clinton's lobbying of Congress through personal conversations, his prowling the corridors of the Capitol, and his repeated phone-calling were major news stories across the nation. After all, most recent presidents had stayed aloof from senators and congressmen. It had been more than a quarter of a century since a president had tried to work so tirelessly with legislators, and even back then, President Lyndon Johnson was known more for his "do-it-my-way-or-else" methodology.

Clinton, however, tried something altogether different. He attempted to persuade and lobby rather than dictate and coerce. While this was news to the nation as a whole, it was old stuff to people in Arkansas who had seen him perfect this style while serving as governor.

"Clinton lobbied openly for his programs," recalls Dr. Bobby Roberts, a former legislative assistant to Clinton. "He could be found almost every day standing outside a committee room with a cup of coffee in one hand. There he would buttonhole legislators to ask for their help, or he would go into a committee room and kneel beside legislators to talk about an approaching vote, or he would ask for recognition to respond to a witness who had raised points against a bill in which he was interested."

Arkansas Democratic senator Dale Bumpers also recalled Clinton's days as governor: "He's a very persuasive lobbyist," said Bumpers. "Legislators used to hide from him because they thought he was going to talk them into something they didn't want to do." Carl Whillock, a former political adviser of Clinton's, concurred: "I'm convinced that Bill could persuade two of every three voters to support him if he could have one-on-one conversations with them."

After Clinton became president, there were not too many Democratic members of Congress who would have disagreed with that statement. During the weeks leading up to the votes on the 1993 budget and NAFTA, for instance, Clinton met with scores of congressmen and senators, especially those who were wavering. One Texas Democrat mentioned that he had "not talked with a single member of Congress who had been in the 'no' category [on the budget vote] in the last forty-eight hours who had not talked to the president."

As negotiators in Congress took weekends off, Clinton continued to lobby legislators by speaking to them casually and listening to their concerns while jogging, dining, or playing golf. After meeting with the president just prior to the vote on NAFTA, Ohio Representative David Mann remarked to a reporter that "he's given me plenty of food for thought," and characterized Clinton as a "persuasive spokesman." He also jokingly mentioned that "I'm going to get an artificial socket for my arm," inferring that the president had been tenacious in his commitment to secure Mann's vote.

Nebraska senator Bob Kerrey had a similar experience, as the last undecided holdout on Clinton's budget package. After a telephone conversation with the president, Kerrey explained that "we didn't hang up [the phone] in anger. [Rather], he offered in very passionate terms why he felt [voting no] was wrong and why he felt that would be a terrible mistake." On the day of the final Senate vote, Clinton followed up by inviting Kerrey over to the White House family quarters for a personal conversation that lasted more than an hour. Afterward, the president saw to it that the senator met with Vice President Al Gore and Chief of Staff Mack McLarty. Then, minutes before casting his vote, Senator Kerrey called the Oval Office and informed the president that he would vote for the plan. According to reports, Clinton calmly accepted the decision and thanked him for his support.

So committed was Clinton to persuading through personal conversation that when he wasn't talking business, he was directing, delegating, and deploying top administration officials to do so. "Make three calls. Make twelve calls. Make two dozen calls. For goodness sakes, make however many you can," the president urged his people. In addition to Gore and McLarty's persuasive skills being put to use, Lloyd Bentsen and Leon Panetta constantly stalked the halls of Congress and furiously manned the phones. During the NAFTA campaign, it was Mickey Kantor and Ron Brown, among others, who led the charge. And for health care, it was nearly every member of the administration who swarmed Capitol Hill, with efforts being led by Hillary Clinton, Ira Magaziner, and Dona Shalala.

Lawmakers from the Democratic and Republican parties noted that personal efforts by both the president and members of his administration

made all the difference between success and failure on Clinton's key domestic initiatives and his foreign policy programs. It reinforced all the
more the realization that Bill Clinton was at his very best when he could
look people in the eye and engage them in informal dialogue and conversation. He seemed to have the ability to bond with whomever he came
into personal contact. Take, for instance, his unusual relationship with
Chancellor Helmut Kohl of Germany.

During the European NATO Summit in January 1994, Clinton approached the German leader and said: "I was thinking of you last night,
Helmut, because I watched sumo wrestling on television." As Kohl
looked a bit perplexed, Clinton went on: "You and I are the biggest people here, and we are still a whole 100 pounds too light. We are too
small!" said the president with a big grin.

Many members of the media suggested that Clinton's remarks were
out of place and could have been taken as offensive by Kohl. But Clinton, who was six feet, three inches tall and weighted 210 pounds at the
time, was simply building his personal relationship with Kohl, who was
six feet, four inches and 287 pounds. Moreover, reporters did not recall,
as surely Clinton did, that when the two met previously at the White
House in March of 1993, Kohl had told Clinton that he reminded him of
a "rug merchant" always trying to get what he wanted. Helmut Kohl was
not offended by Clinton's "sumo wrestler" comment, and he built on the
relationship by traveling to Washington two weeks later for more talks
with the president.

Bill Clinton's ability to connect with people like Helmut Kohl (who
did not speak English), was due, in part, to his affable, easy-going manner. He was gregarious, sincere, and engaged with whomever he was interacting. He appeared to be just a regular guy who used down-home
figures of speech. As president, Clinton spoke about being "as nervous as
a cat in a tree" when it came to the final budget vote; about not making
government so burdensome that we end up telling people "how to do
every last jot and tiddle of their job every day"; and that "you don't have
to be as bright as a tree full of owls to figure out that [some things don't]
make a lot of sense."

While this type of common language came naturally to a fellow
who grew up in small-town Arkansas, Clinton very consciously
avoided using language that flew over the heads of the masses. Rather,
he purposefully and strategically remained plain-spoken. "Today, I
think that we still don't speak in a language that ordinary Americans
can understand," he once told William Safire, columnist for *The New
York Times.*

USING STORIES TO PERSUADE

Part of the language all people understand comes in the form of stories and anecdotes. Dating back to the early days of his youth, Bill Clinton was known for his skill at relating stories. "He had the gift of a true storyteller," recalls William T. Coleman, a fellow student of Clinton's at Yale University. "He could take the simplest event and, in retelling it, turn it into a saga complete with a plot and a moral. By simply being himself," said Colemen, "Bill Clinton became a regular and welcome member of [our group]."

Clinton's gift for storytelling served him well in the political arena, especially in his years as governor of Arkansas. Phyllis Anderson, who for a decade served as his administrative assistant, recalled how Clinton strategically employed storytelling to influence others, even if he wasn't the one telling the story:

> Clinton developed what I think was a unique strategy for educating people. He first tried this strategy with other governors at a meeting of the National Governors' Association in Washington, D.C. We gathered a few Arkansas people who had been involved in literacy programs or who had made the break from Welfare dependency to work. It was daunting for some of those who were called upon because a few of them had never even been to Little Rock, much less to the nation's capital. So it wasn't surprising that when one of the first speakers began to tell why she and her children were happier since she had left Welfare and had gone to work, she faltered and couldn't go on. After only a few seconds, during which an uncomfortable silence filled the room, Clinton leaned into the microphone, looked directly at her, and asked if she was nervous. She said she was very nervous. He said he understood that because the room was full of governors, staff members, and television lights.
>
> "Why don't you just tell our story to me?" he said softly. She did and there was not a dry eye in the room. Everyone there "got it" in a way that they never would have from the dry discourse of a policy expert. Clinton's sensitivity to the woman and his ability to put her at ease made the session memorable. He often asked citizens to come to legislative hearings and conferences to see first-hand the problems that other people faced.

Clinton naturally brought this strategy of telling stories with him to the White House. In his first State of the Union Address as president, to illustrate the need for welfare reform, he told a story that apparently happened at this same governor's conference: "I once had a hearing when I was a governor and I brought in people on Welfare from all over America who had found their way to work," said Clinton. "The woman from my state who testified was asked this question: 'What's the biggest thing about being off Welfare and in a job?' Without blinking an eye, she looked at forty governors and said, 'When my boy goes to school and they say, "what does your mother do for a living," he can give an answer.'"

On every initiative Bill Clinton proposed, from the earned income tax credit to welfare reform, when he wasn't telling stories to illustrate his side of the equation, he brought in ordinary Americans to tell their own stories. The most striking examples came in his campaign to reform health care in the United States. In order to change the health care system, Clinton knew that he not only had to overcome pharmaceutical and insurance special interest groups, he had to persuade people in businesses, both large and small. He had to persuade members of the health care industry and members of Congress. But most of all, Clinton realized he had to persuade the vast majority of the American people. So he strategically turned up the volume on telling health care stories, on a direct, consistent, and ongoing basis.

Through hundreds of thousands of letters received by the White House, and from his own personal conversations with people, Bill Clinton and members of his administration told many horror stories experienced by average Americans from across the country. In so doing, Clinton successfully increased the nation's moral awareness. For millions of Americans, the issue of health care reform turned into nothing less than a difference between right and wrong.

The president spoke of personally meeting an elderly couple in New Hampshire who "broke down and cried because of their shame at having an empty refrigerator to pay for their drugs"; and of a divorced woman he met who had to quit her $50,000 a year job to go on public assistance because it was the only way she could secure health care for her desperately ill child. The administration also highlighted the story of a man who was billed $24,000 for a pair of crutches; of a sixty-one-year-old woman who ran a small business having to give up her health coverage because her premiums went through the roof; and of thousands of Americans who were denied insurance coverage because of preexisting conditions. After telling similar stories caused by absurd government regulations, Clinton stated more than once: "That's not just bad policy, it's wrong. And we ought to change it."

In September 1993, just before his address on health care to a joint session of Congress, the President invited people to the White House to read the letters they had written. A stage was set up in the Rose Garden, where Clinton hosted people from California to Maine; and there were another one hundred or more people in the audience who had also written letters to the White House. He staged a similar event two weeks later in Queens, New York, at the Future Diner, where he personally engaged in conversation with more than fifty people who had also written in about their health care problems. Some of the stories told there left many of the people in the room with tears in their eyes—including Clinton, himself.

These two events, in the Rose Garden and at the Future Diner, elevated the concept of persuasion by storytelling to a level seldom seen in presidential leadership. Both events were televised live, and later rebroadcast in whole by C-SPAN; or, in part, by all the major networks and CNN. People all around the country heard the horror stories and saw their president empathize with the people. It is small wonder, then, that polls taken in 1994 showed that more than 75 percent of the American public believed that, indeed, there was a health care crisis in the United States.

Clinton took advantage of those poll findings when, during his State of the Union Address in January, he referred back to the messages that had been coming forth from stories that had surfaced during the prior six to nine months:

> I know there are people here who say there's no health care crisis. Tell it to Richard and Judy Anderson [a couple forced into bankruptcy]. Tell it to the fifty-eight million Americans who have no coverage at all for some time each year. Tell it to the eighty-one million Americans with preexisting conditions—those folks are paying more or they can't get insurance at all, or they can't ever change their jobs because they or someone in their family has one of those preexisting conditions. Tell it to the small businesses burdened by the skyrocketing cost of insurance. Or tell it to the seventy-six percent of insured Americans, three out of four whose policies have lifetime limits. And that means they can find themselves without any coverage at all just then they need it most.

Bill Clinton also related moving stories when trying to persuade voters of the merits of other major issues. When it came to NAFTA, he frequently rattled off the names of companies who would benefit from new markets in Mexico, and how much they would increase numbers in terms of revenues and new jobs. While discussing the administration's Reinventing Government initiative, both Clinton and Vice President Al Gore effectively told stories of the government wasting taxpayer dollars by paying exorbitant prices for computers, bottles of aspirin, and customized bug spray.

Clinton was at his most eloquent, however, when he tried to build support in tackling violent crime in America. In Tennessee, he spoke about an eleven-year-old child in Washington, D.C., who was planning her own funeral; and of a teenager in California whose bother was shot dead while they were standing in line to register for classes at a new school. In Wisconsin, Clinton brought in a police officer to tell about a thirty-year police veteran who was killed with an assault rifle. And in Louisiana, he told the heart-wrenching account of a nine-year-old New Orleans child named James Darby, who had written the president asking him to stop the killing in the city, because he was "afraid I might be killed." "Just nine days later," said Clinton, "walking home from a Mother's Day picnic, James Darby was shot in the head and killed."

Frequently, Clinton told the same story more than once, especially if it was one he particularly liked, and if it had an unusually strong affect on an audience. One such story was about the family of a critically ill little girl he had met in the White House on Sunday morning, September 26, 1993. A few minutes past noon on the same day, Clinton opened his remarks at the Future Diner in Queens, New York, by relating this incident:

> I want to tell you a story. I got up this morning and went out for my morning run. When I came back in, I was on the ground floor and I looked down the hall, and [noticed] a family taking a tour of the White House, which is quite unusual for a Sunday morning. It was a father and a mother and three daughters. The middle daughter was in a wheelchair desperately ill with cancer. I went over to shake hands with them and my staff member said, "Mr. President, this is one of those Make-A-Wish families. This little girl's wish was to come to the White House, take a tour, and meet the President."
>
> So I went over and shook hands with the little girl and her family, and we talked awhile. I apologized for being in my running clothes. I went upstairs to change, came back down, and looking more like my job, I then had a proper picture with them. And again a nice visit with the wonderful child.
>
> As I was walking off, her father grabbed me by the arm, and I turned around and he said: "You know, my daughter is probably not going to make it. And because of that, these last three weeks I've spent with her are the most important times of my while life. And because of that family leave bill, I didn't have to lose my job to spend that time. But if you hadn't passed that law and signed it, I literally would have had to choose between losing my job and spending this time, or supporting my family and giving up what was the most important time of my life. Don't let anybody ever tell you it was bad for the economy!"

In the following four months, Bill Clinton told this story at least six more times in major addresses across the country. Each time, it was told in substantially the same detail. Yet, Clinton tailored the father's last line to make it most relevant to whatever audience was hearing it. For example, to members of the Democratic Party, he said: "Don't you ever think it doesn't make a difference who wins elections and what they do." At Yale University, he said: "Don't ever believe it doesn't matter what decisions are made in Washington." And to the members of Congress (and a prime time television audience), Clinton said: "Don't you people up here ever think what you do doesn't make a difference."

Whatever the father of that little girl said to him at the end, it is apparent that Bill Clinton was very moved by the realization that his work had some positive effects on average citizens. Clearly, he wanted to share the experience with others and have them feel the way he felt—and he did so in a masterful storyteller's manner.

CONVERSATION AND STORYTELLING AS TOOLS OF PERSUASION

Leaders tend to possess the skills and talents necessary to convince others that a certain undertaking is worthwhile, and to motivate them to take action on their own initiative. And not surprisingly, both conversation and storytelling, when applied skillfully, are two of the most time-honored and effective means of *persuading* people.

Because they can relate detailed information through personal conversation, some people view leaders as having status and power, because it exhibits knowledge and skill. Others regard the very same thing as a sign of connection and rapport. Either way, personal conversation can be used as a strategic tool to influence thoughts, viewpoints, and patterns of behavior. Storytelling is also a powerful motivational tool that can spread loyalty, commitment, and enthusiasm. People tend to remember stories more than they do mountains of information. As a result, they are often more influenced by a well-told story than with any other means of communication.

Bill Clinton was naturally adept at the arts of both conversation and storytelling. Throughout his tenure in office, he avoided playing the dictator or using pressure. He believed that national leaders had little hope of fundamentally changing the government unless they could change the thinking of the people who elected them. "One of the president's most important jobs is to consistently explain to the American people what we're doing and why," said Clinton in 1993. "If the people don't have the facts before them, all they can do is operate on what they know." Accordingly, Clinton played the role of communicator—"constantly, directly, and emotionally," as he once stated. He talked to people as often as he could. At every opportunity, he held a conversation, or told a story so that public opinion stayed on course. He knew that a good storyteller could significantly shape the public's view on any issue. Moreover, his easy-going, affable manner reinforced his image as a "regular guy" from Hope, Arkansas. By telling stories and speaking casually with others, Clinton connected with millions of average citizens.

Curiously enough, he also seemed to be able to rekindle his own energy and provide himself sustenance with a well-told story. For instance, during an interview with *The Wall Street Journal* printed just before Christmas 1993 (in the midst of slanderous accusations about his role in the Whitewater development scandal), Clinton related a story that his eighth grade science teacher used to tell: "The teacher wasn't a particularly handsome man," he recalled. "[But he told all of us] students that each morning he splashed water on his face, shaved, then looked in the mirror and told himself: 'Vernon, you're beautiful.'"

"We've got a lot of walls still to tear down in this country, a lot of divisions to overcome, and we need to start with honest conversation, honest outreach, and a clear understanding that none of us has any place to hide."

—Clinton, in remarks at Howard University
January 17, 1994

"I want to close by telling you a story."

—Clinton, in remarks to the National Governor's
Association in Tulsa
August 16, 1993

*In **October 1994**, Arkansas state trooper L. D. Brown corroborated David Hale's accusation about pressure from Bill Clinton to lend $300,000 to the McDougals. Specifically, he stated that he had heard a conversation between Clinton and Hale in which the governor said: "You're going to have to help us out. We're going to need to raise some money." Independent Counsel Kenneth Starr immediately secured a statement from Brown and leaked it to* The Washington Times, *which reported the accusation in its **October 19, 1994**, issue. Other outlets of the mainstream press (including* The Washington Post *and the* Arkansas Democrat-Gazette *among others) quickly picked up the story.*

Back in the spring of 1994, L. D. Brown had volunteered to back up the original TrooperGate story with renewed accusations of his own. The American Spectator *ran an article in which Brown stated he had arranged more than a hundred sex liaisons for Governor Clinton, that he had solicited women for that purpose, and that Hillary Clinton was having an affair with Vince Foster. The truth is that L. D. Brown had resigned his position when Clinton refused to appoint him to an executive position with the Arkansas Crime Laboratory, and that Brown's wife, who had been a former babysitter for the Clintons, left him. According to files released later, Brown was paid $10,000 by the Arkansas Project. There was never any evidence to substantiate his accusations. However, the entire event was labeled TrooperGate II, and added significantly to the American public's negative perception of President Clinton.*

↝

*In the **November 8, 1994**, midterm congressional elections, the Democratic Party lost control of both the House of Representatives and the Senate for the first time in forty years. In the stunning turn of events, Republicans took control of the House (230–204) and the Senate (52–48). Americans clearly regarded this election as a general repudiation of Bill Clinton's presidency. Political analysts attributed the change to the failure of Clinton's national health care initiative, and to mainstream media coverage of the various pseudo-scandals, including: Whitewater, Vince Foster's death, TrooperGate, the Paula Jones lawsuit, and the religious right's various anti-Clinton videos. As a result of the elections, Newt Gingrich became Speaker of the House and Bob Dole became Senate Majority Leader (in **January 1995**).*

↝

*On **April 9, 1995**, Larry Nichols and Citizens for Honest Government introduced a new video entitled* Unanswered: The Death of Vincent Foster. *Among other things, it alleged that members of the White House staff had* *lied about both the time and place of Foster's death, that he died in his car in a parking lot outside the White House, and that his body had been moved to Fort Macy Park after the fact. Arkansas troopers Larry Patterson and Roger Perry were reportedly paid a $1.00 per video royalty. In addition, other right wing organizations continued promoting various Vince Foster murder theories. Some of these groups included: Accuracy in Media, the National Taxpayers Union, the* Pittsburgh Tribune-Review, *the Western Journalism Center, and, of course, the* American Spectator.

⤫

In **May 1995**, *Gennifer Flowers published a tell-all book entitled* Passion and Betrayal. *In it, she alleged numerous illicit rendezvous with Bill Clinton over an extended period of time—and Clinton's use of both marijuana and cocaine.*

⤫

In the **July 1995** *issue of the* American Spectator, *Arkansas state trooper L. D. Brown made another startling series of accusations about Bill Clinton. Claiming that he was working part-time for the CIA, Brown alleged that in 1984, he had been involved in covert weapons and drug smuggling at Mena Intermountain Regional Airport (located near the town of Mena, in rural Western Arkansas). The airport, he said, had been used by the CIA as a staging area for its secret Contra support activities in Central America. Not only did Governor Bill Clinton know all about it, alleged Brown, but he drew quite a bit of money from the sale of the illegal drugs. Brown further stated that Clinton was a frequent user of those smuggled drugs (mainly cocaine) at parties that included young girls. Even though there was no evidence of Clinton's involvement in any illegal activities at Mena, after the* American Spectator *published the story, it was picked up by both* The Washington Post *and* The Wall Street Journal.

*"Our obligation and our power flows out of two simple lessons
I was taught many years ago. One is that the future can be
better than the present. And the second is that each of us has a
personal, moral responsibility to make it so."*

—Clinton, to the National Baptist Convention
in New Orleans
September 9, 1994

*"I didn't get hired [to be] America's chief mechanic. I got
hired . . . to set forth a vision."*

—Clinton, quoted in *Time*
September 27, 1993

CHAPTER EIGHT

VISION AND HOPE

At a televised town hall meeting in Moscow, Russia, in January 1994, Bill Clinton made the following statement to the Russian people, who were looking for a new direction after the fall of the Soviet Union. "I know the present is difficult," he said. "But if you choose hope over fear, the future will reward your courage and your vision." It was a poignant remark to a people that had suffered for seventy years under the tyranny and oppression of communism.

Six months later, in the summer of 1994, Clinton addressed delegates of the American Legion Boys Nation in Washington, D.C. "My simple vision is to make sure that the American dream is there for you in the 21st century," said Clinton. This was the same Boys Nation national event where, thirty-one years earlier (during the middle of the cold war), sixteen-year-old Bill Clinton had stood as a delegate on the White House lawn and shaken the hand of President John F. Kennedy. Now President of the United States himself, Clinton was keeping the hope of America alive by passing it on to the youth of the nation.

Both vision (a mental image of what the future could or will be like) and hope (to believe, desire, or trust in a favorable outcome) were two key elements of Clinton's leadership style. Not only did he understand that effective visions are important for any leader to convey (whether in Russia or the United States), he also intuitively knew that the greatest visions always imply hope for a better tomorrow.

THE MAN FROM HOPE

As a candidate for the presidency, millions of Americans related to Bill Clinton because he grew up in lower-middle-class Arkansas neighborhoods (born in Hope, raised in Hot Springs). Clinton realized the political significance of his "common man" beginnings, and made it part of his campaign rhetoric with a number of captivating phrases, including, "I still believe in a place called Hope," and "The future can be better than the past."

As the 1992 presidential campaign season progressed, a skeptical media called upon the new candidate to lay out specifics of what he would do if elected president. And Clinton demonstrated that he was far from an unsophisticated small town politician, by laying out his vision and goals in great detail—for everything from health care to the environment, crime to campaign financing, and welfare to education. Clinton called his vision for America a "New Covenant," and then effectively mass marketed it in the book *Putting People First,* coauthored with Al Gore.

Some people argued, however, that Clinton was a bit too specific for his own good. He was so detailed in his plans that he appeared to be making a plethora of campaign promises, which simply added fuel to the fire that he was nothing more than a "slick" politician.

In the end, however, it became apparent that Bill Clinton had run a brilliant political campaign emphasizing a new direction for a nation struggling with economic recession in a changing world. The United States had surrendered unquestioned global economic leadership. While other nations were on the way up, America's old-guard leaders seemed to be simply riding the wave rather than leading in their own time. Clinton's vision sounded the trumpet. It was time for a change.

Few people would disagree that Bill Clinton assumed the presidency with a strong and well-defined vision of where he wanted to take the United States of America. "I came into office with a very clear idea of what I wanted to do," he said in August 1993, "and the sense that I had to try to push a lot more than [had] been pushed in a very long time."

Before taking action, Clinton paused to consider both the big picture and the long-term view. He knew that it had taken more than a decade to create the economic problems plaguing the nation, and he reasoned that it would take more than just his first term to get out of it. So he encouraged the public to step back themselves and look at the long-term effects of his proposals rather than judging him by short-term fix-me-ups, which he had no intention of proposing.

During his opening five minutes of remarks to the Little Rock Economic Conference in December 1992, Clinton used the phrases "long run" or "long term" at least half a dozen times. In Detroit, he stated: "We cannot afford to ever, ever, ever forget about the fact that politics can never be about what works in the moment. We have to be thinking about tomorrow." And in Kansas City, Clinton quoted former Speaker of the House Sam Rayburn, who once said: "Any old jackass can kick down a barn, but it takes a carpenter to build one." And then he added: "It often takes longer to build one than it does to kick one down."

Polls taken after Clinton's first six months in office indicated that nearly 70 percent of the American people believed he possessed a worthy vision for the nation. In addition, a solid majority of citizens were appreciative of the fact that he was making a dogged effort to reduce the budget deficit, to reinvent government, to create new markets for American corporations, to overhaul the welfare bureaucracy, and to reform a troubled health care system. With this new president, the American people garnered hope that things would get better.

TURNING VISION INTO REALITY

Most of President Clinton's plans for key domestic issues were laid out well before he took office. He framed his plan for health care reform, for instance, over a period of months, and involved nearly all of his senior advisers, and hundreds of other experts in the field. Then he set out clear goals to pursue, including:

1. Cap national spending to control costs.
2. Take on the insurance industry.
3. Stop drug price gouging.
4. Establish a core benefits package.
5. Develop health networks.
6. Guarantee universal coverage.

After the goals were set, Clinton turned the entire effort over to his health care reform task force. While formulating their recommendations, the group addressed the president's six goals by seeking advice from insurance experts and health care providers. Essentially, the final plan they proposed filled in the details of Clinton's original vision, including an idea to pay for the entire program principally through reduced paperwork and government cost-control measures.

With respect to health care reform, Bill Clinton had done what was expected of a good leader: He had provided a grand vision along with specific goals designed to accomplish the task. After that, it was easy for people on the team to mobilize, focus their efforts, and follow through. "Almost all the major decisions were made before the administration started," noted Donna Shalala, Secretary of Health and Human Services. "By the time Clinton talked to me about the job, he was already clear on what he wanted to do and how [he wanted to do it]. It was pretty much ruffles and flourishes after that."

Another major strategy employed by Clinton was to combine his various initiatives and paint them as part of a larger canvas. The soaring costs of entitlement programs, such as Medicare and Social Security, could not be fixed unless health care, "the real culprit," as he put it, was first reformed. National problems with violent crime could not be solved, he said, without also addressing the nation's problem of illegal drugs. And the welfare system had to be fixed in tandem with health care reform, because so many welfare recipients refused to get a job due to the resulting loss of health insurance coverage.

Clinton "linked" his initiatives together, in part, to break human nature's natural resistance to change. In doing so, he was able to focus the nation's efforts on issues in which even the most resistant citizens had some sort of personal interest. He was also fairly successful at linking his domestic vision of America with his view of America's new role in the world of foreign affairs. "More than ever our security is tied to economics," he said in November 1993. "Our place in the world will be determined as much by the skills of our workers as by the strength of our weapons, as much by our ability to pull down foreign trade barriers as our ability to breach distant ramparts."

From the moment he took office, Bill Clinton was conscious of the fact that he was to be the first president to serve a full term in the aftermath of the cold war. He was also the first president born after the United Nations was founded. But having elected him largely on the basis of his domestic platform, the American public was uneasy with Clinton's plans for foreign policy. After all, just one of the thirty-two chapters in *Putting People First* dealt with the subject. And the national media constantly posed such questions to the new administration as: "Did the President have a vision for the role of the United States in a post cold war world? Or would he simply play it by ear, and handle whatever came along—as George H. W. Bush had asserted in the 1992 presidential campaign?"

On September 27, 1993, Clinton erased many doubts about his in-
tentions when he formally addressed the United Nations General Assembly and comprehensively articulated his vision. In part, this is what
he said:

> I know many people ask whether the United States plans to retreat or
> remain active in the world and, if active, to what end. Many people
> are asking that in our own country as well. Let me answer that ques-
> tion as clearly and plainly as I can. The United States intends to re-
> main engaged and to lead. . . . In a new era of peril and opportunity,
> our overriding purpose must be to expand and strengthen the
> world's community of market-based democracies. During the Cold
> War, we sought to contain a threat to the survival of free institutions.
> Now we seek to enlarge the circle of nations that live under those
> free institutions. For our dream is of a day when the opinions and
> energies of every person in the world will be given full expression, in
> a world of thriving democracies that cooperate with each other and
> live in peace.

By the close of his first term in office, Clinton had succeeded in shifting
the direction of U.S. foreign policy away from military and ideological
confrontation with those nations still embracing communism, and toward one of economic competition in a new global economy. "I have a
vision, a mission, a strategy for how we can move forward in the 21st
century," he told a group of global businessmen. By then, the president
had chalked up an astounding string of tangible achievements aimed at
fulfilling that vision.

In an extraordinarily hard-fought battle, Clinton secured passage of
the North American Free Trade Agreement (NAFTA), which not only
created an open market with Mexico and Canada, but also set the stage
for an expansion into Central and South America. As a matter of fact, it
was only one year later that Chile was admitted as a full partner in
NAFTA. And at the Summit of the Americas, hosted by Clinton in
Miami in December 1994, thirty-four nations agreed to create a new
"Free Trade Area of the Americas," no later than the year 2005.

The ratification of NAFTA also fueled bold new U.S. initiatives in
both Europe and Asia-Pacific. America, for instance, took an active role
in shepherding Europe's Global Agreement on Tariffs and Trade
(GATT). And in 1994, Clinton's January and July trips to Europe reassured a jittery European Community that the United States was determined to avoid any inclinations toward isolationism.

The president's strong and early support of Boris Yeltsin and democratic reform in Russia also resulted in major agreements that reduced the threat of nuclear proliferation in Eastern Europe. Not only did Russia and the U. S. agree to stop aiming their nuclear missiles at each other, the administration secured an accord in December 1994 with Ukraine, Kazakhstan, and Belarus to completely eliminate and dismantle their formidable nuclear arsenals. "I have sought to ensure," said Clinton, "that the breakup of the Soviet Union does not result in the birth of new nuclear states, which could raise the chances for nuclear accident, nuclear terrorism, or nuclear proliferation." Moreover, while in Europe, Clinton forcefully pushed for an expansion of the North Atlantic Treaty Organization (NATO) by proposing a "Partnership for Peace," which called for the inclusion of formerly communist-dominated Eastern European nations.

Closer ties and an open market in Europe were only part of Clinton's grand vision. He also had his eyes on the most dynamic markets for U.S. goods and services—Asia and the South Pacific. The day after NAFTA's approval in the House of Representatives, Clinton flew to Seattle to host leaders from fifteen Pacific Rim nations. There, at the APEC Conference, he boldly proposed a "New Pacific community," and Pacific-wide zones that would link together jobs, trade, and economies. The President's plan took the other leaders by surprise. "No one expected such a comprehensive vision, or such lofty goals," said one member of the Japanese delegation.

In essence, Clinton had set the stage for future cooperation and action. And when the leaders met again the next year in Bogor, Indonesia, the group was ready to enter the next phase. There they released what was dubbed the Bogor Declaration, which stated, in part, that all the member nations had agreed to create the world's largest free trade zone within the next quarter century. *The New York Times* noted that the leaders' "declaration of common resolve went far beyond the vague vision of their meeting in an Indian long house on a windswept island near Seattle just a year ago."

Both the United States and Japan, as the leading developed nations in the Asia-Pacific region, agreed to eliminate all trade barriers by the year 2010. Other developing nations would follow suite by 2020. Moreover, all the leaders agreed to spend the next year building a road map that would detail concrete actions needed to achieve the goal. That plan would be discussed when they reconvened a third time in Osaka, Japan, in 1995.

As if all that wasn't enough, Clinton also brought Secretary of Commerce Ron Brown to the Indonesian APEC conference where Brown witnessed the signing of more than a dozen business deals that included an energy joint venture between Exxon USA and Pertamina, Indonesia's state-owned oil company. In other strategic moves in Asia-Pacific, Clinton lifted the decades-old trade embargo against Vietnam and acted to impose tough trade restrictions on Japan for failing to open its own lucrative market to American goods as promised.

Elsewhere in the world, Clinton moved forcefully to ease trade restrictions on South Africa, China, and Russia. He revived stalled Mideast peace talks and personally lobbied King Fahd of Saudi Arabia to grant a multibillion dollar order for U.S. airplanes, which came through in February 1994. And in early 1995, the United States signed $1.4 billion in new business agreements for the construction of power plants, telecommunications infrastructure, and aircraft sales with firms based in India.

All of these specific moves were initiated in the context of Clinton's grand vision for the role of the United States in a post cold war world, which was to be a front-runner in creating jobs for Americans. "We must go into the 21st century," declared Clinton, "convinced that the only way to preserve the American dream is to be involved with the rest of the world."

VISION AND HOPE IN LEADERSHIP

In leadership, a vision is commonly defined as a mental image of what the future could or will be like. Once the image is crystallized, a leader will usually develop a strategic plan comprised of itemized steps, or goals, designed to realize that vision. Good leaders almost always imbue a strong sense of hope in their visions, because the feeling of expectation that hope brings is grounds for people in the organization to believe that something good is going to result from their own individual efforts. Therefore, great visions can be effective tools for achievement, because they motivate and inspire people.

From the moment he took office, Bill Clinton seemed to be infused with a permanent sense of commitment. "Every day I try to get up and think about whether what I do will or will not help to improve the lives of most Americans," he said. Perhaps that's why he continually preached and reaffirmed his vision—wherever he went, to whomever he met, and by whatever means necessary. "Let us give our children a future," he said 1994. "Let us take away their guns and give them books. Let us overcome their despair and replace it with hope. Let us weave these sturdy threads into a new American community that can once more stand strong against the forces of despair, because everybody has a chance to walk into a better tomorrow."

There is quite a bit of evidence to suggest that Clinton's constant focus on hope for the future tapped into the hearts of millions of young people who, at the time, felt that good jobs were not available to them. But when the President of the United States told them that "if you work hard and play by the rules, you should be given a chance to go as far as your God-given ability will take you," many felt for the first time in their lives that someone in government was really concerned about them. And tens of thousands signed up for the president's national service and jobs training programs.

Bill Clinton's ability to provide a lofty vision for America was especially suited to a turbulent, rapidly changing world. More than once, he stated that "when so much is threatened and so much is promised, we need to beat back the threats and seize the promise," and that, in such times, the government should "keep people thinking positively and looking toward the future."

As president, Clinton was driven to do all he could to make the future better than the past for future generations of Americans. His remarks in January 1994 provided some insight into his overall sense of mission. When asked what he would like future historians to say about his time in office, Clinton replied:

I would like them to say I restored a sense of hope and optimism to my country, that I strengthened the economy, and made it possible for my people to lead the world economically into the 21st century and, that I restored the sense of community in America, that we came back together as a people even though we are very diverse now. And I would like it to be said that I helped lead the world to more peaceful cooperation, into a future very different from the bloody and divided past of the 20th century.

"As certainly as it was true 200 years ago, yesterday is yesterday. If we try to capture it, we will only lose tomorrow."

—Clinton, at the University of North Carolina
October 12, 1994

"I still believe in a place called Hope."

—Clinton, Democratic National Convention
July 16, 1992

*During the **summer of 1995**, the new Republican-controlled Congress conducted special hearings looking into Whitewater, Vince Foster's suicide, and
potential obstruction of justice and corruption by the Clinton administration. It began in **July 1995** with the Senate Special Whitewater Committee,
chaired by New York senator Alfonse D'Amato and aided by his chief counsel, Michael Chertoff. Time after time, Republican senators, such as Lauch
Faircloth of North Carolina and Richard Shelby of Alabama, accused President Clinton and many of his associates of unethical and illegal activities.
Witnesses who testified to events that were not what the senators wanted to
hear were harassed and lambasted for lying. Hillary Clinton's chief of staff,
Maggie Williams, for instance, was accused of taking a box of files out of
Vince Foster's office immediately after his body was discovered. In response,
she testified that she had transferred the files only after investigators had
searched and cleared the office. Susan Thomases, a friend of both Foster
and Hillary Clinton, was also ridiculed when she stated that her telephone
conversation with Mrs. Clinton following Foster's death consisted of consoling each other's grief and talking about the funeral.*

*In **August 1995**, the House Banking Committee began its own hearings into charges that the federal Resolution Trust Corporation had obstructed or manipulated the results of its investigation of Madison
Guaranty. The committee was chaired by ranking Republican James Leach
of Iowa, who continued his personal Whitewater crusade against the Clintons. Congressional hearings in regard to Whitewater were to last for three
years. All the while, national television and the mainstream press regularly
reported on the proceedings. Hundreds of witnesses were called, hundreds
of depositions were taken, and tens of thousands of documents were reviewed. In the end, there was no reliable testimony and no documented evidence to suggest that Bill or Hillary Clinton did anything wrong with
regard to any of the matters investigated. As a matter of fact, most of the evidence, along with special FBI and Justice Department findings, completely
exonerated the Clintons.*

❧

*After Kenneth Starr was appointed independent counsel, he went to
Arkansas to conduct investigations. Focusing on individuals close to the
Clintons, his apparent plan was to indict key people, gain a conviction, and
then attempt to get them to testify against the Clintons in return for light
sentences or no prison time. Approximately one year after he became independent counsel, Starr issued a series of indictments, most of which were
based on the testimony of David Hale. The first to be indicted, on **June 7,
1995**, was Arkansas governor Jim Guy Tucker, who, as lieutenant governor,
had succeeded Bill Clinton upon his election as president. Starr charged*

Tucker with three counts of conspiracy to commit bankruptcy and tax fraud. The charges were not related to any aspect of Whitewater or the Clintons. After the indictments were announced, Tucker accused Starr of a "politically driven . . . taxpayer funded invasion of Arkansas."

Jim and Susan McDougal were indicted next, on **August 17, 1995.** *They were charged with twenty-one separate counts of bank fraud. Starr accused them of conspiring to loan money to a third party, who shared the money with David Hale. Those funds were subsequently used to obtain a $1.5 million loan from the Small Business Administration. When the initial indictments were filed, both Jim and Susan McDougal denied the charges and asserted that the Clintons had done nothing wrong.*

On **September 5, 1995,** *U.S. District Judge Henry Woods threw out the charges against Jim Guy Tucker, because they had nothing to do with either the Clintons or Whitewater, which Starr was charged with investigating. In his decision paper, Woods stated that Starr had exceeded his lawful authority and that "to gloss over and shortcut the requirements of criminal statutes is the first step toward tyranny." Immediately after the decision was announced, Judge Woods was attacked in* The Washington Times *as being corrupt, engaging in past improprieties, and, worst of all, being a friend of Bill Clinton. Similar charges were leveled in both the* Arkansas Democrat-Gazette *and* The Wall Street Journal. *Kenneth Starr quickly filed an appeal and asked the court to have Woods removed from the case, because "information in the public domain [gives] an unmistakable appearance of bias."*

On **December 18, 1995,** *The Resolution Trust Corporation released a preliminary report on its investigation into the Whitewater matter. According to its findings, the Clintons had told the truth. They were passive investors who lost just over $43,000, and their partner had looted the money without their knowledge. That same day,* The Wall Street Journal *printed an accurate account of the report's conclusions. But other major newspapers buried the news. The next morning (***December 19, 1995***),* The New York Times *ran a front-page story reporting that, according to anonymous sources, Independent Counsel Kenneth Starr was preparing a case to indict Hillary Clinton on felony counts of perjury and obstruction of justice. Later that day, ABC's* Nightline *aired a special segment on the new story and accused the First Lady of being less than truthful.*

The Times' source reportedly was Hickman Ewing, deputy counsel in the Office of the Independent Counsel. Ewing had leaked the story of the possible "indictments" in order to counter the conclusions of the RTC report. This action appeared to be a violation of Federal Rules of Criminal Procedure, which forbids giving the press information that might be used in a grand jury investigation.

PART III
ACTION

"It is not enough in life to have feelings. It is not enough in life to have convictions. You must act on them. You must act on them. You must move. You must do. You must make things happen."

—Clinton, to members of the American Boys Nation
June 7, 1993

"When you live in a time of change, the only way to recover your security and to broaden your horizons is to adapt to the change, to embrace it, to move forward."

—Clinton, in remarks supporting the North American Free
Trade Agreement (NAFTA)
September 15, 1993

"If you'll go out on a limb, I'll go with you."

—Clinton, urging Democratic Congressmen to support his
deficit reduction plan
May 19, 1993

CHAPTER NINE

CHANGE AND RISK-TAKING

Bill Clinton returned to the White House at 1:00 A.M. on May 19, 1993. He had been in New Mexico and California holding town meetings and other open forums in a concerted effort to build public support for the budget deficit reduction proposal that was being debated in Congress. But by 10:00 A.M., he was charging up Capitol Hill to reassure wavering Democratic members of Congress that his economic plan was worth supporting, that it was a necessary change.

While he had been away, a mini-rebellion had occurred in which conservative House Democrats argued that Clinton was both going too far and not going far enough. They wanted more spending cuts, fewer taxes, and more caps on entitlement programs. Over in the Senate, David Boren of Oklahoma was leading an all-out effort to scrap the BTU energy tax and implement greater spending cuts. Nearly all the members of Congress were concerned about the risk involved in supporting Clinton's program. Clearly, prospects for reelection weighed heavily on their minds.

When the president arrived to speak to the Congressional Democratic Caucus and House Democratic leaders, he found that former independent presidential candidate Ross Perot was just down the hall meeting with freshman Republicans and attacking both the president and the budget proposal. But buoyed by a strong show of support from Senate Majority Leader George Mitchell and House Speaker Thomas Foley, Clinton was able to calm the dissenters.

He reassured them that his proposal was worth supporting, that change never comes easily, and that they were not the only ones at risk. Clinton reasoned with them, pleaded with them, and, in the end, inspired them. When he closed by asserting, "If you'll go out on a limb, I'll go with you," the congressmen cheered and applauded. The president's personal presence when it counted, and his willingness to place himself at risk along with his colleagues, may well have made the difference between success and failure—as the economic plan eventually passed by the slimmest of all possible margins in both houses of Congress.

Such uprisings in the House and Senate were not uncommon while Clinton occupied the White House. Furious and often frantic attempts to reassure people, narrow margins of victory, and fluctuating approval ratings in the polls were characteristic of Clinton's tenure. Some critics called his a "Perils of Pauline" presidency. In essence, though, it was one of an activist leader attempting to guide a nation through changing times.

A TIME OF WORLDWIDE CHANGE

The root of many of Bill Clinton's political problems stemmed from the fact that he led during a time of major global transformation—a time when people were constantly challenging values; when corporations were going global on one end of the spectrum and out of business on the other; when people were having to transition themselves from one profession to another, because jobs were coming and going like ships in the night; when the entire world was being refocused while, at the same time, being irrevocably linked together.

Communism had virtually collapsed as a major force in world events, which, in effect, ended the cold war between the United States and a now non-existent Soviet Union. Further fueling the rapid transformation of nearly every aspect of people's lives were the rapid advancements in technology that sent news and information around the world in a matter of seconds. Such technological achievements, which manifested themselves in the likes of CNN and what were called at the time "information super highways," created a new economic world order, and advanced the already exploding process of globalization. It was truly revolutionary. No one had ever seen anything like it in the history of the world.

This was a time when many world leaders saw a decline in their popularity, including Vaclav Havel, president of the Czech Republic, who advocated that the modern age was over, and that the world was in a period of transition called "post-modernism." Havel noted that because of advancements in science and technology, this postmodern period created "the first civilization in the history of the human race that spans the entire globe and firmly binds together all human societies, submitting them to a common global destiny."

Bill Clinton clearly understood the impact of such a changing world, both on himself as president and on America as a whole. When asked at a news conference (in August 1994) why his approval ratings were so low, he responded: "Maybe it's partly a function of the times in which we live. Whenever we move from one historic era into another, [such as] now at the end of the Cold War moving toward the 21st century—our people are filled with a mixture of hope and concern. And when people have these balances going on, it is sometimes difficult to get through with the hope and the progress."

Leading newspapers and magazines also acknowledged the public's reactions to the changing times as a major factor in the deterioration of Clinton's public approval ratings. *The Wall Street Journal,* for example, wrote on August 3, 1993: "Voters' economic worries in the 1990s seem to stem not so much from unhappiness with what's happening today as from the underlying anxieties about tomorrow."

If the American public's anxieties about the changing times were part of the reason for President Clinton's waning popularity, it was also what got him elected in the first place. Fear of the unknown, and a lack of action by previous presidents to confront the coming change, drove voters to search for fresh leadership. Americans everywhere were demanding new approaches, and Clinton had the political intuitiveness to take that message directly to the people during the 1992 presidential campaign. He welcomed the wave of change and wove it into the core of his political strategy.

In Clinton's campaign war room, a sign on the wall became famous for its first line: *"It's the Economy, Stupid,"* and it's third line: *"Don't Forget Health Care."* But sandwiched in between those two slogans, and often overlooked, was the phrase: *"Change Versus More of the Same."*

Change was the primary issue that swept Clinton into the White House. He offered a stark contrast to incumbent president George H. W. Bush. Clinton was more youthful, more vigorous, more enthusiastic, and more passionate. In the first nationally televised presidential debate, on October 11, 1992, Clinton addressed Bush directly and forthrightly: "Mr. Bush," he said, "for twelve years you've had it your way; you had your chance and it didn't work. It's time to change."

A plurality of American voters agreed as Clinton won the election. But the vast majority of citizens were unprepared for the staggering number of changes the new president would attempt to implement.

CLINTON TRIES TO CHANGE WITH THE TIMES

"What this nation really needs is a vital center," said Bill Clinton early in his presidency, "one committed to fundamental and profound and relentless and continuing change." Simply put, Clinton believed that the United States had to transform itself if it was to succeed in the new era of postmodernism. That was his never-ending message to Americans. And he backed it up by pushing hard for a pervasive set of changes in domestic policy, foreign policy, and the internal workings of his administration. With his many new initiatives, Clinton aimed higher than any president had since Franklin D. Roosevelt's proposed legislation to end the Great Depression.

On the domestic front, his proposals were staggering. He sought a $500 billion reduction in the federal budget deficit. As part of that package, Clinton tackled a major reduction in the defense budget, which had always been viewed as a sacred cow by both the executive and legislative branches of government. He advocated the shut down of 180 U.S. military installations around the world, arguing cogently that since the Soviet Union had disappeared, there was no need for such enormous expenditures. At the same time, he proposed a $20 billion plan to provide financial aid and retraining to displaced members of the armed forces.

Clinton's administration also reduced the White House staff by 25 percent, proposed sweeping changes in the way the federal government issued regulations, and changed the way federal unemployment benefits were managed. The president tackled changes in the welfare system, campaign finance reform, crime prevention, and curriculum standards for academic achievement in U.S. schools, to name a few. And his cabinet members followed suit. Attorney General Janet Reno, for instance, pushed for a national program for children that included proper nutrition, health care, and education in the area of drug abuse prevention. Secretary of Labor Robert Reich oversaw major changes in job training and unemployment compensation. And HUD Secretary Henry Cisneros revamped troubled federal housing projects.

Clinton's changes in the area of foreign affairs were no less dramatic and comprehensive. He took a much tougher line with Japan on the issue of trade imports, opened doors to Vietnam, and supported Russia with economic aid. Clinton also shifted away from a policy in which the United States independently intervened in world crisis situations at will. Rather, Clinton made a strategic decision early in his presidency in favor of being part of a larger United Nations peacekeeping force, and concurrently pushed for an expansion of the United Nations' role as global peacekeeper.

Clinton received especially strong criticism on this issue from people on the conservative right who remained deeply skeptical about international cooperation in general, and who wanted to have maximum freedom to act now that the United States was the world's only true superpower. Despite that pushback, Clinton never wavered from his position. He refused to invade Haiti, Rwanda, or Bosnia without full support of the United Nations or other critical world organizations. In Bosnia, Clinton took the unusual step of encouraging the first military action in the history of the North Atlantic Treaty Organization.

Even though he was roundly criticized for holding fast to this new military policy, Clinton was widely praised for changing his own long-held position regarding China's status as a "most favored nation." In June 1994, his administration renewed China's MFN status and separated that issue conditionally from a more restrictive human rights accord. During the presidential campaign, Clinton had assailed George H. W. Bush and crusaded against such action. But as president, he came to see it Bush's way and concluded that non renewal would only serve to further isolate China and inhibit progress in the human rights arena. Of this decision, *Time* wrote: "The courage to change is often the very definition of leadership. The President's action was realistic and courageous."

In addition to domestic and foreign affairs, Clinton wasn't afraid to change his personal and political agendas, either. One of the most notable transformations occurred after his first 100 days in office during which he had allowed euphoria and enthusiasm to veer his legislative agenda too far to the left. When the American public showed their disproval with the lowest presidential approval rating in history, Clinton moved rapidly to the more moderate agenda upon which he had campaigned. He offered a compromise on the divisive issue of gays in the military. He began being more cooperative with moderate Republicans, overtly and in private. He proposed more spending cuts and fewer tax hikes. And with time, he reorganized the White House staff, in part, by replacing his communications director, his chief of staff, and his treasury secretary. Shortly thereafter, Clinton's poll ratings went back up.

Two years later (1995), when the Republicans took over both houses of Congress, President Clinton shifted his political agenda once again. He adopted a set of policies that were more liberal than those of the right-wing Republicans, but more conservative than those of left-wing Democrats. With this strategy, Clinton initiated welfare reform, a balanced budget, and Middle Class Bill of Rights (which included tax credits for college education, child exemptions, expansion of Individual Retirement Accounts [IRAs], and a GI worker's bill). Clinton's ability to secure passage of all these proposals played a major role in his reelection to a second term in 1996.

CLINTON THE RISK-TAKER

At one point during the presidential campaign of 1992, Bill Clinton asserted that "people can't imagine what an effective presidency would be like anymore. What really ought to count is: What have you put yourself on the line for?"

In the months after his election, newspaper and magazine headlines reflected the fact that Clinton frequently took risks by attempting to push through Congress many controversial initiatives. *The New York Times* wrote "He's gambling everything on [health care]." Of pushing his crime prevention bill, *USA Today* noted that "Clinton clearly is taking the chance of another failure." And regarding the campaign for NAFTA, *Newsweek* asserted that "Clinton is betting his presidency on a last-minute victory."

Cutting entitlements and proposing new taxes in order to ensure long-term prosperity were among the proposals that cost Clinton dearly in the polls. He took the heat for his support of President Boris Yeltsin and a hefty Russian financial aid package. He endured the criticism from human rights activists after meeting personally with China's president at the APEC Conference in Seattle. And he stood up to the threats of religious fanatics after welcoming to the White House novelist Salman Rushdie, who was condemned to death by Iranian Muslims for writing *The Satanic Verses.*

During the entire time Bill Clinton served as President of the United States, he made it a habit of confronting issues that most politicians viewed as suicidal. Here are only a few of the political risks he took:

- Clinton risked alienating elderly citizens and the American Association of Retired Persons (AARP) by proposing that Medicare (which serves more than thirty million people) be incorporated into an overall health care reform bill. *Risk involved: Losing the support of the largest single lobby in America.*

- He proposed that a higher percentage of taxes be paid by wealthy citizens and, at the same time, advocated a higher corporate tax rate in order to reduce the federal deficit. *Risk involved: Losing the support of big business and wealthy political patrons.*

- He proposed a broad-ranging ban on semi-automatic assault weapons as a way of fighting increased crime in America. *Risk involved: Losing support of the powerful National Rifle Association and those congressmen and senators supported by the NRA.*

- He proposed a major energy BTU tax as part of his $500 billion deficit reduction program. *Risk Involved: Losing support of the oil and gas industry, utility companies, and motorists who would have to pay higher gasoline prices.*

- He proposed cutting aid to prosperous school districts across the country and redirecting federal financial aid to poorer school districts. *Risk Involved: Losing immediate support from at least sixteen states (Idaho, Indiana, Iowa, Kansas, Maine, Maryland, Minnesota, Montana, Nebraska, New Jersey, North Carolina, Oregon, South Dakota, Utah, Virginia, and Wisconsin) that would see all or part of their federal education aid cut.*

Many of Clinton's proposed changes in the federal government had been attempted by previous presidents—almost always to no avail. Theodore Roosevelt, Harry Truman, Jimmy Carter, and Ronald Reagan all introduced efforts to reorganize the way government did business. Their efforts resulted in little effective change even though several initiatives became law. In addition, both Richard Nixon and Jimmy Carter proposed sweeping changes in America's troubled welfare system. But no substantial legislation was ever passed and welfare entitlements continued to grow.

Major health care reform that guaranteed coverage to all Americans was originally part of Franklin D. Roosevelt's New Deal, and later, the core of Harry Truman's presidency. Both failed after their plans were labeled "socialized medicine" by special interest groups. Not surprisingly, Clinton drew parallels between Truman's experiences and his own. Said Clinton:

Most Americans didn't like him too much at the time. He was low in the polls [and] a lot of people wouldn't have walked across the street to shake his hand when he was in office, because he stood up for ordinary people, he told extraordinary truths, and he tried to get us to face the problems of our time. In retrospect, we can see that [Harry Truman] did a good job. Everybody thinks of [him] now as the fount of all wisdom. He was right fifty years ago, and it's still true.

⇜

The fact that other presidents had tried and failed to change these major bureaucratic barriers did not seem to phase Clinton in the least. While American history demonstrated vividly that his odds of achieving so much formidable change in such a short period of time were very low, he plowed right ahead with many similar controversial issues.

Political pundits questioned Bill Clinton's strategy, if not his sanity, in tackling so many things at once. But the same criticism was leveled at many of the world's past leaders who were known for their strong skills and attributes. The truth is that any leader who desires to be successful at implementing vast waves of change must be ready, willing, and able to take risks.

Throughout his political career, Bill Clinton was clearly willing to take the risks and make the mistakes necessary in his efforts to change the country. As governor of Arkansas, he told his staff that "we must take risks to move forward. The saddest people [I know are] those who had dreams but never tried to fulfill them." And as president, he said on May 31, 1994: "I like fighting these fights. I don't mind making these enemies."

RESISTANCE TO CHANGE

Clinton was elected president largely on a mandate for change. But it was a fragile mandate. Because he received only 43 percent of the popular vote, it was logical to think that a majority of voters did not really want the kind of change he was proposing. The fact that he represented both generational *and* philosophical change could also lead one to conclude that at least one third of the U.S. population felt deeply threatened by Clinton's proposed changes. Furthermore, while many voters knew that things had to get better, there was little agreement on exactly what kind of change was necessary. Therefore, from a human nature perspective alone, the stage was set for a massive negative reaction to whatever initiatives Bill Clinton's administration proposed.

Republicans and Democrats alike lined up to protect their pet programs and to fight anything that might adversely affect their states or districts. Senators and congressmen fretted and ultimately resisted Clinton's attempts to alter campaign finance reform, a proposal that directly threatened their livelihood. The chairmen of appropriations committees in both houses of Congress reacted harshly to the administration's proposal of the line item veto and a plan to change the federal budget cycle to a two-year cycle from a yearly one, because these ideas, if implemented, would reduce their year-to-year power.

Predictably, Clinton's reform proposals mobilized intense, almost frantic, activity from entrenched businesses and industries. Special interest groups, for instance, spent hundreds of millions of dollars to derail the administration's plan to reform health care. And even before a proposal could be made to tax alcohol and tobacco to finance the plan, an enormous negative reaction was provoked from lobby groups. Beer maker Anheuser-Busch fought the tax idea by placing signs on its delivery trucks that asked customers to protest by dialing 1–800-BEER-TAX. Nothing resembling what Clinton originally proposed ever came to the floors of either the Senate or House of Representatives.

Additionally, an unusual coalition came together to oppose passage of NAFTA. It included organized labor, consumer groups, environmentalists, and billionaire businessman Ross Perot. And when Al Gore released his initiative to reinvent government, even Treasury Secretary Lloyd Bentsen and Attorney General Janet Reno, prominent members of the Clinton cabinet, both objected to rolling the Drug Enforcement Administration and the Bureau of Alcohol, Tobacco, and Firearms into the FBI. Similar opposition was encountered during the struggles for campaign finance reform, crime prevention legislation, welfare reform, and military base closings.

Bill Clinton understood that a leader will frequently get hit from both sides of an issue as people sometimes react negatively even if the proposed change will actually be helpful to them down the road. "People who will be adversely affected by the change know it and they'll fight you like crazy," he told the Democratic National Committee in June 1994. "On the other hand, the people who will benefit are always somewhat uncertain about what the change will be, and therefore, they won't bring themselves into the fight with the same gusto as those who are afraid of the change."

Because Clinton could not live on the vision created by past presidents, he worked with the American people to forge new plans and to achieve new goals. "The global economy is no longer the wave of the future," he said in October 1993 at the University of North Carolina. "It is here. And like the oceans that surround us, we cannot order it to recede." Virtually no one in America at the time, regardless of political affiliation, was able to argue that Bill Clinton had not effectively changed the debate. The question for Americans to answer was no longer *what* needed to be done. The question was *how* to do it.

"It is clear that we live at a turning point in human history. Immense and promising changes seem to wash over us every day. The Cold War is over. The world is no longer divided into two armed and angry camps. Dozens of new democracies have been born. It is a moment of miracles. The United States must and will serve as a fulcrum for change and a pivot point for peace. I believe—I know that together we can extend this moment of miracles into an age of great work and new wonders."

—Clinton, to the United Nations General Assembly
September 27, 1993

"The urgent question of our time is whether we can make change our friend and not our enemy."

—Clinton, First Inaugural Address
January 20, 1993

On *January 4, 1996*, *White House aide Carolyn Huber (a former office manager at the Rose Law Firm) discovered 116 pages of Hillary Clinton's missing billing records. According to Huber, she had come upon them in August 1995 in a back room of the Clinton's private White House quarters, taken them to her office for filing, and had forgotten about them. Because the documents were under subpoena by the Office of the Independent Counsel, Clinton's lawyer quickly sent the computer printouts to Kenneth Starr. Two days later, the story hit the press and caused a sensation of negative speculation. On* **January 8, 1996,** *William Safire of* The New York Times *published a column entitled "Blizzard of Lies," in which he labeled Hillary Clinton "a congenital liar." Other critics compared the First Lady to Eva Braun, Ma Barker, and Leona Helmsley. Conservative commentator G. Gordon Liddy carped: "I think the woman's been getting away with everything short of murder. . . . It's just amazing to me that this woman is . . . not yet under indictment." The* American Spectator *accused Mrs. Clinton of participating in "an obstruction of justice at the highest level since Watergate." And on* **January 15, 1996,** *Congressional Republicans charged that the billing records had been purposely withheld from their investigation to hide the First Lady's guilt. Even though the documents supported Mrs. Clinton's public statements in the Whitewater matter, Kenneth Starr issued her a subpoena to criminally probe whether or not the records had been intentionally withheld. And on* **January 26, 1996,** *Hillary Clinton answered Starr's questions in front of a grand jury.*

❧

On *Valentine's Day,* **February 14, 1996,** *White House aide (and former nanny to Chelsea Clinton) Helen Dickey was hauled before the Senate Whitewater Committee to testify. A former Arkansas state trooper had charged that she had placed a telephone call to the Arkansas governor's mansion shortly before Vince Foster's body was discovered. She was reported to have stated that Foster had killed himself in his car in a White House parking lot. "That's simply not true," said Ms. Dickey under oath. "I never would have said that because [those were not] the facts as I knew them at the time. I'm absolutely certain of the timing."*

❧

On **March 11, 1996,** *the heavily Republican Eighth Circuit Court of Appeals, based in St. Louis, Missouri, ruled in favor of the Office of Independent Counsel, and reinstated the indictments against Jim Guy Tucker and the McDougals. It also removed Judge Henry Woods from the case. In effect, this court ruling allowed Kenneth Starr to indict almost anybody,* *anywhere, for any violation of federal law, whether associated with White-water or not.*

The Tucker-McDougal joint trial was held during the months of **April and May 1996.** *Although President Clinton was not a party in the case, his name was repeatedly mentioned as having a role in illegal schemes surrounding Whitewater. David Hale, for instance, repeated his testimony that Clinton had been a participant in discussing a $300,000 loan. The jury also heard an FBI agent claim that, out of that money, the Clintons received a "$50,000 benefit." On* **April 28, 1996,** *the president testified via videotape from the White House. He denied David Hale's charges and, in fact, denied ever having had an extensive conversation with Hale. Due to lack of evidence, on* **May 6, 1996,** *the presiding judge dismissed four of the nine counts against Tucker, and four of the eight counts against Susan McDougal. Three weeks later (***May 28, 1996***), verdicts were handed down in the case. Jim Guy Tucker was found guilty of one count of conspiracy and one count of mail fraud. Jim McDougal was convicted on eighteen of nineteen counts of conspiracy. And Susan McDougal was found guilty on four counts involving misuse of Small Business Administration funds and making false statements.*

Tucker immediately resigned as governor of Arkansas, and, although continuing to proclaim his innocence, eventually agreed to a plea bargain in return for a lenient sentence and his potential testimony in future trials. He served eighteen months of home detention. James McDougal, who was faced with a maximum prison term of eighty-four years, agreed to change his testimony and implicate President Clinton in Whitewater. Susan McDougal, however, refused to "flip" when pressured by the Office of the Independent Counsel. On **August 20, 1996,** *she was given a two-year prison sentence. A short time later, after refusing to testify before a grand jury and implicate the Clintons in any crime, she was cited for civil contempt, and chose to serve another eighteen months in jail.*

In the wake of the Tucker and McDougal convictions, the mainstream media had a field day. The Washington Post *reported that Clinton had urged approval of a massive loan to "help my friends."* The Associated Press *wrote that the fraudulent loan benefited the Whitewater development and, thus, the president and Mrs. Clinton.* The New York Post *stated that the president might very well be guilty of a criminal "conspiracy to defraud a financial institution."* The British Broadcasting Service (BBC) *reported that President Clinton was an unindicted co-conspirator. And* The New York Times *columnist William Safire wrote that the Clintons might be "accomplices in stealing $50,000 from the poor," and titled one of his columns, "Jail to the Chief."*

"We can do better. We must! And we're going to bust a gut trying in this administration. We're gong to do our best."

—Bill Clinton, to the annual Convention of the Newspaper
Association of America, in Boston, Massachusetts
April 25, 1993

"I know they are tired. But they ought to draw energy from the tasks ahead.

—Bill Clinton, referring to Members of Congress
August 14, 1993

CHAPTER TEN

DRIVING TO ACHIEVE

In the summer of 1993, after six months in office, President Clinton had just finished visiting St. Louis, where he convened a major task force to aid victims of the summer's Midwest flooding. His term up to that point had been tumultuous. Gays in the military. A last-second, nail-biting victory in Congress for his budget bill. Low approval ratings. Republicans maneuvering to replace him in 1996. Members of the press already speculating that if he didn't get his act together, if there were many more screw-ups, he'd be history, a one-term president, booted out of the White House, gone.

One can almost visualize a scenario in which, upon walking back to his presidential limousine, Clinton suddenly realized that St. Louis was not that far from where he grew up in Arkansas. Then something came over to him. He ripped off his tie, pitched his coat into the car, and yelled, "ROAD TRIP!"

Bill Clinton's next moves were reported by *The New York Times* on July 19, 1993. The president boarded Air Force One and headed straight for Little Rock. Immediately upon landing at the airport, he threw his golf clubs and duffel bag into the trunk of his limo and drove off—Secret

Service agents in tow. His first stop was the local links, where he played a fast-paced round of golf. Then it was back into the car where he changed shoes and headed across town to visit an old high school classmate. Two hours later, he rode out to visit another old friend—after grabbing a clean shirt from his bag in the trunk. This time, however, much to the annoyance of his guards, he stayed for more than four hours. Finally, in the wee morning hours, Clinton arrived at the Little Rock home of Mack McLarty where he spent what was left of the night. After a few hours of sleep, he was at it again bright and early—jumping back into the car to go visit his mother.

Bill Clinton's "road trip" was a release of tension and frustration. He may have had an impulse to leave it all behind and go back to his beginnings; back to a less oppressive and judgmental environment; back to the carefree good old days. Somehow, it seemed metaphoric for a harried, hyperactive leader whose presidency was filled with numerous quick trips to varied places, and many initiatives that appeared to be all over the map and in various states of development.

But this summer excursion was also a way for Clinton to release some of his pent up energy. Other people didn't move as fast as he did, or do as many things. And predictably, a majority of aides, friends, and family reacted with trepidation at his pace. "You're moving too fast," they said. "We're not so sure we should be doing all this."

ENDLESS ENERGY

About two months after Clinton took office, Secretary of the Treasury Lloyd Bentsen (at 72 years, the eldest member of the cabinet) emerged from a meeting on the federal budget that lasted well into the night. He labeled it "an incredible grind," and expressed amazement that the president, who remained fully engaged throughout, did not "seem to feel the need for sleep." Clinton, on the other hand, emerged from the meeting room and said, "That was fun."

Lloyd Bentsen was not the first person to observe that Bill Clinton's energy level was extraordinary compared to that of most people. Physically, Clinton needed only four to six hours of sleep a night. When he did get tired during the day, one could sometimes find him catching a few winks leaning up against a wall or sitting in a chair. Long-time Clinton friend Diane Blair put it succinctly when she noted that: "[Clinton's] down time is less than that of other human beings."

As president, Clinton was at his job ten to twenty hours a day, and did not take off many weekends. "I normally work pretty late," he confided to Larry King. "Last Friday I worked till 8:30 P.M. And then we gathered up whoever was still working late in the White House, and Hillary and I, and Chelsea came down and watched a movie." Clinton also sneaked in so many short naps during the day that, early in his presidency, the press labeled him the nation's "napper-in-chief"—a moniker previously reserved for Ronald Reagan.

When Clinton channeled his energy toward those issues he felt were vital for the nation, he became a formidable and potent force in both national and international politics. And even when he was successful at achieving his goals, he constantly set about attacking the next item on his agenda. "We cannot stand still!" he said upon signing the Budget Deficit Reduction bill. And after signing the North American Free Trade Agreement into law, Clinton pressed for passage of the more comprehensive Global Agreement on Tariffs and Trade: "Don't rest. Don't sleep. Close the deal," he implored Congress.

Clinton's enormous energy was contagious. It flowed from him to the people who surrounded him like bolts of electricity, sparking new action and new activity. For example, during the 1993 G–7 Summit in Tokyo, Bill Clinton met privately with most of the other leaders and urged them to take more definitive action to open up new markets around the world—and they ended up holding sustained trade negotiations that lasted around-the-clock. When the conference concluded, Clinton was on the move again. The day after the summit officially ended, he had a private breakfast and a subsequent news conference with Russian president Boris Yeltsin; then there was a press announcement with Japanese prime minister Kiichi Miyazawa. A few hours later, Clinton was in South Korea having yet another news conference (and a private meeting) with President Kim Young Sam. From there, the president went to Hawaii to spend a week with his family. But he cut short his vacation after only a few days to fly all night and see first hand the disastrous effects of Midwest flooding in Des Moines, Iowa. Afterwards, he flew back to Washington and immediately began lobbying Congress to pass comprehensive disaster relief aid for the area.

But that effort was nothing compared to his actions on December 5, 1994. During that twenty-four-hour period, Clinton flew to Budapest, Hungary, to participate in the Conference on Security and Cooperation in Europe, where leaders from fifty-two nations had gathered. The president had flown more than 9,000 miles, was on the ground barely seven hours, yet still managed to make three speeches, sign a nuclear arms pact with Ukraine, and meet privately with Boris Yeltsin and Helmut Kohl. Finally, upon his return to Washington, he hosted an evening Christmas reception for 400 members of Congress at which he had made another lengthy speech.

While high-energy leaders usually achieve a great deal, they are also apt to experience serious problems. They frequently risk, for instance, personal exhaustion that can cause irritability and lead to mistakes. Bill Clinton sometimes lost his temper and admitted to making his most serious mistakes when he was overtired. Once, after traveling all night to the January 1994 NATO Summit in Europe, he confided to a reporter that he hadn't slept much recently and was "afraid I'd fall over in public." Workers can also get burned out. As a matter of fact, citing "a new standard of intensity," and "professional burnout in a hectic first year in office," several members of Clinton's staff quit after less than a year on the job. Even the president's young, energetic, and enthusiastic aides complained about working long into the night, eating cold pizza, and being tired all the time.

Furthermore, leaders who pursue too many initiatives at one time often jeopardize all their initiatives. Members of Congress, for instance, frequently complained that the president submitted so many new pieces of legislation that they didn't have enough time to adequately evaluate all of them. Perhaps the most politically damaging problem for hyperactive leaders is that they are often perceived as being chaotic and disorganized. This was certainly a criticism of Bill Clinton—so much so, in fact, that some critics actually suggested that he take drugs to help him slow down and focus. White House advisers, on the other hand, urged him to prioritize, concentrate on one issue at a time, and get some rest.

Time reported in February 1994 that "Americans appreciate Bill Clinton's formidable energy and his doughty resilience." Given their choice, people would much rather have a leader predisposed to exerting high amounts of energy than one who is lethargic or of average vitality. They want their leaders to get things done for them—or at the very least *try* to get things done. The bottom line is that people value effort.

Ronald Reagan, America's eldest president, was criticized for not being involved enough in the day-to-day affairs of government. But Bill Clinton, the third-youngest American president, was accused of being *too* involved. Clinton made it quite clear to anyone who would listen that his style was that of a very active, hands-on person who was can-do, open, and flexible. "You've got to show others you're working harder than they are," he often said.

A STRONG BIAS FOR ACTION

Bill Clinton proposed more major initiatives in the early going of his presidency than any other new president had in the previous half century. Not since the days of Franklin Roosevelt and the Great Depression had a leader been so bold in attempting to change the status quo. Clinton, however, was not acting in a time of national crisis, which made attempts at change all that more difficult. But as justification for his aggressive agenda, Clinton referred to the people who put him in office. "We were elected to govern," he told his fellow Democrats. "We were elected to end gridlock. I don't know how many people I heard [during the campaign] tell me, 'Even if you make me mad, do something. Do something. Move this thing. Break us out. Get something going.'"

And get something going he did. In a little more than a year and a half, he secured passage of such major legislation as: The Family Leave Bill, the Motor Voter Bill, a $500 billion deficit reduction budget package, a national service program, NAFTA, the Brady Bill (which was the first major federal gun control legislation in a quarter of a century), and a $33 billion bill to fight crime in America.

Over the course of his presidency, Clinton also tackled such sensitive, divisive issues as health care reform, welfare reform, abortion rights, and campaign finance reform. With regard to abortion, he ended a twelve-year restriction on federally funded abortions and eliminated the so-called gag rule that involved counseling patients.

In the areas of science and the environment, Clinton promoted the Safe Drinking Water Act, a reformed Superfund program, and the Kyoto global warming accord. He created the national Sustainable Development Commission on the environment, proposed a plan for controlling the release of harmful pollutants into the atmosphere, offered a settlement in the long-troubled Northwest timber dispute, funded research and subsequent development of a national information superhighway, and proposed a comprehensive national technology initiative.

The media annually chronicled Clinton's ambitious agendas. Of his second-year plans, for instance, *Time* reported: "[The president] limited his top priorities for 1994 to seven initiatives, eight if you count the information superhighway, but couldn't resist adding a dozen or so secondary and tertiary items, amounting to an enormously ambitious and detailed to-do list by any standard." But when some members of the media derided him for what was perceived as a shotgun approach to government, Clinton defiantly responded: "I've been criticized for doing more than one thing at once. I believe you'd rather see us err on the side of effort than on the side of just preserving the status quo."

Clinton also justified his extensive political agenda by eloquently speaking about the importance of periodic renewal. "Our ability to recreate ourselves at critical junctures is why we're still around after all this time. . . ." he said. "Our founders clearly understood that every generation would have to reinvent the Government. Thomas Jefferson said that laws and institutions must go hand in hand with progress of the human mind as that becomes more developed, more enlightened, as new discoveries are made and new truths discovered and manners and opinions change. With the change of circumstances, institutions must also advance to keep pace with the times."

Bill Clinton went a step further by trying to turn his rhetoric into reality. "Make no mistake about this," he said regarding his plan to reduce waste in government. "This is one report that will not gather dust in a warehouse. There are a lot of places in this report where it says 'the President should.' Well, let me tell you something, I've read it, and where it says 'the President should,' the President will."

A LEADER'S BULLY PULPIT

When Clinton issued a call for action, it often set off a flurry of activity at the state level. While some state legislators thought Clinton's initiatives were good ideas, others decided to implement their own plans before the federal government imposed regulations on them. Whatever the reasoning, there was definitely a "ripple" effect generated when Clinton cast the first stone in the water. The administration's Reinventing Government initiative and the 1993 deficit reduction budget bill, for instance, set off a wave of deficit lowering at the state and local levels. By May 1994 (fifteen months after Clinton took office), hundreds of cities across the United States had cut their budgets similarly—chopping nearly all areas except police protection.

When Clinton proposed financing health care reform with so-called "sin taxes" on alcohol and tobacco, four states (Connecticut, Massachusetts, Rhode Island, and Washington) immediately increased taxes on cigarettes; and fifteen other states considered the idea. When the president convened a task force to fulfill his campaign pledge to "end Welfare as we know it," a dozen or more states began to experiment with their own version of reform. Wisconsin asked the White House for permission to proceed with a two-year limit on welfare benefits—something that Clinton had previously proposed. Arkansas, Georgia, and New Jersey immediately reduced their payments to mothers who had new children, as did California to *all* welfare recipients. In addition, New Jersey, Maryland, Florida, New Hampshire, and other states began revamping their own systems.

For a variety of reasons, a president's actions can also spur congressmen into action. Some write their own legislation because they want their particular views included in the bill; some do it for purely partisan political reasons; and some because they want to move faster than the president can or will move. Impatient members of the Democratic Party's Mainstream Forum, for instance, led by Oklahoma representative. Dave Mc-Curdy, submitted their own Welfare plan in May 1994, simply because the president's agenda had been tied up with health care and other major initiatives. In this case, the legislators were trying to spur action.

The same thing happened with health care reform, only on a larger scale. Within a month after Clinton's address to a joint session of Congress, there were no less than five different health care plans put forward by various Congressmen and Senators. A year later the Clinton administration's plan was unveiled, and more alternative proposals were offered, including those from Senate Republican Leader Bob Dole of Kansas and Senate Democratic Leader George Mitchell of Maine.

Dozens of states also began experimenting with, or improving upon, their own versions of health care reform before the federal government became involved. Health care plans in such states as Connecticut, Iowa, Kentucky, Minnesota, New Jersey, Oregon, Tennessee, and Washington varied from complete and unequivocal universal coverage to encouraging the formation of HMOs and other similar alliances. "Unable to wait any longer for federal reform," wrote *Time* on June 28, 1993, "states and companies are launching their own programs to cut costs and extend coverage to more of those now uninsured."

By the end of 1994, Texas, California, and as many as eighteen other states began enrolling citizens in health alliances similar to the ones suggested in Clinton's original plan. Seventy-five percent of all physicians willingly reduced medical fees. Many corporations enrolled their employees in HMOs. And nearly all other states, at the very least, passed laws that protected small businesses from being gouged by health insurance companies. Of such "ripple effect" action, *The Wall Street Journal* observed in August 1994 that, "Many of [the] changes parallel the types of sweeping reorganization sought last year in President Clinton's original health care initiative."

Even with his failure to achieve a comprehensive package of universal coverage for all Americans in one fell swoop, Clinton was still able to call unprecedented attention to the issue. He had successfully elevated health care to a point where everybody was talking about it. And Clinton knew exactly what he was doing. In March 1994, he spoke about his strategy to raise awareness of key issues, and concluded by saying, "Theodore Roosevelt said once that the greatest power of the Presidency was the bully pulpit, the ability to talk about these problems and to give other people the chance to be heard."

Bill Clinton's "bully pulpit" approach was a consistent pattern over the course of his presidency, and usually resulted in success. After the defeat of a motion that kept his proposed crime bill from coming to a vote in the House of Representatives, for instance, Clinton went straight to the American people and told them that special interest groups were trying to kill the bill. Of this approach, *The Wall Street Journal* reported that the president used "his bully pulpit to pummel Republicans and other foes." Clinton's comprehensive crime bill was eventually passed in both houses of Congress.

AN INNATE DRIVE TO ACHIEVE

In one of its annual reviews of Bill Clinton's presidency, *Newsweek* charged that he "tends to mistake achievement for leadership." But *Newsweek* had it wrong. One of the things leaders are supposed to do is achieve things. Many of history's most successful leaders possessed a deep, driving need to achieve. It was part of their physical and chemical makeup. It's what set them apart from the crowd. And in many cases, it was much more than a simple inclination to get things done, it was an obsession. This was true of Mohandas K. Gandhi, Abraham Lincoln, and Theodore Roosevelt, to name a few.

A researcher doesn't have to dig very deep to realize that Bill Clinton was also driven to achieve. "I just try to get up every morning and make a little progress; I think that's what life is all about," he said on *Meet the Press*. "Martin Luther King, Jr. did a lot with the time he had, and I think we should try to do the same," he said on Dr. King's birthday in 1994. "When we [eliminate] insecurities, we will set our people free to create and innovate and achieve, as Americans always have and always will," he told students at the University of North Carolina.

What causes a person to take action while others sit around and watch? Could it be an innate trait, genetically predisposed at birth? If so, there is evidence to suggest that Clinton displayed such a trait at an early age. Margaret Polk, a family friend who lived in Hope, Arkansas, recalled an incident at a playground when a young Billy Blythe (Clinton) was only four years old.

> [A little girl named] Mitzi was about to slide down when the string on her cowboy hat got hung up on the slide. Before we could get to her, Bill climbed up the slide and pushed her feet up in order to free the string. He was such a little thing then, and I think that showed he was thinking beyond his age. Bill just seemed to accept responsibility early—even at the age of four.

Clearly, Bill Clinton's predisposition toward action, combined with his training to be a leader, prepared him for the presidency. When he made it to the White House, Clinton employed his energy, stamina, knowledge, and desire toward taking action on his political agenda. Then he relied on the sincerity of his actions to carry him over with the American public. "The economy was in pretty bad shape during most of Franklin Roosevelt's presidency, until the war started," said Clinton in May 1994. "[But] the perception of the country was that he was working, that he was experimenting, and that he was trying to get things done."

Bill Clinton knew that people will tolerate a great deal if they perceive their leaders are earnestly trying to make things happen. That knowledge, in part, was his sustenance against all the criticism he endured during his Presidency. It was why he vowed to his wife one day during a particularly bad time: "We're going to keep going. They're never going to stop us."

"It's like everything else. You just have to show up every day and try to make a little progress. I think that's what you do in life."

—Bill Clinton, on *Meet The Press*
November 7, 1993

"We cannot be tired today. We have a lot to do."

—Bill Clinton, to an audience in St. Louis, Missouri
June 24, 1994

In the run-up to the 1996 presidential election, a spate of anti-Clinton books were published—evenly spaced over the course of the year for maximum damage. Three notable examples were:

Blood Sport: The President and His Adversaries (**March 1996**), *written by Pulitzer Prize-winning author James B. Stewart, was a massive, error-ridden account of Whitewater. Among other things, the writer contended that the Clintons had not been passive investors, but had played a greedy leading role. Included in Stewart's national book tour was an appearance on ABC's* Nightline, *where Ted Koppel and the author discussed "the Clintons' refusal to abide by financial requirements in obtaining mortgage loans," and the belief that their involvement was a crime.*

Unlimited Access: An FBI Agent Inside the Clinton White House (**July 1996**) *was a hostile, tell-all type narrative about the Clintons and the people who surrounded them. Former FBI agent Gary Aldrich authored the book and charged such things as the president's having "frequent late-night visits to the Marriott Hotel" with a woman, and pornographic ornaments being hung on the White House Christmas tree. Excerpts of the book were reprinted in* The Wall Street Journal.

Boy Clinton: A Political Biography (**September 1996**) *was written by R. Emmett Tyrrell, Jr, the editor-in-chief of the* American Spectator. *Tyrrell charged that President Clinton used drugs heavily and might have been treated for a drug overdose, that Commerce Secretary Ron Brown (who died in a plane crash) might have been murdered, and that Clinton's administration was "the most corrupt and incompetent in American history."*

*One month before the presidential election, in **October 1996**, another pseudo-scandal erupted involving charges that the Democratic Party, and President Clinton's election campaign, in particular, had received illegal contributions from foreign sources. The Washington Post published an article detailing a Justice Department investigation that had apparently discovered evidence that spies for China had tried to donate money to the Democratic National Committee. Two Taiwanese nationals, Johnny Chung and Charlie Trie, were later convicted of various counts of election law violation. That same month, conservatives groups charged that the White House, as a way to raise money for the presidential campaign, was auctioning off sleepovers in the Lincoln Bedroom to wealthy donors. Congressional Republicans condemned the practice as demeaning to the presidency. Bill Clinton adamantly denied that any such thing ever happened.*

❧

*On **November 5, 1996**, Clinton was reelected President of the United States over Republican candidate Bob Dole of Kansas. Clinton won the popular* vote, 49 to 41 percent, and the Electoral College vote, 379 to 351. With that result, Bill Clinton became the first Democratic president to be elected to a second term since Franklin D. Roosevelt in 1936, sixty years earlier.

≈≶

On the steps of the U.S. Capitol building, with Hillary Clinton holding the Bible, Chief Justice of the Supreme Court William H. Rehnquist administered the oath of office for the second time to Bill Clinton (**January 20, 1997**). In the first moments of Clinton's new term, before delivery of the inaugural address, the chief justice turned to the president and shook his hand. "Good luck," said Rehnquist. "You'll need it."

That comment was a cryptic message based on fact. Just one week earlier, on **January 13, 1997**, the Supreme Court had heard arguments in Case No. 95–1853, Clinton v. Jones. The Paula Jones case had been in temporary hiatus after Little Rock Judge Susan Webber Wright's order that the trial be postponed until after Bill Clinton left office. Jones's lawyers appealed to the Eighth Circuit Court of Appeals in St. Louis, which promptly overturned Judge Wright's decision. Subsequently, the U.S. Supreme Court was left to decide whether or not a civil lawsuit against a sitting President of the United States could proceed, even though it was based on an incident that occurred prior to him being elected to office. Chief Rehnquist's comment to Clinton was an obvious warning that the argument had not gone well for him.

≈≶

On **February 17, 1997**, Kenneth W. Starr submitted his resignation as independent counsel, and announced he was accepting the position of Dean of the Schools of Law and Public Policy at Pepperdine University in Malibu, California. The new position had been established, in part, on a generous donation through a foundation funded by Richard Mellon Scaife. Almost immediately, Starr's announcement was met with rage and disgust by conservatives across the country. William Safire's column in The New York Times was a good example. Entitled "The Big Flinch," Safire charged that Starr had brought "shame on the legal profession by walking out on his client, the people of the United States, leaving us alone at the courthouse door." The conservative backlash was so profound that, four days later, Starr reversed his decision, declared that he was staying on the job after all, and went back to his investigations.

"I am going to focus like a laser beam on this economy."
—Bill Clinton, to Ted Koppel of ABC News
November 4, 1992

"I'm sorry the polls are the way they are. But, as President, [I must] take the information I have and do what I believe is best for our national security interests. My job is to make [a] decision and go forward. [And] my decision is that it's time for them to go. We have tried every other option."
—Bill Clinton, on why he would force dictators out of Haiti despite low public support
September 14, 1994

CHAPTER ELEVEN

DECISIVENESS

In mid-June 1993, Bill Clinton was praised by critics for working in tandem with the United Nations to solve ongoing problems in Somalia. On several occasions he defined in specific terms what the UN mission was doing there and how the United States was supporting that plan. In each instance, he was clear, concise, and to the point. No one questioned the UN policy or involvement by the United States. At the time, Somali warlord General Mohammed Farah Aidid was on the run and the UN peacekeeping forces were in firm control.

By early October, however, eighteen U.S. soldiers had been killed and more than seventy-five were wounded during a failed UN combat mission there. Millions of Americans watched in horror as the badly battered body of a U.S. soldier was dragged through the streets of Mogadishu while a crowd of Somalis cheered. Instantly, the president's detractors charged that he had not explained the U.S. presence in Somalia and that he was an irresolute commander in chief. When Clinton sent Defense Secretary Les Aspin and Secretary of State Warren Christopher to meet and discuss the situation with members of Congress, the president was roundly criticized as being nebulous and indecisive. "No clear mission," they charged. "What are we doing over there?" asked the press. "Get us out!" responded the public.

Clinton, who was in California when he received word of the tragedy, did not panic. He immediately got on the telephone, started gathering information, and returned to Washington the next day. When he took three days to obtain all the facts and reevaluate the situation, he was again accused of being indecisive, of wavering, of taking too long to decide.

On the third day, the president spoke to the American people. He specifically described what had happened and reemphasized the American objectives and goals in Somalia. He set a timely target for all American troops to be withdrawn by the end of March 1994. And he forcefully and impressively explained the need for continued involvement and support of the United Nations efforts.

Even though he acted decisively, and in a relatively brief period of time given the situation, the perception of Bill Clinton as indecisive had once again floated to the surface. This time, though, Clinton handled the criticism like a professional. He had been through it before.

CLINTON'S DECISIVENESS

After becoming president, Clinton frequently "thought out loud" when considering various decisions. While the American people were unaccustomed to a president who opened up his thought process for public inspection, the fact that all options under consideration were released by the White House in the order they came gave many people the impression that the president couldn't make up his mind.

While in the process of filling Thurgood Marshall's vacant seat on the Supreme Court, Clinton learned very quickly that many people did not want leading contender Bruce Babbitt chosen because he was viewed as too valuable as Secretary of the Interior. And *The New York Times* revealed that another prospective nominee for that seat, Judge Stephen Breyer, had a potential problem with not paying taxes for a domestic servant—the same issue that sank Zoe Baird's nomination for attorney general. That disclosure, in part, led Clinton to select Ruth Bader Ginsburg because he did not want to risk making the same mistake twice. One year later, however, Breyer (who had resolved his problem to the president's satisfaction) was selected to fill the vacancy of retiring Supreme Court Justice Byron White.

As in the Breyer case, President Clinton often changed his mind or reversed course after a decision had been made. For doing so, he was mocked by critics such as Republican Party Chairman Haley Barbour who charged that the President "shares with the hummingbird the amazing ability to turn 180 degrees in a wink."

When Clinton blundered badly and then corrected his mistakes, he was perceived as wavering and indecisive. As it became apparent that Zoe Baird's nomination as attorney general and gays serving in the military were unacceptable to the vast majority of Americans, was President Clinton acting as a leader by changing his mind—or was he being wishy-washy, wavering, and indecisive? Is it wrong for a leader to change his mind and risk being viewed as indecisive if his original judgment was in error, or should he stand by his first choice on principle and abandon his goals?

While much of the American public perceived Clinton as unwilling to make decisions, a close inspection of his record reveals that he was, in fact, an unusually decisive president. There were not many items that lingered in the Oval Office.

Take, for instance, the flurry of activity leading up to the 1993 Fourth of July weekend. Before leaving for the G–7 Summit in Tokyo, Clinton made the following decisions—all of which were announced nearly simultaneously: He closed 130 military bases around the country, 90 more overseas, and reduced the operations of another 45; he proposed $5 billion in spending to help communities hit hard by military base closings; he extended the ban on U.S. nuclear testing for fifteen months; he opened up a dialogue for restoring international trade to Vietnam; he decided to release a plan to help resolve the Pacific Northwest's spotted owl/timber dispute; he made the decision to fire FBI Director William Sessions; and he ordered the military bombing of Iraq. "It was like hell week around here," Clinton told a *Newsweek* reporter. "Line them up and knock them out."

Except for the times that Clinton went on vacation or traveled abroad, such a rapid-fire decision-making pace was not unusual. He consistently pressed for action on his own initiatives and reacted swiftly to changing events. Nor did he hesitate to countermand orders from subordinates that conflicted with his overall goals and objectives. In August 1993, he rescinded a command issued by Marine Corps Commandant General Carl Mundy, who had announced that, as of September 30, 1995, the Marines would no longer accept married recruits. Neither Clinton nor Defense Secretary Les Aspin had been consulted and both realized the paradoxical situation of allowing neither homosexuals nor married men into the service. The order was revoked instantly, but not before Colorado representative Pat Schroeder made her searing comment: "If they are not allowed to be homosexuals and they're not allowed to be married, what are they supposed to do—take cold showers?"

During the 1992 presidential campaign, Republicans painted Clinton as weak in foreign affairs, especially compared to the more experienced George H. W. Bush. But Clinton had studied international affairs while at Georgetown University and, as president, he became remarkably adept when it came to performing on the world stage. Take his handling of a crisis in Bosnia-Herzegovina, for instance. In February 1994, Clinton initially resisted retaliation with force after a brutal Bosnian attack on Sarajevo killed dozens of people and wounded several hundred. But within hours of the assault, the president convened a meeting of his national security team in which he ordered the American military to help evacuate casualties from the city, asked Warren Christopher to gauge the pulse of North Atlantic Treaty Organization member nations, and delegated to UN Ambassador Madeleine Albright the responsibility of working with the United Nations to determine specific responsibility for the offensive. The next morning (Sunday, February 6), in his private residence, the president reviewed the findings of the previous day and considered a variety of options.

A few days later, Clinton decided that, rather than act alone, he'd press for military action through NATO and begin peace negotiations. He also agreed to a modified proposal made by France to create a demilitarized zone of 20 kilometers around Sarajevo. Then Clinton got on the phone and spoke personally with John Major of Britain, Francois Mitterrand of France, and Jean Chrétien of Canada, and pressed for military action if the Serbs did not comply.

The president's next moves were to fulfill his commitment under the War Powers Act by sending a statement to Congress notifying them he might order U.S. warplanes to bomb Bosnia and Herzegovina. For the public, Clinton defined the nation's interests in taking part in NATO's action in Bosnia, which included: maintaining the credibility of NATO, preventing a broader European conflict, stemming the flow of refugees, and halting the killing of innocent women and children. On March 1, 1994, in what was the first NATO military action in its forty-five-year existence, American planes shot down four Serbian jet fighters in response to their bombing of a Bosnian munitions plant. And a month later, bombs were dropped near the city of Goradze when Serbs ignored demands from the United Nations to pull back.

On another front, Clinton never wavered in his resolve to restore democracy to Haiti. Early on, he supported a series of steps by the United Nations designed to return exiled President Jean-Bertrand Aristide to power by October 31, 1993. But when the first ship carrying

American troops tried to dock at Port-Au-Prince, violent armed demonstrations staged by the Haitian military prevented a safe landing. And Clinton immediately ordered the vessel to return to the United States. He then pressed to impose economic sanctions against the tiny island nation.

Nine months later, when sanctions were clearly not working, Clinton built a coalition of Western Hemisphere nations who approved a military invasion. But by September 1994, 70 percent of the American public were against using force in Haiti. Clinton, on the other hand, was adamant that action had to be taken.

He deployed nearly 20,000 troops on battleships off the coast of Haiti and, in a live address from the Oval Office, he meticulously laid out justification for his plans—and also took the opportunity to deliver a stern warning to leaders in Haiti: "The message of the United States to the Haitian dictators is clear," said Clinton. "Leave now or we will force you from power."

Finally, in a last-ditch effort to avoid a forced invasion, Clinton sent a delegation to negotiate with General Raoul Cedras. Jimmy Carter, fresh from a successful effort in North Korea, was selected to go, along with retired General Colin Powell, who represented the American military, and Senator Sam Nunn, who led congressional support for an invasion.

While the trio was in Port-Au-Prince, Clinton monitored activity on CNN and took several phone calls from Carter and Powell, who called seeking the President's direction. As the talks stalled, Clinton asked Carter to tell Cedras that the invasion was starting. When the Haitian general confirmed that sixty-one airplanes were already in the air and on their way south, he quickly worked out a deal for amnesty and agreed to leave power no later than October 15, 1994. On that date, Aristide returned to Haiti, which was almost exactly one year after the target date Clinton had originally set.

Lesser known to the American public was that, from 1995 to 2000, Bill Clinton made a wide-ranging series of forceful decisions designed to fight and prevent terrorism. In the legislative arena, among other things, he proposed new laws to provide additional enforcement officials to combat terrorism, boosted counterterrorism resources for both the CIA and FBI (including a new FBI counterterrorism center), and increased overall counterterrorism funding by 43 percent.

Through executive directives, Clinton established the position of National Coordinator for Counterterrorism and Infrastructure Protection, and appointed Richard A. Clarke to hold the position. He established a National Infrastructure Protection Center to prepare a comprehensive plan to protect the nation's transportation, water system, and telecommunications networks. And he approved the use of military experts to aid in threats and incidents involving chemical, biological, and nuclear weapons. President Clinton also signed executive orders to allow greater law enforcement access to financial records and to implement extensive electronic surveillance on suspected terrorists. He levied sanctions against firms that did business in the energy sector with Iran and Libya, and imposed economic sanctions on the Taliban, Al Qaeda, and Osama bin Laden.

On the diplomatic front, after the Senate refused to attack Al Qaeda's financial roots, Clinton forged an agreement with twenty industrial nations to close the terrorist organization's tax havens. He also urged Sudan to expel Osama bin Laden (which they did), and Saudi Arabia not to take him (which they didn't). When the terrorist accepted refuge from the Taliban in Afghanistan, Clinton met with and pressured the president of Pakistan, Pervez Musharraf, to fight and try to apprehend bin Laden. Clinton also authorized both covert action and outright military bombing against terrorist targets. In addition to giving the CIA the go-ahead to kill or apprehend bin Laden, the President ordered air strikes against Al Qaeda training camps in Afghanistan and a terrorist weapons factory in Sudan.

In the long run, the Clinton administration was given credit for having stopped a number of terrorist attacks, including plots to blow up a dozen planes leaving the Philippines for the West Coast of America; planned attacks on the United Nations and the Lincoln and Holland tunnels in New York City; and the famous "Millennium" plots against the Space Needle in Seattle, hotels in Jordan, various holy sites in Israel, and Los Angeles International Airport.

CLINTON'S DECISION-MAKING PROCESS

Bill Clinton's open-minded style of decision making was called informal by some because he regularly relied on a small group of trusted advisers with whom he frequently met. His overall methodology was often misinterpreted as wavering or waffling. In May 1994, for instance, *The New York Times* reported that the president had "tried and failed again today to decide on a nominee for the Supreme Court." Press Secretary Dee Dee Myers, however, immediately responded that he was "in the final phase of the decision-making process."

As president, Clinton used a much more formal process than was generally recognized. Whether it was selecting a new justice for the Supreme Court or bombing Baghdad, all his major decisions were made with the same, classic four-step decision-making process. It was a method that listened to the voices of different people, weighed various options, and measured impact. While many interpreted his process as a weakness, it was actually one of Clinton's greatest strengths as a leader.

Let's examine his response to the 1993 crisis in Somalia as an example:

Step 1: Gather Information and Understand All the Facts

Monday, October 4: Clinton, in San Francisco, learned of the seriousness of the situation in Somalia after returning from his regular morning jog. The president decided to stay in California, finish his schedule, and begin to gather the facts.

Among numerous calls and briefings, the President had a telephone conference call with Defense Secretary Les Aspin and three advisers to accumulate all early information. As a precautionary measure, Clinton immediately ordered several hundred reinforcements to Somalia to do "everything we can to protect the young Americans [who] are putting their lives on the line so that hundreds of thousands of Somalis can stay alive."

Step 2: Discuss and Review a Variety of Solutions and Try to Arrive at a Consensus

Monday, October 4: Clinton sent Aspin and Secretary of State Warren Christopher to Capitol Hill to brief congressional leaders and seek their opinions. Members of Congress denounced Clinton, Aspin, and Christopher, saying that if they have to ask Congress what needed to be done, then they had no policy in Somalia and weren't effective leaders.

Tuesday, October 5: Flying back to Washington on Air Force One, Clinton made numerous phone calls to confer with advisers. He received a ten-page fax concerning facts and possible options.

At 6:30 P.M., the president met with his top advisers in the White House to review all the options and hammer out a consensus. It was decided not to pull out of Somalia immediately. Rather, the United States would send in reinforcements, set a deadline for removing American troops, and change its policy of hostility toward General Aidid. Clinton adjourned the ninety-minute meeting by stating that he wanted "to think more about the alternatives," and asked that they meet again on Wednesday morning.

Step 3: Consider the Consequences and Impact of the Decision and Assure Consistency with Administrative and Personal Policy Objectives

Wednesday, October 6: Clinton conducted three separate meetings with advisers, the first beginning at 8:45 A.M. that lasted through the afternoon and late evening. At these meetings, details were delineated and dialogue took place about the merits and repercussions of each part of the plan. Impact was considered on the events currently taking place in Russia (where legislators had taken over the Parliament building). Discussions were held regarding the administration's goal of accomplishing the original mission of ending hunger in Somalia. This personal policy goal was weighed against mounting pressure from congressional leaders and the public for a total withdrawal.

Meanwhile, members of Congress continued to pressure the president. House Minority Leader Bob Michel sent him a letter signed by seventy-five Republicans. "The Somalia policy your administration has pursued is a failure," they declared. "America's international standing must not be jeopardized by an indecisive and naïve approach to foreign policy."

Thursday, October 7: In the morning, President Clinton met with thirty-four members of Congress to brief them of his decision.

Step 4: Effectively Communicate the Decision and Implement

Thursday, October 7: At 5:00 P.M., Clinton spoke live via television to the American people and communicated goals and objectives involved in his decision regarding Somalia. "Let us finish the work we set out to do," said the president. Accordingly, Clinton announced that he would send an additional 5,300 soldiers as reinforcements—a higher-than-expected number. He called for a general withdrawal of all Americans by March 31, 1994. Meanwhile, he relayed four key goals for immediate implementation:

1. Provide protection for U. S. troops.
2. Keep lines of communication and flow of food and supplies open via roads and the port at Mogadishu.
3. Keep the pressure on Somalia's insurgents.
4. Help the Somalis "reach agreement among themselves so that they can solve their problems."

Clinton also announced that he had directed Ambassador Bob Oakley to lead efforts with nearby African countries to help Somalia preserve order. He forcefully defended his decision not to pull out of Somalia immediately. "Our leadership in world affairs," said Clinton, "would be undermined at the very time when people are looking to America to help promote peace and freedom in the post Cold War world. And all around the world, aggressors, thugs, and terrorists will conclude that the best way to get us to change our policies is to kill our people. It would be open season on Americans."

THE IMPORTANCE OF DECISIVENESS

The American public's perception of Bill Clinton as indecisive was due, in part, to society's view of an ideal leader in a male-dominated command and control hierarchy. Take, for instance, the question put to Clinton in a September 1993 interview by columnist William Safire. Safire asked the president if, after eight months in office, he leaned "more toward exercising leadership or toward exercising the ability to build coalitions."

"I don't believe the two things are inconsistent," Clinton quickly responded. "In America today, I don't think you can govern effectively unless you build coalitions."

And when Safire commented that the president seemed "to be all carrot and no stick," and then asked: "When do you exercise power . . . [and] try to impose discipline?"—Clinton said, "In the end, on the domestic front, the only stick a President has is whether the people will or will not hold those who are obstacles to progress accountable at the next election."

This interchange is a perfect example of how Safire *perceived* leadership—and how Bill Clinton *understood* leadership in its purest form. Clinton knew that "command and control" is not necessarily leadership. Rather, if power is wielded without control, it can be more akin to dictatorship. Women, in general, understand this fact and intuitively see things a bit differently from the majority of men. Author Deborah Tannen noted that "women expect [and prefer] decisions to be discussed first and made by consensus. They appreciate the discussion itself as evidence of involvement and communication. But many men feel oppressed by lengthy discussion about what they see as minor decisions, and they feel hemmed in if they can't just act without talking first."

Women by nature, therefore, gravitate more toward Bill Clinton's four-step decision-making process than do men. This may be one reason why Bill Clinton, as president, was consistently given higher approval ratings by women. On the other hand, most men perceive asking for information as a weakness. And what happens when a leader is perceived to be weak and indecisive by others in power, especially when they tend to be male? Others will often try to usurp his power—just as some members of Congress attempted to do with President Clinton. A perfect example occurred in October 1993 during the Haitian crisis. Sensing a perceived weakness in Clinton's order for American ships to turn back and impose a blockade, Senate Majority Leader Robert Dole tried to introduce a constitutional amendment restricting the president from deploying American soldiers in Haiti (or anywhere else) without the approval of Congress.

Clinton immediately fired off a letter to both Dole and Senate Majority Leader George Mitchell saying, in part: "It is wrong and even dangerous to allow the questions of the moment to undercut the strength of our national security policies and to produce a fundamental shift in the proper relationship between our two branches of government."

"Clearly," Clinton wrote, "the Constitution leaves to the President, for good and sufficient reasons, the ultimate decision-making authority." Then, to reinforce his beliefs, Clinton ordered U.S. ships "to move closer to [Haiti's] shore, so they will be in plain sight" while enforcing the arms and oil embargo. He also froze assets of the Haitian military and barred entry into the United States of either the military leaders or their supporters. When Clinton took these bold actions, many members of Congress jumped to his defense. And lacking enough votes, Dole backed down the day after receiving the president's letter.

Senator Dole's actions were reminiscent of criticism by members of the press around the 100-day benchmark of Bill Clinton's presidency. When the president stated that he would definitely consult with Congress before taking action in Bosnia, it was written that Clinton "apparently believes protecting his presidential prerogatives is less important than obtaining political cover by sharing the responsibility with Congress."

Had Dole and the press misinterpreted presidential strength for weakness? Did they not realize that it often takes more courage and self-confidence to work with people and persuade them than it does to dictate or simply issue orders?

Another important point Clinton recognized was that the United States Constitution explicitly grants Congress the power to declare war, which they have done only five times (War of 1812; Spanish-American War; Mexican-American War; World War I; World War II). However, presidents have ordered troops into combat on more than 100 occasions—and countless times since 1945, including Korea, Vietnam, Grenada, Panama, Somalia, Afghanistan, and Iraq. With the end of the cold war, a new philosophy regarding the deployment of American troops abroad was being presented. The majority of Americans backed Clinton's belief that it should be done in coordination with United Nations sponsorship and that the American people should be consulted in the process. Paradoxically, Clinton also steadfastly maintained the power of the presidency in the event of a dire emergency that put the nation in jeopardy and required immediate action.

Bill Clinton's natural tendency to include others in decision-making was uniquely suited to the times. This was the beginning of an era in which technology brought information and events into every person's home instantly. In reality, therefore, nearly everyone was already involved in the decision-making process. The majority of the American people garnered the facts of many events just as fast as he did, either through television or the Internet. So they were intimately involved in the first step of the decision-making process. *They've gathered information and understood all the facts involved.* Additionally, most people were also well engaged in the second step as they sat around the dinner table or the office and *discussed a variety of possible solutions and actions.*

A sitting President of the United States, therefore, must act quickly or face criticism from those who are impatiently waiting for the decision. However, it is the president, alone, who must consider the consequences and impact of every executive decision. The president, alone, must bear the responsibility. Time and time again, Bill Clinton assumed this lonesome burden. He made the decision that needed to be made at the moment, and then moved on to the next one. And of the judgments that were finalized, Clinton felt the same way another 20th century leader felt. "Once a decision was made," said Harry Truman, "I did not worry about it afterward."

> *"I like to get everybody together around a table, let everybody say what they want, and [then] argue and debate. That's the way ideas get fleshed out . . . . When you consult broadly, think about it, and are personally involved, you tend to make the right decision. And that's [what] really counts."*
>
> —Bill Clinton, discussing his decision-making process
> May–June, 1994

> *"I don't have to win them all. But let's make decisions. This institutional delay and gridlock is bad for America."*
>
> —Bill Clinton, in Chicago, encouraging Congress
> to act on Midwest flood relief.
> July 25, 1993

*While the Jones lawsuit was on hiatus in the courts, fund-raising and public relations within the anti-Clinton network continued. Newsweek ran a cover story in **January 1997** timed to coincide with the argument before the Supreme Court. Through writer Michael Isikoff, Newsweek would continue to keep the story in the public eye, although Jones's version of her encounter with Clinton would change with time, become more explicit, and raise conflicting details. Funding for the Paula Jones Legal Fund would both continue and increase. Some of the conservative organizations that aided Paula Jones included, the Legal Affairs Council, the Fund for a Living American Government (FLAG), the Landmark Legal Foundation, the Independent Women's Forum, and the Federalist Society. Paula Jones, herself, reportedly received $100,000 for signing a contract with a fundraiser who was granted the right to use her name in a direct mail campaign. And like Gennifer Flowers, Jones later received a fee for posing nude in* Penthouse *magazine.*

Meanwhile, the Jones lawyers tried to negotiate a settlement with a big payoff funded by Clinton's insurers. Their hope was that the lawsuit would become such a distraction for the president that he would come to the bargaining table. As a matter of fact, in August 1996, Jones's lawyers thought they had an agreement for $700,000, but Paula Jones refused the deal, because it did not include an admission of wrongdoing by Clinton. She also reportedly feared losing a potential book deal if the case were to go away. This was good news to the "elves," the conservative attorneys who had organized to help in the legal effort. As one of those lawyers, Ann Coulter, was reported to have said, "We were terrified that Jones would settle. It was contrary to our purpose of bringing down the President."

⚜

*On **May 27, 1997**, the United States Supreme Court ruled unanimously for Paula Jones and against Bill Clinton. The president, the justices stated, had no constitutional right of immunity from a civil lawsuit, temporarily or otherwise. This decision sent shock waves throughout the national legal community, which widely interpreted it to mean that the Office of the Independent Counsel now had the right to pursue any and all elements of the president's past private life.*

*Jones v. Clinton was quickly remanded to the federal district court in Little Rock, where Judge Susan Webber Wright scheduled discovery. By **September 1997**, when the case would go to trial, Paula Jones had secured a new team of lawyers from Dallas, Texas, who worked on a contingency fee basis. Litigation costs were underwritten by the Rutherford Institute, a conservative think tank. According to later reports, Jones's lawyers planned to question President Clinton under oath and, hopefully, catch him in a lie* about relationships with other women. Then they would leak the embarrassing information to the media and expose him as a liar. The Jones team began using subpoena power and the deposition process to pursue people who might have knowledge of Clinton's personal life.

By *June 1997*, within a month of the Supreme Court ruling, Kenneth Starr's staff was in Arkansas questioning eight Arkansas state troopers about their knowledge of possible Clinton extramarital liaisons. "All they wanted to talk about was women," said one trooper. "Whether I had ever seen Bill Clinton perform a sexual act." The Office of the Independent Counsel also hired private detectives to identify and locate women who might have been involved with Clinton. According to public records, approximately $2.45 million was spent for these investigators between 1996 and 1999. Starr's office justified this activity as "perfectly appropriate" in attempting to identify possible witnesses in whom Bill Clinton might have confided information about Whitewater.

The wide fishing net cast by Kenneth Starr eventually attracted Kathleen Willey, a volunteer aide in the White House social office. Willey alleged that on November 29, 1993, President Clinton had sexually assaulted her in the private study of the Oval Office. Her claims were first reported on *July 28, 1997*, by reporter Matt Drudge as a "World Exclusive" on his Internet-based Drudge Report. There was a major follow-up article in an *August 1997* edition of Newsweek, written by Michael Isikoff. That kind of mainstream media exposure caused a sensation, eventually leading to Willey's appearance on CBS's 60 Minutes, which, according to reports, was arranged by the Office of the Independent Counsel. Starr granted Willey immunity from any potential prosecution, and had her testify before a grand jury. But in his final report, Starr listed her as a witness who was likely not to be believed.

It turned out that Kathleen Willey and her husband had been experiencing financial problems and were heavily in debt. The morning after the alleged assault by Clinton, Willey returned home to find that her husband had committed suicide. Some observers speculated that after losing her job several years later, she believed her charge against the President might result in a book deal that would solve her monetary difficulties. But New York publishers were not interested. President Clinton, through a spokesman, denied that he had assaulted Kathleen Willey.

"One of the reasons more people voted in the Presidential
election of 1992 . . . is because of all the debates, all the town
meetings, all the open forums, all the ways that people found to
say this is your place, not the politician's place. This is your
country. This is your government; take it back."

—Bill Clinton, to the League of Women Voters
June 7, 1993

"Every single piece of evidence shows that when people know
what we're trying to do, a majority will see it as fair, sensible,
and progressive."

—Bill Clinton, to Democratic Congressmen
July 20, 1993

CHAPTER TWELVE

KEEPING THE CAMPAIGN GOING

Bill Clinton did not wait for the 1996 presidential election to
begin his first campaign as an incumbent president. Rather, it
began within a month of taking office when, on February 17,
1993, he addressed a joint session of Congress. That forum officially
started the campaign for passage of the president's ambitious $500 bil-
lion deficit-reduction plan.

The day after Clinton's speech, which was judged a success by most
analysts, members of his administration hit the road selling the proposal
directly to the American people. While the president, himself, was in St.
Louis speaking with several thousand Missourians, the rest of the cabinet and top advisers fanned out across the country—many venturing
back to their home territory.

Overall, fifteen states were covered in one day—an event unprecedented in the annals of the American presidency. Lloyd Bentsen (Treasury)

was in Texas speaking at an Austin high school auditorium, where his remarks were broadcast on satellite television throughout the state. Henry Cisneros (HUD) lobbied for the plan while on a bus tour of federal housing projects in Flint, Michigan. Mike Espy (Agriculture) visited a department store and addressed a joint session of the Mississippi state legislature in Jackson. Donna Shalala (Health and Human Services) was at a children's hospital in Cleveland at the same moment Jesse Brown (Veterans Affairs) toured a veteran's hospital in Chicago. While Bruce Babbitt (Interior) visited Tucson and Albuquerque, Hazel O'Leary (Energy) was in New Jersey, Richard Riley (Education) was in his home state at the University of South Carolina, and Federico Pena (Transportation) was in Denver at a joint session of the Colorado state legislature. Meanwhile, Ron Brown (Commerce) and Robert Rubin (Assistant to the President for Economic Policy) were both in New York; Mickey Kantor (Trade Rep.) and Laura D'Andrea Tyson (Council of Economic Advisers) were assigned to California; Madeleine Kunin (Deputy of Education) was speaking at the University of Vermont; and Deputy Treasury Secretary Roger Altman was in Boston.

Journalists needed a program to keep up with everybody. But only the White House "war room" had all the details. Staff members there aided in keeping the speeches consistent from official to official, from state to state. And throughout the campaign, members of the administration continually coordinated their efforts through the war room to ensure consistency.

The idea behind this campaign was to have all members of the team working both individually and collectively to do everything possible to secure passage of the ambitious and controversial deficit reduction plan. As far as American presidential leadership was concerned, no one had ever seen anything quite like it.

THE FIRST CLINTON LANDSLIDE

Clinton's budget campaign was to last nearly six months. During that time, he attended dozens of events designed to reach citizens through personal human contact. The day after his appearance in St. Louis, the president continued on to Chillicothe, Ohio for a morning question-and-answer session at a local high school. In the afternoon, he delivered a speech at Hyde Park, New York home of Franklin D. Roosevelt. Two days later, he was in California and Washington holding special sessions in Silicon Valley and at a Boeing plant, respectively. The president's travels and town halls continued every month right up to the budget votes in Congress.

Clinton also sought the help of high-profile individuals to endorse the plan. He rounded up leaders of both large and small businesses, discussed the matter with them, and included them in press events where their support for the plan was announced. He also conferred frequently with leaders in Congress and with the governors of any state who would work with him.

Nearly every appropriate opportunity was used to sell his message to the American people, including press conferences, speaking engagements, impromptu remarks, and the president's regular Saturday morning radio addresses. Just as in the election campaign of 1992, staff members took every criticism or detrimental remark seriously. Threats were addressed and countered head-on Clinton, himself, frequently went on the attack to fight fire with fire.

The new administration also made efficient use of the mass media and information technology. There was an 1–800 number for people to call in and ask questions. Better yet, citizens could order the budget plan on a computer diskette, or simply download it from the new electronic mail system the White House had installed. In late February, Clinton held a widely acclaimed "Kids Town Hall" broadcast live by satellite from the East Room of the White House, moderated by ABC News anchor Peter Jennings. On March 24, he was interviewed for prime time by CBS News anchor Dan Rather, and later by Tom Brokaw of NBC. On August 3, barely a week before the final votes in the House and Senate, the President addressed the nation again urging passage of the plan— only this time he did so from the Oval Office.

Bill Clinton's campaign ended with a budget bill passing by the barest of all possible margins in both houses of Congress. On August 5, 1995, the House of Representatives approved his budget plan by a tally of 218 to 216. Had one "yes" vote been switched to a "no" vote, the measure would have failed, because tie votes there are treated as defeats. Two nights later, voting in the Senate ended in a 50–50 tie and Vice President Al Gore had the opportunity to cast the final deciding vote in favor of the plan. In the end, every single Republican in both houses of Congress voted against the proposal.

White House staff members jokingly called the win a "Clinton landslide." But no one disputed the assessment that it was Clinton's personal campaign that made the difference. However, many members of Congress said that he couldn't keep such an energetic pace going. And, indeed, the president was exhausted.

Few people could have known at the time that the budget fight was just the beginning. Not only would Clinton keep the campaign going with the same intensity, he would keep it going forever. And virtually no one could have guessed that he would *increase* campaign efforts when it came to health care, NAFTA, anti-crime legislation, and every other major initiative he would propose.

HOW THE CAMPAIGN WORKS

There were hints that something new was coming to the American presidency when Clinton announced that the three architects of his phenomenally successful electoral campaign would stay on at the White House. George Stephanopoulos would become White House Director of Communications (later senior presidential adviser). And James Carville and Paul Begala would maintain a close consulting relationship with the president.

When the people stayed on, so did the campaign style that proved so effective in the election. It was a campaign strategy that had consisted of: countless speeches filled with personal stories; making the most of radio and television talk shows; unusually open and informal town hall meetings where more audience interaction was not only allowed but encouraged; strategic use of the mass media and information technology; the "floating" of ideas ahead of time to gauge the public's reaction; jumping over the conventional press to converse directly with Americans; and putting Clinton in front of the people. All the strategies and new techniques were continued in the White House. Only now there would be more clout behind every event. Also, a more streamlined, fluid, and consistent process would emerge—one suited to a mobile and highly energetic president and his administration.

Clinton's White House was the first to establish a specifically designated policy war room—an idea that had been used in business for some time. The war room was staffed with highly knowledgeable and energetic members of each department in the administration. Experts on specific initiatives were brought in as consultants and activists. The staff disseminated information, ensured consistent and repetitive communications, kept tabs on negative criticism, and responded to attacks. A major goal of the war room was to generate grass-roots support from average Americans—thereby putting pressure on their representatives in Washington. But the staff also gave special attention to members of Congress, specific lobby groups, and nearly anyone in the city with influence over the outcome of legislation.

People in the war room ensured the continuous development of key messages that were communicated with consistency by all parties. An excellent example was the clarity of the administration's six-word message regarding health care: "Security, simplicity, savings, choice, quality, and responsibility." After Clinton introduced this easy-to-remember, hard-to-forget message, it was trumpeted by every member of the administration.

Clinton's campaign process began almost immediately after he made a decision to move forward. Initial actions involved choosing the right people to carry out the mission, such as a high-profile leader. Once the right people were in place, actions preliminary to the formal campaign began. The Clinton administration started to plant the seeds of change, to set a new tone, to let people know what was coming—so they could think about it for a while and get used to the idea. Later, when the initiative was formally proposed, the public reacted to it as more of a familiar idea than a radical change.

During his campaigns, Clinton made a special concerted effort to reach young people, which had always been one of his goals. In the 1992 presidential campaign, he had played his saxophone on Arsenio Hall's talk show and had given his impression of Elvis Presley during an interview with New York shock radio's Don Imus. As president, Clinton continued the tradition by giving live interviews to Imus and MTV's Tabitha Soren. He also dispatched all the members of his cabinet to do the same thing. One notable example was Vice President Al Gore, who put on something of a one-man media blitz after launching the Administration's Reinventing Government initiative. Over a two-day period, he appeared on such national television shows as *Larry King Live* (CNN), *The Today Show* (NBC), *Donahue* (syndicated), the *MacNeil-Lehrer NewsHour* (PBS), and *Late Night with David Letterman* (CBS).

Gore's appearance with David Letterman was a defining moment for the Clinton administration in that it set a new government precedent of recognizing the communications impact of popular television. As he and Letterman wore protective goggles, Gore used a hammer to break a glass ashtray "the government way." Mocking the bureaucracy that he wanted to change, the vice president announced that if the ashtray didn't break into exactly thirty-six pieces, it was unsuitable for government use. As a result of that appearance, he was able to reach millions of young viewers who distrusted big government and had no interest in its operations. As Gore departed, Letterman seemed to sum up the reaction of a younger, disinterested generation when he casually remarked: "Good luck with this government thing."

NAFTA: 12 STEPS TO A PERFECTLY EXECUTED CAMPAIGN

When analyzed on a broad scale, the 1993–1994 NAFTA campaign provides unique insight into a process that changed the mechanics of

American presidential leadership. With obvious exceptions and more entailing complexity, every Clinton campaign consisted of a dozen fundamental steps, many of which were interchangeable with regard to timing.

Step 1: Plant the Seeds of Change

Within a month of taking office, Bill Clinton was candid about his support of NAFTA. For the first eight months of his tenure, he fielded questions and made public statements about the agreement in a variety of forums, including: A town hall meeting in Chillicothe, Ohio; a press conference with Canadian Prime Minister Brian Mulroney; radio interviews in Los Angeles and Chicago, and with the Texas media. He also discussed it in some detail during his six-months-in office interview with Larry King and in formal meetings with leaders of Caribbean nations in late August. In general, though, much of the preliminary work had been accomplished the previous year when the Bush Administration initiated and signed the proposal. Clinton's task now was to gain public support for its passage in Congress.

Speaking about NAFTA in public forums helped prepare people for the president's support of the issue. By gradually presenting bits and pieces in a preliminary fashion, he eliminated surprises and helped pave the way for a smoother acceptance in the future. Everyone knew President Clinton's position when, on August 13, 1993, he issued a formal statement endorsing the North American Free Trade Agreement. The stage was set for the campaign to begin.

Step 2: Appoint One Person to Lead the Campaign—and Staff the War Room

On August 19, President Clinton formally announced the appointment of William M. Daley of Chicago as NAFTA task force chairman. In early September, he selected Brookings Institute scholar and former twenty-year Minnesota congressman Bill Frenzel as a special adviser to the president on NAFTA. Coupled with Daley's political connections, Frenzel's experience as a member of the House Ways and Means Committee provided instant insight and credibility for the leadership team.

The staff at the war room immediately began to formulate and create messages. The administration stressed the vast amounts of jobs and new markets that NAFTA would create. In October, the argument was advanced that should the U.S. turn down the agreement, Japan or Europe would step in and set up their own trade agreements, leaving the U.S. out in the cold. In early November, the message shifted to warnings that a defeat of NAFTA would endanger and undermine America's foreign policy plans. Clinton and Gore emphasized that the NAFTA vote was a choice between "hope and fear," "the future and the past," "openness versus isolationism."

In October, the war room staff helped coordinate the visit to Washington each week of more than 100 businessmen, who would be shown the merits of the trade agreement. Many of them met with members of Clinton's economic team, including, Lloyd Bentsen, Al Gore, Mickey Kantor, and Bob Rubin. Follow-up notes and phone calls were sent out after the businessmen returned home.

Step 3: Hold A Major Kick-Off Event

On the morning of September 14, Bill Clinton delivered an impassioned speech at the White House as he was flanked on stage by former presidents Gerald Ford, Jimmy Carter, and George H. W. Bush. The invited audience was comprised of more than a hundred supporters of NAFTA, mostly members of Congress and leaders in the business community.

At the time, however, the prospects for the passage of NAFTA looked bleak. Fewer than 100 House Democrats supported the agreement. One hundred fifty were undecided and sixty had already declared their opposition.

Step 4: Hit the Road and Get in Front of the People

The next day, Clinton traveled to New Orleans, where he gave a rousing speech and answered questions on the merits of NAFTA. Sharing the stage were Louisiana governor Edwin Edwards and local business and civic leaders.

On October 4, Clinton traveled to San Francisco to speak to the annual convention of the AFL-CIO. The response of the labor organization was understandably cool toward the president's remarks. But that didn't slow him down. Three weeks later, on October 28, he spoke at the *Wall Street Journal* Conference on the Americas in New York City. At this event, the president admitted that he did not anticipate the public's slow reaction to NAFTA. "I really believed that the votes would rather quickly line up," he said. "It is no secret that has not yet happened."

The following afternoon, Clinton visited the corporate offices of Gillette in Boston, Massachusetts, where he delivered remarks on NAFTA to the employees. On November 5, he was in Lexington, Kentucky, speaking to workers at Lexmark International, a computer firm that exports to Mexico. And on November 15, he pitched the merits of NAFTA in Memphis, Tennessee.

Step 5: Deploy Members of the Team

The war room staff supplied members of the cabinet with the names of undecided congressmen and, during the heat of the campaign in mid-October, cabinet officials met each week with those on the list. They also traveled to the home districts of the undecided House members. For example, Federico Pena journeyed to the Maryland district of representative Ben Cardin and spoke to employees of a company that manufactured dredging equipment. Lloyd Bentsen was in representative Sam Johnson's Texas district and told people employed at Texas Instruments that NAFTA would help create new jobs. White House economist Laura Tyson went to Georgia to speak to business leaders, hoping to persuade voters represented by representative Buddy Darden. And on November 10, Al Gore was in Colorado speaking to employees at a company called StorageTek.

Step 6: Hold Special Events that Draw Attention to the Initiative

The most spectacular of the NAFTA campaign's special events took place the morning of October 20, 1993, on the White House lawn, when Bill Clinton held the "NAFTA Jobs and Products Day Trade Fair." Under two large tents, companies that either did business with Mexico and/or supported passage of the North American Free Trade Agreement showcased their products, which included everything from clothing to computers, and from steel to hot dogs. In the audience were lobbyists, members of Congress, and key members of the cabinet that included the secretaries of Labor, Treasury, Commerce, Education, and the U.S. Trade Representative. The administration also sponsored similar events in designated congressional districts across the nation.

Step 7: Enlist the Help of High-Profile People

Unlike the campaign for his economic plan, Clinton was able to muster extensive and wide-ranging bipartisan support for NAFTA. In an effort to counter the negative position of Ross Perot, the president persuaded Lee Iacocca to be a spokesman for the initiative. The former Chrysler chairman responded with successful television advertisements of his own.

On November 2, Clinton hosted numerous high-profile leaders who endorsed NAFTA, including former secretaries of state Robert McNamara, Henry Kissinger, Cyrus Vance, Ed Muskie, and James Baker. One week later, General Colin L. Powell announced his support. In a final White House campaign event held the day before the House vote, Clinton appeared with fifteen of forty state governors who supported NAFTA. On the same day, all former living presidents (Nixon, Ford, Carter, Reagan, and Bush) issued a formal letter endorsing the trade agreement.

Step 8: Use Every Opportunity to Sell the Initiative

From the kick-off NAFTA speech to the final vote in the House of Representatives, Bill Clinton spoke about NAFTA at numerous events that were not specifically designed to promote the trade agreement. These included four formal press conferences, three of which were held jointly with foreign leaders (Prime Minister Paul Keating of Australia; President Hosni Mubarak of Egypt; and Israeli Prime Minister Yitzhak Rabin of Israel). He also plugged NAFTA at speeches to the National Hispanic Caucus Institute, Yale University, the Conference of Business for Social Responsibility, and at the dedication of the John F. Kennedy Library Museum in Boston.

Step 9: Take Every Threat Seriously and Fight Fire With Fire

On Sunday morning, November 7, President Clinton appeared on NBC's *Meet the Press*. While a variety of subjects were discussed, he also spoke passionately about NAFTA. For the first time, however, Clinton accused organized labor of using "naked pressure" and "real roughshod, muscle-bound tactics" in trying to defeat the trade agreement. The president further acknowledged that he was still approximately 30 votes short of gaining a majority in the House of Representatives.

At this point (ten days before the scheduled House vote), it still did not look good for the passage of the agreement. Supporters were anticipating defeat. Organized Labor, members of Congress, and Ross Perot felt confident of victory. Something needed to be done to shake things up. So President Clinton, at the suggestion of Al Gore, challenged Ross Perot to debate the vice president on CNN.

On the evening of November 9, the vice president debated Perot live on Larry King's television show. During the discussion, Gore went on the attack. The highlight occurred when he presented Perot with a framed picture of former congressmen Smoot and Hawley, who sponsored isolationist legislation in the 1930s that worsened the Great Depression. Gore gave Perot the black and white photograph and invited him to take it home and hang it on his wall.

Clinton defied conventional thinking when he invited Perot to debate Gore. Critics said that such a thing was demeaning to the White House and the office of both president and vice president. The public, however, thought differently. The Gore-Perot NAFTA debate on CNN garnered the largest audience for a regularly scheduled program in cable television history. It was the turning point in the campaign. The next morning, NAFTA was on every newspaper front page in America and nearly every radio and television talk show were discussing the debate's outcome. Gore was a nearly unanimous choice as the winner. By contrast, Perot was viewed as whiny and arrogant. This portrayal gave those members of Congress who were seeking to get Perot and organized labor off their backs the courage to vote for the agreement. The success of the debate also served to shift public attention away from recent Republican pivotal victories that were touted as having the potential to hurt NAFTA's chances for safe passage.

As of November 12, three days after the debate, opponents of NAFTA still claimed that they had enough votes in committee to defeat the agreement in the House of Representatives.

Step 10: Take Advantage of the Media

At lunch hour on the first of November, Bill Clinton left the White House and went across the street to the United States Chamber of Commerce, where he participated in a televised conference that was broadcast by satellite to more than 1,000 locations around the country. Giving a speech and interacting with the audience via questions and answers, Clinton predicted that if NAFTA wasn't passed, Japan and Europe would jump on it "like flies on a June bug."

During the two weeks leading up to the House vote, Clinton arranged two teleconferences from the Oval Office, gave an interview to Connie Chung of CBS News, and conducted a media roundtable interview. The president also devoted four of his weekly radio addresses specifically to NAFTA—one each in September and October, and two in November.

Step 11: Employ Personal Lobbying Efforts

During the formal campaign for NAFTA's passage, President Clinton met personally with all the undecided members of the House of Representatives (more than 150). He invited some to go jogging, others to play golf, and most to have dinner at the White House. During the six weeks leading up to the vote, the president held no less than fourteen "official" visits with members of Congress during working hours. On November 8, Clinton was reported to have spent all day and most of the night meeting with congressmen in small groups, in pairs, or one-on-one. And when he couldn't meet with them personally, he constantly worked the phones. The day before the vote, Clinton complained to a group of visitors that his "ear hurt from talking on the phone all week to members of Congress."

Step 12: Cut Deals, Make Bargains, Twist Arms

As the campaign came down to the wire, Clinton enthusiastically participated in the time-honored political tradition of bartering for votes. He offered Florida representatives protection for citrus fruit, sugar, and winter vegetables. Texas congressmen Esteban Torres won a commitment to start up a North American development bank at a cost of $225 million. Congressmen from Pennsylvania and Ohio secured protection for steel imports from Japan. Clinton also offered deals on wheat, sugar, and textiles to gain sorely needed votes. Two days before the final vote, Clinton even assured Republicans that he would come to the defense of any congressman voting for NAFTA who was attacked by a Democratic opponent in upcoming elections. That assurance was put in writing and sent to Republican House leader Robert H. Michel.

⌘

On the evening of November 17, 1994, the United States House of Representatives voted to approve the North American Free Trade Agreement by a vote of 234–200. The 34-vote margin of victory was larger than expected. Shortly afterwards, it passed easily in the Senate and the agreement became law upon the president's signature.

Immediately after the House vote, President Clinton went before the media. "Tonight's vote is a defining moment for our nation," he said. "At a time when our people are hurting from the strains of this tough global economy, we chose to compete, not to retreat, to lead as America has done in the past. . . . We have not flinched. Tonight, the leaders of both parties found common ground in supporting the common good. We voted for the future tonight. Our people are winners."

Then, in what *The New York Times* called "the political equivalent of lighting a victory cigar," Bill Clinton went over to the war room to thank and congratulate the staff who had worked so hard to secure NAFTA's passage.

Clinton didn't take much time to celebrate his victory, though. He chose to ride the wave of success by seeking to open even more markets.

On November 18, he was in Seattle, Washington, hosting the APEC conference of Pacific Rim leaders. By seeking to open new markets for American products in the world's Asia-Pacific region, Bill Clinton was, in effect, beginning a brand new campaign.

IMPORTANCE OF THE CAMPAIGN

Bill Clinton's efforts in the NAFTA campaign did not go unnoticed by either the public or the press. An article in *The New York Times* noted that the Free Trade Agreement had been approved "after a Herculean display of Presidential persuasion." And Speaker of the House Thomas B. Foley, who had previously stated that he honestly believed that there was no way NAFTA could pass in the House of Representatives, remarked on the day of the vote: "I cannot recall any President with whom I have served where there has been a greater personal effort than has been exerted by President Clinton in support of NAFTA."

While Clinton's campaigning ability garnered interest from the nation as a whole, it was nothing new to the people of Arkansas. Ernest Dumas, a former reporter for the *Arkansas Gazette,* observed that Clinton "had what seemed to be a compulsive need to meet people, to know them, to like them, to have them like him. These natural inclinations along with Clinton's love of politics seemed to coalesce into one major activity—the campaign."

So it was not unexpected when Bill Clinton moved his idea of a permanent campaign into the White House. Nor was it surprising that he was the very first President of the United States to successfully apply all the elements of a political campaign to a particular piece of legislation brought before Congress.

While the American presidency still remained the strikingly decisive executive branch of government it was always meant to be, Bill Clinton renewed the intent of the founding fathers to make it a position of communication and persuasion. His entire campaign process represented a major shift in modern-day presidential leadership. With Clinton, securing the passage of initiatives was no longer only about convincing, cajoling and coddling the members of Congress. It was also about educating and selling the American people on new ideas. That's how Washington, Jefferson, Franklin, Madison, Adams, and all the other early leaders of the United States wanted the process to work.

And in truth, that's really what leadership, itself, is all about. This principle applies not only to the presidency, but to all leaders, of every organization, everywhere. In the end, a leader must have followers—and the only way people will follow for any extended length of time is to be well-informed of the direction in which they are heading and the reasons for going there.

For President Bill Clinton, whose constituency was composed of more than 250 million Americans, leading effectively demanded a full-fledged campaign. Yet many people, who had been used to command and control management, were slow to grasp the merits of Clinton's style. In the aftermath of the 1993 budget vote, for instance, Senate Republican Leader Bob Dole stated that Clinton "[acted] as if the last presidential campaign was still in progress." This mocking remark was actually more of an unknowing compliment.

However, General Colin Powell, who endorsed the NAFTA pact in the waning days of the administration's campaign, was more visionary in his comment about Clinton's ongoing campaign style. "I think it's the wave of the future," he said.

> "We must speak to the millions who are not here—who do not even watch us on television or listen to us. Who do not care. Who will not bother to vote, or if they do, will probably not vote for us."
>
> —Bill Clinton, at the 1988
> Democratic National Convention

> "I think there is still a continuing job to do to make sure the American people know again exactly what is in this program and why I think it is good for the country."
>
> —Bill Clinton, in an informal
> exchange with reporters
> August 3, 1993

Throughout the year 1997, there was a steady movement to impeach President Clinton—one that was below the radar screens of most of the American public. The **January 1997** newsletter from Citizens for Honest Government (producer of The Clinton Chronicles), featured an article by William Dannemeyer. Titled "Why Congress Must Impeach Bill Clinton," the former Republican Congressman wrote, among other things: "I for one believe that both Bill and Hillary Clinton know where, when, why, and by whom Foster was killed, and it was no suicide." Two months later, on **March 11, 1997**, Georgia congressman Bob Barr sent a long letter to Henry Hyde of Illinois, the House Judiciary Committee Chairman, formally requesting an impeachment inquiry. As justification for the probe, Barr cited an "alarming pattern of abuse" of the "political system by this Administration," a "series of criminal law violations," and violations that point "precisely toward theories of impeachment law [used] in the matter of President Nixon." A dozen more conservative Republicans soon joined Barr's call for impeachment.

In **June 1997**, people who purchased The Clinton Chronicles began receiving telephone messages from a Christian telemarketing firm that featured Bill Dannemeyer labeling President Clinton a "liar and a criminal," pointing out that "Henry Hyde is already studying the law on impeachment," and stating that "we're in the process of impeaching Bill Clinton [and] are planning the same process for [Vice President] Al Gore." Dannemeyer then asked people to show their "support for the impeachment of Bill Clinton" by joining "committees of impeachment," signing petitions demanding that Congress impeach, and sending in contributions to help pay for the effort.

Things really started to heat up in **October 1997** with the release of another book written by Bob Tyrrell entitled The Impeachment of William Jefferson Clinton. Coauthored by "Anonymous," Tyrell wrote that impeachment hearings would begin in 1998, be run by Henry Hyde of Illinois, and would be prompted with a special report to Congress by Kenneth Starr. That same month, The Wall Street Journal featured an editorial by neoconservative Mark Helprin that featured the one-word title, "Impeach." Helprin called Bill Clinton "the most corrupt, fraudulent, and dishonest president we have ever known." The president, he said, had "purloined FBI files, used the IRS to intimidate opponents, plotted to cage government business, met with drug dealers, arms traders, and mobsters, raised illegal campaign money, sold influence, and shook down the Chinese." Shortly thereafter, one of the producers of The Clinton Chronicles joined an anti-abortion leader and a conservative talk show host to lead an impeachment rally on the steps of the U.S. Capitol building.

In **November 1997**, lawyers helping Paula Jones were contacted about the story of Linda Tripp, a former White House employee who had testified in the Office of the Independent Counsel's investigations of Vince Foster's death, the Travel Office firings, and Whitewater. According to Tripp, Bill Clinton had recently engaged in an affair with a twenty-three-year-old intern named Monica Lewinsky. The Jones team had heard of Linda Tripp through a chain of conservative contacts that sensed that her story, if true, could result in significant political damage to the president. Advised to secretly tape her private conversations with Lewinsky, Tripp was eventually put in contact with the Office of the Independent Counsel, with whom she shared her story and evidence. By **December 1997**, Bill Clinton's lawyers received a new Jones trial witness list that included the name of Monica Lewinsky. Shortly thereafter, Lewinsky herself received a subpoena from lawyers for Paula Jones. The day after the witness list was received, President Clinton told his lawyers, his closest associates, and his wife that he had not engaged in an affair with the young woman.

After the holidays, on **January 7, 1998**, Monica Lewinsky signed an affidavit denying a sexual relationship with Clinton. The next week (**January 13, 1998**), the Office of the Independent Counsel wired Linda Tripp with a recording device for her lunch with Lewinsky at the Ritz-Carlton in Arlington, Virginia. In what was later widely reported by the media as a "sting operation," Tripp asked Lewinsky explicit and leading questions about her relationship with the president. Kenneth Starr's staff spent most of that evening and much of the next day reviewing the tape. They also reportedly shared it with two of the "elves," who analyzed its legal impact. Also on **January 14, 1998**, Lewinsky wrote and provided Linda Tripp with a list of suggestions for how to prepare an affidavit in the Paula Jones case. This document would later come to be known as the "Talking Points" memo.

The next day, **January 15, 1998**, one of Kenneth Starr's deputies met with the Assistant Attorney General of the United States to request authority to expand the Whitewater investigation into the possibility that Monica Lewinsky or others had obstructed justice or suborned perjury. According to later accounts, Starr's deputy assured the assistant attorney general that the Office of the Independent Counsel had no conflicts of interest nor had they any contacts with attorneys for Paula Jones. However, Kenneth Starr apparently had spoken by telephone with one of Jones's lawyers a day or two before the request, and certainly Starr himself had worked on behalf of the Jones case prior to accepting his appointment. Analysts who later reviewed the entire scenario suggested that, because Starr had been unable to find any evidence that the President had committed any crimes, he was forced to spend millions of dollars on an element of Clinton's personal life that was totally unrelated to Whitewater.

On the morning of **January 16, 1998**, the attorney general granted the Office of the Independent Counsel's request to expand its investigation.

Starr wasted no time in dispatching his people to utilize Linda Tripp in setting up Monica Lewinsky for another lunch at the Pentagon City Mall's food court in Arlington. When Lewinsky arrived, she was met by two FBI agents and escorted to Room 1012 of the Ritz-Carlton Hotel next door. Present in the room were six deputy prosecutors, a private investigator from Arkansas, and Linda Tripp. In an attempt to get Lewinsky to "flip" against the president, the prosecutors threatened to charge her with up to five federal crimes (obstruction of justice, perjury, subornation of perjury, conspiracy, and witness tampering) that could result in a total of twenty-seven years in prison. Her only way out, they said, was to cooperate by giving a full statement implicating Clinton, and agreeing to wear a wire and covertly tape conversations with him. After repeated requests from the young woman, one of the FBI agents finally phoned her attorney's office, but it had closed for the Martin Luther King, Jr. holiday weekend. Lewinsky was then permitted to call her mother in New York. Without agreeing to any of the prosecutor's demands, the young woman was finally allowed to leave the hotel at 12:23 A.M., almost twelve hours after she had been detained.

*One of the reasons for keeping Lewinsky so long was that a deposition of Clinton was scheduled for the very next day. There was apparent intent to spring a perjury trap on the president. If Clinton did not know about the existence of a tape with Lewinsky discussing their relationship, he was more likely than not to try to evade, mislead, or even lie under oath. So on **January 17, 1998**, during a six-hour deposition, when Clinton was asked specifically about his relationship with the young woman, he responded, "On [a technical] basis, I have never had sexual relations with Monica Lewinsky. I've never had an affair with her."*

PART IV
CHARACTER

"It's a legacy my grandparents left to me: if you get beat down,
just get up again. Find something to be grateful for every day."
—Clinton, in a radio interview with Bill Moyers
July 7, 1992

"Ultimately, the test of leadership is not constant flawlessness. Rather, it is marked by a commitment to strive for the highest standards, to learn honestly when one falls short and to do the right thing when it happens."

—Clinton, to cadets at the U.S. Naval Academy
May 25, 1994

"We need a system of lifetime learning in which a young person, who will change jobs on average seven or eight times in a lifetime, will know that he or she can always get the training, the skills, the knowledge that [they] need to make a change."

—Bill Clinton, to the American Legion Boys Nation
July 29, 1994

CHAPTER THIRTEEN

CONTINUAL LEARNING

Upon assuming the presidency, Clinton was the ultimate Washington outsider. As governor of a relatively small state, he had few personal relationships with key members of the U.S. Congress, and fewer still with the city's press corps. At first overwhelmed by the massive Washington bureaucracy and relentless media coverage, Clinton's administration blundered badly in a number of areas.

One of Clinton's first mistakes was to close the hall leading to the White House pressroom, essentially freezing members of the media out of their accustomed space near the Oval Office. This move was a knee-jerk reaction to negative press coverage, and members of the media clearly did not like it. Even Richard Nixon, who openly voiced his hatred for the press, did not shut them out.

The Clinton administration also made several strategic political errors in dealing with the entrenched Washington establishment. For example, when faced with the threat of a Republican filibuster in the

Senate over the administration's first major piece of legislation (a proposed $15 million jobs stimulus bill), Clinton's team essentially ignored the warning and described the opposition as "irrelevant." That sentiment served only to unify and motivate Republican senators into mounting a successful filibuster that resulted in killing the bill.

And barely a week into his presidency, Clinton allowed the press and gay rights groups to push him into announcing his intention to end the ban on gays in the United States armed forces. The explosiveness of the issue started him off on very bad footing with the military, with conservative factions in Congress, and with most of the American public, who believed that they had elected a "New Democrat" rather than a member of the liberal faction of the Democratic Party. This disastrous controversy overwhelmed Clinton's initial months in office, essentially wiping out any "honeymoon" he may have been accorded as a rite of passage.

In a statement that seemed to sum up Clinton's first 100 days in office, *The New York Times* reported that his administration suffered from "poor communication, lack of focus, inadequate staff work, unfortunate timing, conflicts among the President's aides, and lackluster liaison work with Congress."

Rather than brooding or sulking, Clinton accepted responsibility and reflected on his mistakes. "There is a permanent government here," he said not long after the defeat of his jobs stimulus bill, "but there's also a permanent political culture. And I have to learn. It is my job as President to make the most of that instead of letting it make the most of me. I hope I can learn something."

CLINTON THE LIFELONG LEARNER

At an early age, Bill Clinton displayed an innate hunger for learning. He could read by the age of three and, throughout his youth, was almost never without a book on his bedside table. This was a passion clearly recognized by family and friends. In high school, his pals used to joke about going "over to Bill's house to watch him read." And one of his roommates in college recalled that Clinton "had an intense intellectual curiosity about every conceivable topic and discipline. I would go to bed, get up at six o'clock, and find him on the same couch reading a completely different book.

"I came from a family that had no money, no influence, and no particular interest in politics," Clinton once remarked to an aspiring young leader. "My advice to you would be: One, get the best education you can; and two, involve yourself in politics and figure out what you believe. [America's] greatest President was Abraham Lincoln. When he was a young man, Lincoln wrote in his diary, 'I will work and get ready, and perhaps my chance will come.'

At the age of sixteen, Bill Clinton set his sights on becoming President of the United States. After high school, he left Arkansas to gain experience. He went to Georgetown University to acquire knowledge about foreign affairs and learn the ways of Washington. And he made it a point to practice politics by working on the staff of U.S. Senator J. William Fulbright and by volunteering in the campaigns of a state senator, a mayor, a U.S. senator, and in George McGovern's 1972 presidential bid. All this knowledge and practical experience was purposely engineered by Clinton so that, upon returning to Arkansas, he would be better prepared to enter the profession of politics.

After being elected governor in 1978, it quickly became apparent that Clinton's intellectual abilities played a major role in his leadership of the state. "Even with a staff of bright people, Clinton set the standard," recalled one of his assistants. "All of us who worked there marveled at his ability to juggle many issues and remember large concepts and minute details on almost any subject."

As an adult, Clinton loved to browse through bookstores and frequently emerged with an armload of books. He often read four books a week, sometimes two or three simultaneously. The subjects varied widely and included murder mysteries, business books, classics, and biographies. In later years, when someone asked him if it was true that he had once read 300 books in one year, he laughingly responded: "Yes, that was in 1982 when I didn't have much else to do."

This remark referred to the hiatus Clinton experienced after having been voted out of the governor's mansion on his first try for reelection in 1980. He used the next two years as a time for reflection and learning. In an effort to improve himself, he read hundreds of books and performed numerous post-mortems of his two years as governor. It became a focused effort to learn where he had gone wrong.

Clinton concluded that there were three major reasons for his election defeat. First, his agenda had been too ambitious. He had simply made too many legislative proposals and the people could not keep them all straight, nor were they inclined to change so fast. Curiously, this would be a lesson that Clinton largely ignored a decade later when, during his first few years as president, he proposed an unprecedented amount of legislation.

Second, Clinton realized that he had been a bit too dictatorial in pursuing many of his initiatives. In his zeal to achieve, he had pushed and prodded many of the legislators rather than trying to work with them by building consensus. And third, because his opponent in the

1980 reelection bid had run a very negative campaign, Clinton realized that he must be certain in the future to immediately counter negative advertising. That lesson was later reinforced for him after observing the effects of unanswered accusations against Democratic nominee Michael Dukakis during a failed 1988 presidential campaign.

Through perseverance and learning from past mistakes, Clinton regained office by a solid majority in 1982. In general, his twelve-year tenure as governor of Arkansas provided valuable learning experiences that would aid him during his future presidency. These included skills such as: dealing with Congress, compromising, building consensus, and staying in touch with the people.

LEARNING WHILE ON THE JOB

Similar to what he had done after being voted out of the Arkansas governor's mansion, in the wake of his disastrous first 100 days as president, Clinton performed a formal detailed evaluation of events that had occurred up to that point. Among other things, he analyzed White House lines of communication with Congress, his relationship with the press, and his strategies for gaining passage of key legislation.

Learning much from the findings of that study, Clinton began a series of changes that included a major shake-up of his White House staff. He brought in Roy Neel, a former aide to Vice President Gore, to assist White House Chief of Staff Mack McLarty and made Washington insider David Gergen the new Director of Communications. Gergen immediately reopened the White House halls and pressroom to reporters, which instantly improved relations with the media.

Clinton also determined to never again ignore the Republican opposition. "We want to improve our ability to communicate what we believe and what we're doing," he said. In a concerted effort to improve relationships, Clinton frequently invited Senate Majority Leader Bob Dole to the White House for discussions. He and his advisers also held bipartisan briefing sessions on all new initiatives. Republican members of Congress quickly noted the change and complimented the president, even though they still expressed opposition to most of his proposals.

When the public's perception of a lack or organization and discipline in the White House didn't improve with time, and it became a political liability, Clinton made further changes. He replaced White House Chief of Staff Mack McLarty with Budget Director Leon Panetta. Clinton had told McLarty that things were not working as smoothly as he would like, and moved him into a presidential adviser role with access to the Oval Office. Such a move not only preserved McLarty's dignity but also better utilized his individual skills and talents. If McLarty, an Arkansas businessman known to the Washington establishment as "Mack the Nice," was the quintessential Washington outsider, Leon Panetta was exactly the opposite. He was a consummate Washington politician who was also viewed as more of a firm disciplinarian. Panetta had been a member of the U.S. Congress from California for sixteen years, and he knew the players on Capitol Hill. In addition, his eighteen months as Clinton's Director of the Office of Management and Budget had increased his working knowledge of the government. Panetta quickly reorganized management of day-to-day operations in the White House, which improved both internal efficiency and the public's perception of how business was conducted.

Not all of the lessons Bill Clinton learned as president were as painful as removing his friend Mack McLarty. Often, he would host scholars from around the world to help prepare for pending presidential activity. For example, in early November 1993, Clinton invited about a dozen political experts to the White House for a candid assessment of his presidency. Of this conference, *The New York Times* noted: "This group of political scientists, intellectuals and Presidential scholars, like Richard Neustadt of Harvard and William Julius Wilson of the University of Chicago, gathered in the White House dining room. According to participants, it was a no-holds-barred session, with the President taking notes on the back of his dinner menu." Just two months later, in January 1994, Clinton assembled twenty more people to help him prepare for his upcoming trip to Europe. As *Time* reported: "After cocktails in the Red Room, guest experts talked while the others ate, giving prepared comments on the future of NATO, post-election politics in Russia, and the economic stagnation across Europe." Such preparation later led an impressed Russian college student to note of Clinton: "He is a very informed man on Russian problems." And prior to traveling to Normandy to participate in D-Day fiftieth anniversary ceremonies, Clinton convened a White House seminar where historians and veterans educated him and his staff on the events of that historic World War II invasion. At this session, one scholar present recalled the president muttering under his breath: "God, I'm learning a lot!"

Clinton's interest in learning, and his ability to learn while on the job, did not go unnoticed by the American public. One poll conducted in June 1993 reported that "sixty-nine percent said Mr. Clinton was learning from the problems he has encountered and will do better."

When he made a mistake, Clinton tried to find out what went wrong, fix the problem, and prevent it from happening again. The process he employed is not an easy one to accept, even for the most advanced leader.

It requires great introspection and solicitation of critical feedback from peers and advisors, as well as from subordinates. The results of this self-analysis, however, help leaders develop strong philosophies and ways for handling similar situations in the future.

Before ordering American troops to Haiti, for example, Clinton considered the loss of lives involved when American troops were left in Somalia for an extended period of time. As a result, concrete actions were taken to ensure similar tragedies were not repeated in the Haiti occupation.

President Clinton, in October 1994, also deployed American forces to Kuwait in response to Iraq's troop buildup at the Kuwaiti border. Four years earlier, the world community did not respond forcefully to a similar movement of Iraq's army, which subsequently invaded and took possession of the smaller country. Remembering that experience, Clinton immediately sent troops, armaments, and warnings to Saddam Hussein that any threat to Kuwait would not be tolerated. In response, Iraq withdrew its forces in less than a week.

APPLYING ACQUIRED KNOWLEDGE

During the time he occupied the Oval Office, Bill Clinton usually began each day perusing newspapers such as *The New York Times, The Wall Street Journal, The Washington Post,* and *USA Today.* In addition, his staff provided him with summaries of the previous evening's television news reports. And whenever there was a fast-breaking story, such as Iraqi troop movements along the Kuwait border or events in Somalia or Haiti, in addition to internal governmental reports, the President usually monitored the situation on CNN.

Clinton's personal acquisition of information and knowledge was, he believed, strategic to performing his job properly. "That's what good leaders do," he said. He also believed that someone had solved virtually every problem somewhere before. So he was constantly foraging around for past solutions to similar issues by reading widely or by speaking to people from specialized disciplines. When his administration announced a plan for a $382 million government fund for loans, for instance, Clinton cited a lesson learned from "a remarkable man named Mohammed Yunus, who told me how, through the Grameen Bank, he had made market-rate-interest loans to poor village women in Bangladesh, most of whom had paid the loans back." (In 2006, Bill Clinton was a strong supporter and vocal advocate for Muhammad Yunus, who, that year, was awarded the Nobel Peace Prize.)

Clinton was also a great admirer of the German Apprenticeship Program and, while president, proposed a number of similar government education and retraining programs. "If the USA doesn't do a better job educating its children and training its workers," he said, "society will continue splitting into haves and have-nots. And a weakened economy won't be able to compete globally."

For a leader, intellectual curiosity alone does not guarantee the ability to learn. Information must be retained, absorbed, and analyzed. Policies must be formulated and then set into motion. This was a process that Clinton frequently thought about. "In order to visualize, to imagine the future," he stated in May 1994, "you [must] have some structure in your head, some way of organizing all the things that are coming in."

While Ronald Reagan was often described as a "3x5 note card" president, Bill Clinton was repeatedly called the "CD-ROM" president, because of the vast amount of data he was able to retain. Several former associates remarked that Clinton "had an encyclopedic knowledge" and "could absorb facts and analyze complicated information with computer-like precision." And when it came to explaining the details of his many initiatives, Clinton could talk for hours without notes. Regarding health care, for instance, *The New York Times* reported that the president "was deeply involved in explaining things about comprehensive benefits, long term care benefits and basic benefits, and about model forms for doctors, variations on the model forms, and variations on the variations . . ."

Issue after issue, day after day, and year after year, Clinton responded to questions with the same impressive command of details. When a reporter asked him about the status of Subchapter S corporations in a pending budget proposal, Clinton responded with a barrage of statistics: "Well," he said (without notes), "there are seven million Subchapter S corporations in America. Of those, 400,000, or far less than ten percent, will not have any income tax increase at all under this program. All of them will have the expensing provisions of the Code [and] will be able to write off $20,000." Another time, in response to a comment about how important California was to the economic recovery of the nation, Clinton off-handedly pointed out that "California has twelve percent of the country's population, twenty-one percent of the country's defense budget [and] took about forty percent of the cuts in the last round of base closings."

Such performances had a decided effect on people who heard and saw his skill firsthand: "I was impressed, and I'm a Republican," said a woman in the audience at one of Clinton's town hall meetings. "He has so much information on the top of his head, and I like his easy manner of communicating with people."

On the other hand, however, Clinton was frequently criticized for too often becoming bogged down in details, to the point where his answers were so complex that people had trouble filtering out an answer to their questions. Near the end of one town hall, hosted by newsman Ted Koppel, for instance, a woman expressed her disapproval of taxes being used to fund abortions. In the middle of the president's extensive response, Koppel interrupted with what he called "a curious criticism." "Sometimes I think you're so specific in your answers or so detailed in your answers," he lectured the president, "that it's a little hard to know what the answer to the question was." Although Clinton seemed a bit annoyed, he ignored Koppel's remark and continued his response to the woman who had asked the original question.

More than just talking about everything he had learned, Bill Clinton displayed an uncanny ability to transform knowledge into something innovative and useful. Because he believed that the process of globalization required a new and different perspective on pursuing business, for instance, Clinton embraced the rapid advancement of information technology. As a matter of fact, he deserves a great deal of credit for leading the United States into the Information Age.

In addition to being the first president to use e-mail as a means of communicating with the American people on a national basis, Clinton signed the Government Printing Office Electronic Information Access Enhancement Act of 1993, which provided online computer access to two of the major source documents that informed the American people about new laws and regulations: *The Congressional Record* and *The Federal Register*. He also instituted the National Technology Initiative (to further strengthen the building and implementation of new electronic information highways), spearheaded government spending for high-tech research and development, and offered $17 billion in tax breaks over a five-year period for corporations who embraced new information systems. And with input from both private industry and government agencies, the Clinton Administration proposed the creation of the National Information Infrastructure (NII)—a seamless web of communications networks, computers, databases, and consumer electronics to which every American would have access.

LEARNING IN LEADERSHIP

As leaders grow into their jobs, they participate in continued intellectual study, investigate and ponder, and engage in personal self-analysis and self-criticism. This sustained acquisition of knowledge or skills through experience, practice, and study is of profound importance in leadership for three reasons. It helps leaders:

1.   *To enhance decision-making.*
     By gaining a deeper understanding to the question at hand,
     leaders are able to make better, more informed decisions.
2.   *To persevere after setbacks and failure.*
     Because leaders are agents of change, they are likely to
     experience resistance and pushback. The only way to succeed,
     therefore, is by learning from experience.
8.   *To persuade followers.*
     By communicating a detailed understanding of initiatives and
     proposals, leaders are able to convince people in the
     organization of the merits of their actions.

Bill Clinton had an astonishing ability to absorb information, process it mentally, and discuss it lucidly with others. He also understood the value of continual learning in life, as well as in leadership. And he used his presidential powers to do something about it.

In February 1994, Clinton introduced a seven-point agenda for lifelong learning. "I believe that every child can learn and can achieve," he said. "That is at the heart of our general initiatives on education, the Goals 2000 program, the school-to-work initiative, the reformation of the college loan program. It's at the heart of the national service program. It's at the heart of the reemployment program."

All seven points were aimed at young people:

1.   Help every child begin school healthy and ready to learn.
2.   Set and achieve world-class standards in public education.
3.   Open the doors of college opportunity to every young
     American who is eager and able to do college work.
4.   Expand opportunities to our young people to serve their
     communities and their country while earning money for their
     education.
5.   Provide new learning opportunities for young people who are
     going from high school to work.
6.   Change our unemployment system into a reemployment
     system.
7.   Challenge every sector of our society to accept greater
     responsibility for achieving an environment of lifelong
     learning.

The president strategically targeted this agenda toward young people who did not intend to pursue college and to less fortunate children who had few hopes of making it to a university. For those who were planning to go to college, in December 1994, he proposed tax deductions for college tuition "just as we make mortgage interest tax deductible." These two programs were part of Bill Clinton's strategy to implement a system of lifelong learning in the organization he led—the United States of America.

"I have made my mistakes. And I have learned again the importance of humility in all human endeavor."

—Clinton, State of the Union Address
January 26, 1995

"We've got a lot to learn from each other."

—Clinton to world leaders at the 1994 G–7 Summit
July 5, 1994

The very same night of Clinton's deposition, in the wee morning hours of **January 18, 1998,** *Matt Drudge exposed the Monica Lewinsky story on his website with the headline: "Blockbuster Report: 23-Year Old, Former White House Intern, Sex Relationship With President." His sources were reportedly members of the "elves," and others associated with Linda Tripp. Less than nine hours later, conservative commentator William Kristol appeared on the ABC Sunday morning news program,* This Week, *and exposed details of the story to a national television audience. After that, the media floodgates opened and virtually every major print publication, radio station, and television network across the country reported the item. Much of the information apparently came, directly or indirectly, from the Office of the Independent Counsel.* The Washington Post, ABC News, *and* NBC's Meet The Press, *for example, cited "sources" close to, or associated with, Kenneth Starr's investigation.*

In the wake of what quite literally became a full-fledged media frenzy, Clinton's detractors pounced. The more extreme compared him to the devil, called him "the man from grope," said he was "diseased," and stated that the question now was whether to "impeach or assassinate." Political commentators predicted that Clinton's time in office was numbered in days, that his presidency was dead, and that he simply could not possibly survive such a devastating revelation.

On **January 26, 1998,** *President Clinton, pressured by his advisers to respond, appeared in the Roosevelt Room of the White House to introduce a new federally financed program for childcare. Afterwards, he took a few questions from the press. When asked about the reports, he said: "I did not have sexual relations with that women, Miss Lewinsky. I never told anybody to lie, not a single time, never." The next morning, on* **January 27, 1998,** *Hillary Clinton appeared on NBC's* The Today Show *to defend her husband. "This is what concerns me," she said. "This [inquiry] started out as an investigation of a failed land deal. . . . We get a politically motivated prosecutor who is allied with the right-wing opponents of my husband. . . . This vast right-wing conspiracy has been conspiring against my husband since the day he announced for president. It has not yet been fully revealed to the American public." Predictably, conservative commentators ridiculed Mrs. Clinton for suggesting such a thing. The next day,* **January 28, 1998,** *Kenneth Starr convened a grand jury ostensibly to investigate whether Bill Clinton committed perjury or obstructed justice. Later that evening, the president delivered his State of the Union Address.*

Over the next six or seven months, a steady barrage of accusations and attacks in the media dogged President Clinton. On **February 15, 1998,** *conservative columnist Robert Novak reported that key people on the White House staff were, similar to Richard Nixon, keeping an "enemies list." On*

March 16, 1998, the day after she had testified before Starr's grand jury, Kathleen Willey appeared on CBS's 60 Minutes. *Less than two weeks later, on March 28, 1998, the deposition of an Arkansas woman named Juanita Broaddrick turned up on various right-wing websites. Broaddrick's testimony, taken by lawyers for Paula Jones, stated that Bill Clinton had raped her in an Arkansas hotel room back in 1978. The story was also mentioned in* The Wall Street Journal *despite the fact that years earlier in a sworn affidavit, Broaddrick had denied the incident ever happened. Her turnaround was reported to have been a result of speaking with prosecutors from the independent counsel's office, who promised her immunity from prosecution. On April 30, 1998, Kenneth Starr filed new charges of tax fraud and conspiracy against Webster Hubbell and his wife, Suzanne. A defiant Hubbell, who believed the charges were trumped up in an effort to get him to "flip" and testify against Bill Clinton, reacted angrily. "I want you to know the Office of the Independent Counsel can indict my dog, they can indict my cat," he said in a public briefing, "but I'm not going to lie about the President, I'm not going to lie about the First Lady or anyone else." On June 4, 1998,* The New York Times *columnist William Safire compared White House aide, Sydney Blumenthal, to Charles Colson (convicted felon and Richard Nixon's former White House aide), and predicted Starr would indict him. On July 16, 1998, a report appeared on NBC's* The Today Show *that, according to "people close to Starr," Secret Service agents had facilitated the president's various rendezvous with Monica Lewinsky. In August 1998, Ann Coulter published a best-selling book urging the president's impeachment* (High Crimes and Misdemeanors: The Case Against Bill Clinton). *And in September 1998, conservative author William Bennett released his new book,* The Death of Outrage: Bill Clinton and the Assault on American Ideals, *in which he accused the American public of acquiescence in allowing Clinton to foster "decadence" and "moral rot."*

"I understand and appreciate the fact that compromise and consensus and conciliation will have to be the order of the day. Nothing this difficult and complex can be accomplished without listening to different voices and different ideas."

—Bill Clinton, discussing the
1993 budget bill with congressmen
July 20, 1993

"The reason we had to compromise is we didn't have the votes to get more done."

—Bill Clinton, on the issue of gays in the military; at a town meeting in Sacramento
October 3, 1993

CHAPTER FOURTEEN

COMPROMISE

Six months into his first term, Bill Clinton was seated in Room 459 of the Old Executive Office Building doing an interview by satellite with members of the Wisconsin press. He had just returned from Capitol Hill, where he attempted to rally wavering Democratic members of the House of Representatives to support his budget bill. The president had a similar conference scheduled with the Louisiana press at 5:30, and later that evening he would give Larry King a live interview from the White House.

The loaded question came at about a quarter past five: "Mr. President," the Wisconsin reporter began, "rightly or wrongly, public opinion polls have suggested that a number of people see you as not being a strong leader. They also see your position on gays in the military as having been a bit of a compromise. Would you expect to continue to compromise on important issues in the future, or do you see yourself as becoming a stronger leader on those key issues?"

After a few moments of rambling comments defending his record, Clinton exploded in a verbal tongue-lashing: "I am the first President who ever took on this issue. Is that a sign of weakness? It may be a sign of madness, sir, but it is not a sign of weakness. And I think that we need to get our heads on straight about what is strong and what is weak. When a president takes on tough issues, takes tough stands, tries to get things done in a democracy, you may not get 100 percent. Was I wrong to take 85 [percent]? That's what a democracy is all about. Read the United States Constitution. It's about honorable compromise. And that is not weakness if you're making progress."

The reporter did not understand Bill Clinton's nature. Nor did he understand that Clinton considered the art of compromise a measure of strong leadership. Not only would the new president employ it on nearly every important issue in the future, but compromise, in and of itself, would become a trademark of the Clinton presidency.

LEARNING THE ROPES IN ARKANSAS

Compromise was a skill Bill Clinton had learned during his four-term tenure as governor of Arkansas. He was in a far weaker position than the leaders of the other states largely because Arkansas did not grant its governor much executive authority. So when push came to shove, Clinton had no real power with which he could hammer his opponents. As a result, he was forced to negotiate and bargain.

Dr. Bobby Roberts, a former adviser to Clinton, succinctly summed up Arkansas' complex relationship between the executive and legislative branches of government:

> In Arkansas, the power tactic is hard to employ because the office of the governor is systemically weak. . . . After the Civil War, Reconstruction government in Arkansas was controlled from the governor's office, and when the Democrats finally overthrew the Republican regime, the state ratified the "Redeemer" responsibility. [So] real political power passed to the general assembly. The office remains a weak instrument compared with that of most other states. The governor still has no direct control of the highway and transportation departments, higher education, the prisons, or the state fish and wildlife departments. Powerful independent management boards run them. Any governor who seeks to assert much independent executive authority is headed for trouble with the legislature.

Because of these unique circumstances, Bill Clinton was thrust into a situation similar to a middle manager in a major corporation—one who has little authority but a great deal of responsibility. Being a dicta-tor, or employing a "command and control" style simply would not work in the state of Arkansas. Still, if things didn't get done, the people would blame him. So Clinton was forced to bargain and compromise, because it was the one of the few ways he could get something done. Ac-cordingly, Clinton rarely tried to use power to gain an objective. He pre-ferred to negotiate with the general assembly. "Negotiation rather than muscle," said Roberts, "also is an impulse of Clinton's character. He [found] no satisfaction in defeating opponents."

During his second term as governor, Clinton focused on only one major issue—education reform. He was extraordinarily successful in weaving together a consensus through deals and compromises that led to a sweeping new initiative, making Arkansas's new plan for education a role model for other states. The process he used to get that measure through the state legislature was adept and persistent. "[Clinton] would meet with any legislators who wanted a favor from him or who had a bill that they wanted the governor to support," said Roberts. "[He] would listen and probe for some common ground for agreement. Even if they didn't agree, they usually parted on friendly terms." Employing this type of political give-and-take ensured a victory on education that turned out to be a win-win situation for everyone involved—the people of Arkansas, the legislators, and Governor Clinton, who, because of the bill's success, was catapulted to national prominence.

Bill Clinton's ability to get things done through bargaining and compromise impressed many of his advisers, to whom it seemed unnat-ural. "One thing that I realized too late in my time as a member of Clin-ton's staff was that his approach to conflict and controversy was much more sophisticated than my own," said Stephen A. Smith. "I saw political choices as representing the dialectic between opposites, while he was more sensitive to the nuances or differences and shades of opinion. Where I assumed that zero-sum choices were the only option, he saw the possibility for greater consensus and sought the advantages for compro-mise among competing interests."

On the other side of the coin, however, Ernest Dumas, a former edi-tor of the *Arkansas Gazette*, noted that: "It's always been a criticism of Clinton that he compromised too easily, that he always wanted to get something passed. If he couldn't get the whole loaf, he'd try to get some-thing through. That's his history."

Curiously, this was also a criticism of Clinton after he became presi-dent. He often seemed too eager to please everyone, too anxious to uti-lize appeasement and compromise over conflict. Even Clinton's most fervent supporters criticized him for being too willing to negotiate on key issues. And yet, with time, they also came to realize that he usually would not yield on his overarching mission.

"I have never known him to negotiate away a goal," observed long-time associate Betsey Wright. "I have seen him take less at a given time because it was a step forward and then pick it up and carry it to the next step at the next opportunity. [And] I have also seen him draw the line in the dirt and say, "No, this is so far afield from what the goal is, I'd rather have nothing.""

A COMPROMISING PRESIDENT, OR A PRESIDENT COMPROMISED?

As President of the United States, Bill Clinton repeatedly sought to compromise on major initiatives in order to make some progress. Yet despite all he had learned while governor of Arkansas, Clinton did not begin his presidency with effective negotiations. In fact, he fell flat on his face with his first two major initiatives.

The first, involving the jobs stimulus package, saw Clinton refuse to negotiate with Republicans, whom he viewed as "irrelevant" because the Democrats held a majority in both houses of Congress. When the president's people worked only with the Democrats, Republicans in the Senate became angry and staged the filibuster that effectively killed the bill. Clinton was only able to salvage a smaller program of extended unemployment benefits.

And if former colleague Betsey Wright never saw Bill Clinton negotiate away a goal as governor of Arkansas, she had only to wait until he became president. In the second major issue he faced, which involved allowing gays to serve in the armed forces, Clinton compromised himself to the extent that he ended up totally abandoning his original principle. Clinton had made a campaign promise to end discrimination against gays in the military. And after his election, gay groups immediately pressed him to take action. But the proposal was met with such stiff opposition from the military brass, certain members of Congress, and the majority of the American public, that it had virtually no chance of success from the beginning.

After months of discussions and debate, which included emotionally charged congressional hearings, a compromise labeled "Don't Ask, Don't Tell, Don't Pursue" was put forth. This new policy eliminated a standard recruiting question about sexual preference and further centered on homosexual "conduct," which would still not be tolerated. Gays could still be forced out of the service for being homosexual, especially if they attempted to serve in an open manner. But stronger evidence was necessary; a "pattern of credible information" was required, whereas previously rumor and circumstantial information was sufficient for a major inquiry. That small concession from the military was the best that Clinton could do. It was very early in his presidency and he had too much to risk by being dogmatic about this particular issue. Moreover, Clinton not only risked a significant decline in public opinion ratings, he could have made permanent enemies of certain members of Congress who were key to passage of future legislation. So under great political pressure, Clinton endorsed the proposal. Chairman of the Joint Chiefs of Staff, Colin Powell, called it "an honorable compromise." But Clinton was roundly castigated by the gay community for caving in, and from conservatives for bringing up the issue in the first place. "I got the worst of both worlds," Clinton later lamented.

Clinton followed his defeats on the jobs stimulus bill and gays in the military with a string of legislative successes, nearly every one of which involved compromising on his original proposal.

Here are a few key examples:

1993 Deficit Reduction Budget Bill

One of the most controversial elements of Clinton's 1993 deficit reduction bill was an energy tax proposed as a means of raising revenue. As initially written, the tax was a vague and confusing regulation that centered on the public's consumption of energy as measured in British Thermal Units (hence the name, BTU Tax).

Because of massive resistance to the tax, the Clinton administration offered dozens of compromises. It proposed to exempt coal in order to pacify the steel industry; to exempt ethanol to pacify the farm industry; and to exempt jet fuel for international flights to ease the burden of the airline industry. When local utilities balked, the administration agreed to list the energy tax on a separate line on gas and electric bills, so that every consumer would know how much the federal government was charging them.

In early June, as the energy tax became more and more of a problem. President Clinton set out five broad principles for his overall budget bill that he asked not be compromised. Everything else was fair game. As *The New York Times* reported: "He asked negotiators to leave intact his goal of reducing the deficit by $500 billion over four years, to approve only those new taxes that affect the rich more than the poor, to keep measures for small business and for the working poor, and to retain spending cuts."

One week later, Democratic senator David Boren of oil-rich Oklahoma proposed a compromise bill that totally eliminated Clinton's energy tax, and then personally warned Clinton that his overall plan would face certain defeat if he did not back down on the energy tax. In the end, it became nothing more than a minor sales tax to raise revenue in the larger budget deficit reduction plan. The political reality was obvious: If Clinton had not retreated on the energy tax, he would have lost passage of the entire 1993 budget deficit reduction bill, and his presidency would have been irrevocably damaged.

"I never expected to get 100 percent," Clinton said immediately following passage of the bill in Congress.

National Service Plan

Clinton's National Service Program hinged on one major issue: the student loan program. Many members of Congress did not want to place the federal government in the business of lending money for college educations. They called it "big government run amok." Clinton's compromise included a government lending cap of 50 percent of the total student loan volume. The final bill, which passed only after this compromise was worked out, also included a provision that allowed student volunteers to perform social and environmental work for the government in return for repaying their college educational loans.

Foreign Affairs

Clinton consistently sought to negotiate and compromise regarding both U. S. troop involvement in trouble spots and general military and diplomatic strategies to solve problems. In Haiti, for instance, Clinton encouraged exiled President Jean-Bertrand Aristide to compromise on his demands for punishment of the military officers who deposed him, so that he would have a better chance of returning to power.

On another front, Clinton repeatedly sought a compromise strategy for dealing with the ethnic crisis in Bosnia. Rather than an all-out invasion or doing nothing, he agreed with the United Nations to institute food drops and a blockade of certain cities.

Clinton also forged a compromise that brought American troops in Somalia home by March 1994. He agreed to an early withdrawal, in part, to satisfy irritated congressmen because he had other major and controversial issues that needed to get through Congress. Health Care, NAFTA, and Reinventing Government initiatives all were significantly important enough that he decided not to risk alienating legislators.

North American Free Trade Agreement

In order to get NAFTA passed, Clinton not only cajoled, persuaded, twisted arms, and compromised, he cut deals in exchange for votes. The administration offered to limit Canadian shipments of peanut butter and wheat to the United States; it promised cuts in tariffs on numerous fruits and vegetables entering the United States; it tightened rules on beef and cattle shipments; and it accelerated the elimination of Mexican tariffs on wine. Clinton's administration even agreed to influence Mexico into speeding up the extradition of a man accused of raping a four-year-old American girl. All were made in exchange for "yes" votes in Congress.

During the political process of deal-cutting and compromising over NAFTA, Clinton was heard to say in the Oval Office, "God, I love this."

Health Care Reform

During the full year that health care reform was under consideration, Bill Clinton repeatedly offered to compromise on key elements of his plan in order to secure passage of a bill that adhered to his basic underlying principles. The president started out strong on September 22, 1993, when he addressed a Joint Session of Congress. "If you send me legislation that does not guarantee every American private health insurance that can never be taken away, you will force me to take this pen, veto the legislation, and we'll come right back here and start all over again," he vowed.

However, earlier that same day, Clinton had already offered to compromise on the proposed three-year phase-in of universal coverage. By the time the official written proposal was submitted to the House and Senate in late October, several dozen changes had been made in response to suggestions and criticism from special interest groups and members of Congress. Those changes included an even longer transition to the new system, more generous dental benefits, and expansion of mammography coverage, among other things.

Due to the many special interest groups who were sure to voice opposition, the President and Hillary Clinton had realized at the outset that they had little chance of seeing their proposal pass through Congress exactly as written. Accordingly, they had viewed their initial bill as more of a broad direction-setter than a detailed road map. It was a guide for arriving at the final destination, which was coverage for all Americans. Flexibility in how to get there was key for the Clintons. "We have no pride of authorship," they repeatedly stated.

Sure enough, within weeks of announcing the plan, lobbyists were sparing no expense to fight the proposal. Groups such as the Health Insurance Association of America, the American Hospital Association, the American Medical Association, the American Association of Retired Persons, and countless others were either running major advertising campaigns or raising significant doubts about the Clinton health plan. That organized opposition caused the administration to offer a variety of alternatives over an extended period of time.

For example, in late January 1994, the Administration conceded that participation in proposed health care alliances could be voluntary rather than compulsory, as originally proposed. In March, Clinton reiterated to a Boston group that a slower pace of change in the health care initiative was agreeable to him. In May, he told Democratic senators: "We are going to keep open, keep flexible, and reach out to Republicans." Indeed, Clinton met with Republican members of the Senate and assured them he was ready to compromise to keep the bill alive. And in June, Clinton conferred with more than 100 Congressional members from oil- and gas-producing states who were hoping to cut some deals in exchange for their support for Clinton's health care bill. He also began working closely with Senate Majority Leader George Mitchell and Speaker of the House Thomas Foley to forge a compromise bill. "When I put my ideas out," said Clinton, "I made it clear that I was very flexible on how to get there."

By mid-July 1994, health care reform was in serious trouble and the various proposals still on the table were significantly different than Clinton's original plan. But the president still pushed for action. He spoke to the National Governor's Association and suggested that Congress postpone its August recess and work to complete a compromise bill. Among other things, he agreed to abandon the notion of employer mandates if another way could be found that would guarantee universal health coverage. For the first time, Bill Clinton admitted that "universal health coverage" might mean insuring less than 100 percent of the people. "We know we're not going to get right at 100 percent," he said, "but we know that you've got to get somewhere in the ballpark of 95 [percent] or upwards so that you stop the cost shifting." At the same time Clinton pointed out that recent polls confirmed that the vast majority of Americans backed his goal of universal health coverage.

Within days of his speech to the governors, leading Democrats in both the House and Senate announced they were working with the president to draft a compromise health care bill that would pass Congress. The president's plan, they said, had essentially been scrapped. While his overarching principles would still be left in place, universal coverage would be phased in over a longer period of time. After Clinton met with the congressional leaders on July 23, he recapped the meeting in a news conference: "I have been saying for four weeks that we have agreed to dramatically change this plan. We're going to string it out, we have to have a longer phase-in, we have to have less bureaucracy, we have to have totally voluntary small business alliances, and we have to give a bigger break to small businesses to get them to buy into it."

By the fall of 1994, the idea of reforming the nation's health care system had completely collapsed in Congress. Special interest groups had spent hundreds of millions of dollars to fight it, Republican senators and congressmen maneuvered to delay it; public opinion waned; and President Clinton finally refused to compromise for less than his basic goal of universal coverage for all Americans.

COMPROMISE IN LEADERSHIP

Even though Bill Clinton was able to secure passage of the majority of legislation he proposed, much of the public complained about his style. "He's a waffler," they said. "He's namby-pamby. He'll fold at crunch time."

Many of Clinton's political allies, however, valued his skill at compromise. Speaker of the House Thomas Foley, for instance, strongly supported the president's tactics, and pointedly addressed those who criticized him for negotiating with Congress. "I don't understand the charge that he's not acting on principle," said Foley. "Most of what's happened that's good in this country in public policy has been achieved over the years, even decades, by compromise, by adjustment, by partial success, and not by total victory at one moment."

Foley was right. Creative compromise has always been a part of American political leadership. The Constitution, for example, would not have its current structure had not the founding fathers agreed to work together in 1787 to establish two houses of Congress. In the 1820s, the Missouri Compromise was established to maintain a balance between slave and free states. And in 1962, President John F. Kennedy avoided nuclear war by compromising with Russian Premier Nikita Khrushchev, agreeing to remove American nuclear weapons from Turkey in exchange for removal of those in Cuba. That action embodied Kennedy's famous comment: "Compromise need not mean cowardice."

History has also demonstrated that *not* having the ability to compromise, or lacking the will to do so, can harm a leader. President Jimmy Carter, for instance, was frequently criticized for not compromising on key issues. And George H. W. Bush chose to lambaste Congress over "gridlock," a tactic that only broadened divisions among the legislative and executive branches of government. Both Carter and Bush were voted out of office by sizeable margins after only one term, largely because they failed to achieve very much.

While the path of negotiation and compromise can often yield results, it is also fraught with serious risks. First of all, both sides invariably complain that they didn't get everything they wanted. When Bill Clinton proposed a compromise in the dispute over logging and the environment in the Northwestern United States, for example, he was immediately attacked by environmental groups and the timber industry. "This plan is like 'kissing your sister,'" they said. "Clinton gave too much to the other side." And this was after he had been hailed as a hero for convening a special conference in Oregon to examine the issue in the first place.

Second, because Clinton set his sights high on every issue, and then ended up settling for less, he gave the appearance that he was always *retreating* rather than always moving forward. As a result, much of the public perceived that he was accomplishing very little, and that he would easily give in. Clinton was also frequently misinterpreted for selling out his personal principles, in that much of the public perceived he would compromise on any given issue and simply take whatever he could get. With time, such a perception can result in a lack of trust and credibility from people within the organization. In Clinton's case, it caused Americans to ask a fundamental question: "When is compromise appropriate and when is it the abandonment of principle?"

Philosophically, Clinton once tried to answer that question by explaining that he preferred to follow the advice of golfer Tom Watson, who upon handing the president a club, said: "Now look at your grip, Mr. President. If you move your [hands] too far to the left, it gets you in trouble on the right. But if you move [them] too far to the right, it gets you in trouble on the left. The trick is to keep your grip balanced in the center."

Bill Clinton's "compromising" style of leadership was clearly a double-edged sword. On one end, it was a weapon for thrusting legislation through Congress. On the other, it was a sharp blade upon which he fell on from time to time. But that was a paradox he didn't seem to mind. By being willing to accept the risks that go along with negotiation and compromise, Clinton demonstrated a certain strength of character that included both self-confidence and internal personal security. He was not afraid to be viewed negatively, nor was he afraid to lose. And it was precisely such fearlessness that propelled him forward and allowed him to achieve so much.

Still, whenever it came to the issue of compromise, Americans wondered whether Bill Clinton believed in Edmund Burke's viewpoint, which was: "All government, indeed every human benefit and enjoyment, every virtue, every prudent act, is founded on compromise and barter"—or whether he gravitated more toward Nikita Khrushchev's point of view, which was articulated in 1958, four years before the Cuban Missile Crisis: "If you cannot catch a bird of paradise, better take a wet hen."

"The process we begin today will not be easy. Its outcome cannot possibly make everyone happy. Perhaps it won't make anyone completely happy. But the worst thing we can do is nothing. As we begin, [let's all] admit that there are no simple or easy answers."

—Bill Clinton, opening remarks at
the Forest Conference in
Portland, Oregon
April 2, 1993

"I'm not the tooth fairy."

—Bill Clinton, on health care
September 21, 1993

After more than six months of positioning, haggling, and threatening, the Office of the Independent Counsel finally agreed, (on **July 27, 1998**), to give Monica Lewinsky immunity from prosecution in exchange for her testimony against the president. The OIC's plan was to produce a one-witness case against Clinton with the charge that he had lied under oath about his relationship with Lewinsky, and that he had obstructed justice by asking her to lie and withhold evidence. After being granted immunity, however, Lewinsky would only confirm the relationship, and steadfastly maintained that Clinton had never asked her to do anything illegal. She would, however, turn over a dress with a fluid stain on it that DNA testing identified as Clinton's.

Once Monica Lewinsky's cooperation was secured, the president was deposed for the grand jury via videotape. During the three-and-a-half hour session, on **August 17, 1998**, prosecutors asked a litany of questions that could be interpreted as perjury traps. Clearly embarrassed and under duress, Clinton hemmed and hawed and offered a variety of legalistic responses. In one instance, his attorney's statement that "there is absolutely no sex of any kind in any manner, shape, or form, with President Clinton" was brought up, and Clinton was then asked: "That statement is a completely false statement, is that correct?" The president responded by stating: "It depends on what the meaning of the word 'is' is."

After the deposition, Clinton went on national television and confessed to the public. "Indeed, I did have a relationship with Miss Lewinsky that was not appropriate; in fact it was wrong," he said. "It constituted a critical lapse in judgment and a personal failure on my part for which I am solely and completely responsible. At no time did I ask anyone to lie, to hide or destroy evidence, or to take any other unlawful action. I know that my public comments and my silence about this matter gave a false impression. I misled people, including even my wife. I deeply regret that. I was motivated by many factors. A desire to protect myself from the embarrassment of my own conduct. Concern about protecting my family. A politically inspired lawsuit."

After Clinton's mea culpa, a nationwide poll revealed that 69 percent of the American public wanted Kenneth Starr to end his investigation. And while the president's approval ratings remained high, conservative Republicans were merciless in their criticism of Clinton. Now, they believed, they had what they needed to formally move toward impeachment in the House of Representatives.

On **September 9, 1998**, Kenneth Starr presented his final written report to Congress. Totaling 452 pages, with eighteen accompanying boxes of FBI interviews, grand jury testimony, and other evidence, it was filled with explicit details of Clinton's private life, but failed to prove either obstruction of justice or perjury. The narrative amounted mostly to a nonstop negative attack on the president's behavior and character. Placed under the jurisdiction of the House Rules Committee, Starr's report was quickly made public (on **September 11, 1998**), even before most congressmen had a chance to examine it. The massive volume was placed on the Internet and was read by millions of people around the country and, indeed, the world. Ten days later, on **September 21, 1998**, the House Judiciary Committee announced that the videotape of Clinton's August deposition would be released to the public. It, too, was then broadcast on national television, further adding to the president's humiliation and embarrassment.

On **October 8, 1998**, the United States House of Representatives voted, 258–176, to open a formal investigation into the possible impeachment of the President of the United States. The next week, a group of 430 constitutional law professors issued a formal statement concluding that the independent counsel's allegations "do not justify presidential impeachment under the U.S. Constitution," and that "members of Congress would violate their constitutional responsibilities if they sought to impeach and remove the President for misconduct, even criminal misconduct, that fell short of the high constitutional standard required for impeachment." Republican leaders, however, dismissed the statement, saying, in effect, that they could impeach the president for anything they deemed to be appropriate. Accordingly, on **November 19, 1998**, Kenneth Starr testified before the House Judiciary Committee about President Clinton's "criminal" behavior. He was the only witness allowed to testify before the committee. When Democratic members asked that Clinton's lawyers be allowed to speak, their request was denied on a straight party vote.

"We agreed to make next year's session even more informal so that we could focus on a few big things, cut out a lot of the bureaucracy and all the other stuff that goes with these summits, and really try to get things done in a very informal way."

—Clinton, after the Tokyo G–7 Summit
July 8, 1993

"I run a remarkably open presidency. I wanted people to believe that their Government belonged to them again and that we could be more open and accessible to them. I've tried to do that."

—Clinton, during a live interview with Larry King
January 20, 1994

CHAPTER FIFTEEN

INFORMALITY AND OPENNESS

One could only imagine the reactions of leaders of the most important nations bordering the Pacific Ocean when informed of what American president Bill Clinton wanted them to do at the upcoming Asia-Pacific Economic Cooperation (APEC) Summit in Washington State. "Meet me at the Seattle docks at dawn," Clinton essentially wired. "We're going to take a ferry out to an uninhabited island. Dress is casual. No ties. No conference tables. No formal speeches. Oh, and by the way, dress warmly. There isn't any indoor heating where we're going."

Despite the unusual invitation, on November 20, 1993, there they all were: The leaders, whose fourteen nations, when combined, accounted for more than half of the world's total goods and services, gathered in a rustic Indian long house with wooden floors, on Blake Island in the middle of Puget Sound. Chairs were arranged in a circle and the leaders were warmed by nothing more than each other's conversation and a small space heater. Nearly everyone complied with the dress code. Most wore sweaters. Japan's Morihiro Hosokawa wore his aviator's scarf. Fidel Ramos of the Philippines brandished his cigar. Clinton was dressed in a brown leather bombardier's jacket, khaki slacks, and boots. Only the Chinese president showed up wearing a tie. The attire was a first in world summit meetings and *The New York Times* cleverly labeled it the "L. L. Bean diplomatic dress code."

"I don't know if they are going to be holding hands and singing 'Kumbaya'" said a White House spokeswoman, "but this is just what the President had in mind." And Clinton made the most of it, guiding the group in informal discussions and casual conversations. When it was over, the leaders had produced a vision statement that read, in part: "In this post–Cold War era, we have an opportunity to build a new economic foundation for the Asia-Pacific that harnesses the energy of our diverse economies, strengthens cooperation and promotes prosperity. Our meeting reflects the emergence of a new voice for the Asia-Pacific in world affairs." And at a post-summit news conference, a euphoric Bill Clinton announced: "We have agreed that the Asia-Pacific region should be a united one, not divided. We have agreed that our economic policies should be open, not closed."

Many of the leaders had never before met each other, but the informal nature of the event created an atmosphere that made it easier for them to get to know one another in a way that a more rigid formal meeting could never have allowed. This casual and open style remained a mainstay throughout Bill Clinton's presidency.

CLINTON THE CASUAL

Just four months prior to the APEC meeting, Clinton had complained to his staff about the undo pomp at the 1993 G–7 Summit in Tokyo. He also expressed a dislike for the rigid structure and "business suit" formality of the event. As the conference wore on, Clinton pushed for an unstructured three-hour meeting (which he got) and constantly lobbied for ways to decrease formality at future G–7 meetings. Afterwards, the president remarked to the press: "We agreed to make next year's session even more informal so that we could focus on a few big things, cut out a lot of the bureaucracy and all the other stuff that goes with these summits, and really try to get things done in a very informal way. So I feel good about it." And indeed, the 1994 G–7 meeting in Naples began with an informal dinner and reception where the leaders gathered on a terrace overlooking the city.

This casual, give-and-take style was one Clinton had adopted during the 1992 presidential campaign. His aides frequently scheduled relaxed town hall meetings, because Clinton excelled in such a setting. When one of the three presidential debates was held in an informal give-and-take venue, President George H. W. Bush and Ross Perot looked uncomfortable, while Clinton appeared as at ease as if he was in his own living room.

Clinton continued the town hall format after winning the presidency and was quick to dismiss even the slightest hint of aristocracy. Just prior to a meeting in Detroit, for example, when a plush, nicely upholstered chair in the center of the stage was noticed, Clinton's advance team asked that it be removed. The president, they said, preferred a plain wooden stool. During the meeting, Clinton sat on the edge of that stool, or stood up, or walked around and interacted with the audience as much as possible. He used no notes, spoke extemporaneously, and took all questions. A year later, *The New York Times* reported that during a similar event in Moscow, Clinton "shed all pretense of formality, leaving his podium behind to walk down a ramp and onto a platform that extended into the crowd."

During his two terms as president, Clinton projected the confident and trustworthy image of someone who had nothing to fear, nothing to hide, and everything to share. His casual style was not limited to the office. He displayed it with nearly everyone he met, virtually anywhere he went. While vacationing on Martha's Vineyard, Clinton showed up at a party at Vernon Jordan's home wearing loafers but no socks. On a plane trip from California to Texas, he casually interacted with reporters while dressed in a track suit. He held one press conference while wearing a sweater and jeans; and he frequently talked to reporters just before and after his morning jogs, still dressed in his workout clothes. Clinton's casual appearance sent the message that he was always approachable, at ease with people, and willing to listen and engage in conversation.

Garry Trudeau, creator of the cartoon strip *Doonesbury*, spent a week at the White House in 1993 and described President Clinton one early morning, "clad only in a nightshirt, schmoozing with reporters in the press room. 'Hey, Phil,' said the president, 'how's the wife and kids. Still big Red Sox fans?' When the reporter responded with a quip, [Clinton] laughed heartily and got off a few self-deprecating haircut jokes," wrote Trudeau.

U.S. presidents previously did not interact in such an informal manner with the public. It simply wasn't done. Bill Clinton changed the standard. He also changed the operational style of the White House from one of rigid formality to one that appeared sporty and freewheeling. He encouraged his administration to be on a first-name basis as much as possible. He opened the White House cafeteria to include all employees and staff, and frequently ate there himself. Clinton also allowed a more casual dress code where many of the people who worked in the White House did not wear ties. And on weekends, rolled up shirtsleeves, sweaters, and coffee mugs were the order of the day. Actually, Clinton's casual presidency was sometimes referred to as "coffee cup" in nature, which may have started on May 27, 1993, when Paula Zahn of CBS's early morning television show introduced the president at 7:05 A.M. during a live broadcast from the White House by simply stating. "Here comes President Clinton, cup of coffee in hand."

Critics of the administration had a field day with Bill Clinton's new style. They complained that he allowed a dozen or more people access to the Oval Office at a time and that guests frequently wandered the halls unattended. There were also too many meetings, they said, where details were debated endlessly with no decisions being made. National carping about White House operations eventually reached a crescendo when Bob Woodward released his book *The Agenda,* which chronicled a chaotic if not activist administration.

While many people in the press and federal bureaucracy grumbled about Bill Clinton's informality, private industry was embracing it. Casual interaction was becoming the order of the day in corporate America. Executives such as Jack Welch at General Electric wanted "on-the-spot answers" as opposed to formal written reports. Microsoft's Bill Gates created "open" office spaces that were furnished with living room furniture, which were intended to encourage informal discussions. And there were also major trends in business and industry to relax dress codes, loosen up on formal structures, and give employees more contact with their leaders, whether it was at an informal luncheon or a town meeting. In addition, many forms of public communication, such as television news programs and political press conferences, became more informal, with extemporaneous discussion rather than prepared texts.

OPENNESS EVEN WHEN RISKY

Almost immediately upon taking office, Clinton initiated a series of steps designed to make the federal government more open and accessible. On April 26, 1993, he issued an executive directive that ordered a comprehensive review of rules designed to keep government documents secret. Clinton's move was aimed at millions of government reports filed away during the cold war. Six months later, he called on "all Federal departments and agencies to renew their commitment to the Freedom of Information Act." In doing so, Clinton rescinded a rule put in place during the Reagan years that ordered the government to hold back key documents if an agency deemed that there was a "substantial legal basis" to do so. "I remind agencies that our commitment to openness requires more than merely responding to requests from the public," said Clinton. "Each agency has a responsibility to distribute information on its own initiative, and to enhance public access through the use of electronic information systems."

Simultaneously, the White House relaxed its control on federal agencies and gave them more authority to act on their own. When combined, these two actions, along with Clinton's personal encouragement, resulted in certain cabinet members releasing documentation of previously secret and unpleasant government actions in their own departments. Energy Secretary Hazel O'Leary garnered the most attention when, in December 1993, she made public the U.S. government's radiation experiments on humans, along with details about the United States nuclear arsenal.

The president, of course, was severely criticized by conservative Republicans, who argued that such information was a matter of national security and shouldn't have been disclosed. Despite the negative feedback, Clinton continued his efforts to make the federal government more open. He released millions of secret documents associated with the John F. Kennedy assassination, and created the Assassination Records Review Board to review and make them public. He also took the unusual step of telling the American public that the government method for estimating the unemployment rate was flawed, and that he was changing the system to make it more realistic. Calculations with the new method increased the unemployment figure by 0.5 percent, which was a significant political liability.

Clinton's openness policy extended to working with members of Congress, whom he encouraged to cut down on closed-door, backroom bargaining. "Do not let us pull another Washington, D.C. game here and let this crime bill go down on some procedural hide-and-seek," he lectured in 1994. "If we're going to have a shoot-out, let's do it [at] high noon, [in] broad daylight, where everybody knows what the deal is."

Clinton also continued to seek advice before making most decisions, which resulted in leaks to the press about his prospective appointments and nominations, and criticism that he couldn't make up his mind. When questioned about the openness of his decision-making process regarding a Supreme Court appointment, Clinton essentially acknowledged that his open style invited problems: "If you seek advice, you will have leaks," Clinton noted. "I decided that I would pay the price of the leaks, even the wrong ones, to follow the duty of the Constitution."

With time, as the impact of his presidential decisions could be determined, Clinton often discussed the mistakes he had made. And that particular habit began right at the beginning of his presidency. He spoke openly, for instance, about the botched nominations of Zoe Baird for attorney general and Lani Guinier for civil rights chief in the Justice Department. In Guinier's case, Clinton assumed full responsibility for his actions and was startlingly frank in discussing the issue. After reading her writings in great detail, he had concluded that some of her ideas were simply not consistent with his views. So he decided to withdraw her nomination. He met with Guinier, talked it out, and told her of his decision. Clinton then faced the press, announced his action, and fielded a barrage of questions. Most startling of all was the fact that Clinton even stated that he would not have nominated her for the Justice Department had he read her writings in the first place and, in retrospect, he wished he had done so.

Such a candid admission was unusual for a sitting President of the United States. Predictably, the press and members of the opposing Republican Party railed at his error. Clearly, Clinton realized that such openness was a political risk. Yet he continued admitting his mistakes, and the number of those occasions became too numerous to list. Just take a look at a few of the open admissions during the first two years of Clinton's administration: The White House released a written report acknowledging serious errors by White House personnel in the firings of several members of the Travel Office; Clinton abruptly broke off discussions with Japanese Prime Minister Hosokawa in Washington by declaring their trade talks a failure. "We could have disguised our differences with cosmetic agreements," said the president, "but the issues between us are so important for our own nations and for the rest of the world that it is better to have reached no agreement than to have reached an empty agreement"; The administration admitted publicly that its stance regarding Haiti had failed and that the entire policy would be reevaluated and reformulated (six months later American troops occupied Haiti and President Aristide was back in office); and Henry Cisneros, Secretary of Housing and Urban Development, admitted flat out that his department's management of public housing had been an abject failure. Such admissions from the executive branch of the federal government were rare, if not totally unheard of. And yet, it seems as if the Clinton administration lived with two contemporary adages: "There are no secrets in successful organizations."

CLINTON AND THE ISSUE OF PERSONAL CHARACTER

In the immediate years after Bill Clinton left office, a majority of Americans believed he had done a good job as president, but also perceived him to be a flawed individual in terms of personal character. There were two major reasons for this unusual dichotomy. First and foremost was the ongoing and relentless character assassination perpetuated by right-wing extremists and neoconservative members of the opposition political party. After nearly a decade of constantly being told that Clinton was a bad guy, many people came to believe it. And others, while unsure what to believe, felt that if there were so many complaints about Clinton, he must have done something wrong. In other words, where there was smoke, there had to be fire. Second, Clinton's entire handling of the Lewinsky affair—the one major time he was less than candid—harmed him immeasurably. His supporters were extraordinarily disappointed, and his detractors were able to say, at last: "I told you so."

Important to note, however, was that nearly all of the extreme attacks on Bill Clinton were related to his personal life. On the other hand, criticism of Clinton's job performance as president was relatively normal in scope for a sitting president. Legitimate detractors merely disagreed with his programs, which is expected in the modern political arena.

Most analysts agree that there are at least four primary elements with which to judge an individual's personal character (hard work, ethics, integrity, and honesty). In Bill Clinton's case, it's relevant to consider all four in making a determination as to how he performed, in terms of character, while he was President of the United States.

1. Hard work

Hard work is just what it sounds like—reliable, energetic, and determined physical and mental effort in pursuing any endeavor. By virtually every standard, Bill Clinton had an extraordinary capacity for doing exactly that. In fact, he thrived on hard work. He showed up every day at the office, stayed up late, didn't take off weekends, tackled controversial issues, drew energy from important tasks, and derived great satisfaction in helping people.

Clinton was constantly in the field meeting with constituents, asking their opinions, listening to their wants and needs, and responding to natural disasters. He traveled the world building relationships, alliances, new global agreements, and new economic partnerships. Before he had left office, Clinton achieved more new legislation than any president since Franklin D. Roosevelt had during the Great Depression. And Clinton did it in the 1990s, largely a time of peace and prosperity, which made his achievements all the more remarkable.

2. Ethics

Ethics can be defined as: "An incorruptible code of conduct that governs a person's or a group's behavior." As president, Clinton consistently initiated executive actions and orders aimed at making government more efficient, more trustworthy, and more responsible to the needs of its citizens. On his very first day in office, for instance, Bill Clinton signed an executive order instituting a higher standard of ethical behavior to which every high government official was obliged to abide by. This code included a five-year ban on lobbying by former aides, and a lifetime ban on representing a foreign government by those aides. "[This] will uphold the highest possible ethical standards," said the president, "and guarantee that the members of this administration will be looking out for the American people and not for themselves."

As president, Clinton was constantly confronted with determining what *was,* and *was not,* ethical behavior on the part of his cabinet secretaries and other high officers in the government. Clinton stood by Secretary of Commerce Ron Brown when he was accused by a Vietnamese businessman of extorting money in return for opening trade to the United States. "He's told me that he hasn't done anything wrong," said the president. "I have no reason not to believe him." But a year later, Clinton prodded Secretary of Agriculture Mike Espy to resign when it became clear that there had been some ethics violations. "Although Secretary Espy has said he has done nothing wrong," said the president, "I am troubled by the appearance of some of these incidents and believe his decision to leave is appropriate." (Mike Espy was later cleared of wrongdoing.)

From 1993 through 2000, twenty-nine people occupied the fourteen major positions in President Clinton's cabinet. With the exception of the Espy situation, and an unsubstantiated claim about Energy Secretary Hazel O'Leary (for which she was quickly cleared by the attorney general), there was never even a hint that Clinton's cabinet secretaries conducted themselves in anything but an incorruptible, trustworthy, and upright manner. And that's the way the president wanted it. "We regard good ethics as the basis of good government," said Clinton.

3. Integrity

In leadership, integrity refers to the soundness, reliability, dependability, and dedication of an individual to consistently do the right thing. There are countless examples of Bill Clinton, while president, giving credit where credit was due, and accepting blame and responsibility when things went wrong. Here are just two:

During the signing of the Israel-PLO peace accord in September 1993, Clinton let the attention focus on Yitzhak Rabin and Yasir Arafat. He also stated the facts leading up to the agreement and gave former presidents Jimmy Carter and George H. W. Bush full credit for making it happen. Clinton called Carter "wise" and Bush "skillful," invited both to the ceremony, and had them spend the night at the White House. As *Time* noted:

> It was a triumphant but curious time for Bill Clinton. He deserved credit not for what he had done but for what he had not done. This agreement was the work of others over decades. Clinton stayed out of the way in the last act and let it happen naturally. He did not posture or seek personal acclaim, but paid tribute to those who had long carried the heavy burden. Such acts are far too rare in the presidency, but they are just as much a measure of honor. Bill Clinton enhanced himself as well as those who had braved the road to the South Lawn by the courage of his restraint.

That same year, Clinton delegated responsibility to Attorney General Janet Reno for the Branch Davidian standoff in Waco, Texas. Initially, when she was praised for her efforts, he was content to stand on the sidelines and let her bask in the glory. But a few months later, when Reno was criticized for ordering the final assault on the compound that led to the murder-suicides of eighty-six cult members, Clinton stepped forward and publicly held himself accountable for the raid.

"I was informed of the plan to end the siege," said the president, "[and I accept] full responsibility for the implementation of the decision."

4. Honesty

Honesty in leadership is the same as it is in everyday life. It is the quality of being honest, sincere, and free of deceit or untruthfulness.

In matters related to his job as president, there is no evidence that Bill Clinton ever lied about anything. On the contrary, he was unusually candid and straightforward when it came to explaining to the American people the problems that confronted his administration and the nation as a whole. He told people the truth about health care, about crime, about welfare, about NAFTA, about Haiti, Bosnia, Somalia, and Iraq. When he discovered that the government's formula for estimating the unemployment rate in America vastly underestimated the real numbers, he told the truth to the public and revised the system. As soon as he discovered that the government's inaccurate calculations hid $50 billion of the federal deficit, Clinton informed the public, added the $50 billion to the official tally, and changed the formula. In doing so, the president said simply: "Folks, we are telling you the truth for a change. We're telling you the truth."

In matters of private behavior in Bill Clinton's personal life, few people will ever know the full truth regarding his public statements. In the constant onslaught of political attacks and vilification, there were times when he seemed completely straightforward and truthful. During the Whitewater land deal controversy (which extended over the course of his entire two terms), Clinton consistently denied that neither he nor his wife had done anything wrong. And the record has proven that to be true. There were other times, however, when he seemed to walk a fine line, shade the truth, or be evasive. And of course, there was one very public, glaring lie that was simply indefensible.

In regard to the issue of Bill Clinton's personal character, the American people were left to answer several paradoxical questions: If flaws in a president's personal character do not impact positive job performance, should they be held against him? Do such personal flaws inevitably permeate job performance, or can they be compartmentalized and held in check? How should a president be judged—on performance only, on personal behavior only, or both performance and personal behavior? Was Bill Clinton a good president or not?

CHARACTER IN LEADERSHIP

Personal character is of paramount importance in leadership quite simply because, in the long run, people will not follow a leader who does not establish trust and exhibit the highest mental and moral qualities representative of the culture of the organization as a whole. Character is the foundation of leadership. All other traits, skills, qualities, and attributes related to effective leadership rest upon it.

That is precisely why so many of Clinton's adversaries chipped away at his personal character so relentlessly. If their actions were flawed, their reasoning was not: Find a crack in the foundation of leadership, and the entire structure could come crashing down.

If Bill Clinton could run again for President of the United States, would a majority of the American people vote for him? There's good reason to indicate they would.

Despite the vicious and relentless attacks over the course of his tenure as president, and despite his one big mistake, when Bill Clinton's words, actions, and general behavior are closely examined, the picture of a real leader emerges, one who exhibited extraordinary fortitude and character. Most Americans recognize that he attempted to do the right thing in his public life, if not always in his personal life.

⁓

One spring day, President Clinton left the White House and drove a few miles north to visit the Martin Luther King, Jr. Middle School in Beltsville, Maryland. To the 500 or so students gathered in the school's gymnasium, Clinton asked: "Is there still racism in America today?"

"Yes," they yelled back.

"Of course there is," he said. "Is there too much violence?"

"Yes," they responded.

"Are there still too many people who don't think they're going to get a fair shake in life?" asked Clinton. "Of course," he answered rhetorically.

"So what are you going to do about it? What am I going to do about it? What we should say is we're going to build on the things that have gone before that are good," advocated the President of the United States.

When he spoke to young people in instances such as these, Bill Clinton was using his position as president, not for self-aggrandizement, nor to increase his personal wealth, but to encourage others to act responsibly, to do the right thing, and to help make the world a better place in which to live.

"Do not let us pull another Washington, D.C. game here and let this crime bill go down on some procedural hide-and-seek. If we're going to have a shoot-out, let's do it [at] high noon, [in] broad daylight, where everybody knows what the deal is."

—Clinton, one week before a procedural maneuver
prevented his crime bill from coming
to a vote in the House
August 5, 1994

"The central tenet of every democracy in the end is trust. It's trust."

—Clinton, to employees of the federal government in
Franconia, Virginia
September 8, 1993

*On **November 3, 1998**, American voters expressed their unhappiness in the mid-term elections by voting five Republicans out of their House seats, which cut the majority to eleven. House Speaker Newt Gingrich subsequently announced his plans to resign from Congress. Ten days later, on **November 13, 1998**, a settlement was announced in the Paula Jones case. Many analysts expressed surprise at this development, because Bill Clinton had apparently won the case when Judge Susan Webber Wright issued a summary judgment in April dismissing the charges as being without merit. The independent counsel's office, of course, appealed the decision. And when it was made public that the three-judge panel was headed by the same conservative judge who had overturned Judge Henry Woods on Whitewater, the President and his lawyers opted to pursue a settlement. As Clinton later wrote in his memoirs, "I hated to do it because I had won a clear victory on the law and the facts in a politically motivated case . . . But I had promised the American people I would spend the next two years working for them; I had no business spending five more minutes on the Jones case." Settlement terms included a payment of $850,000, most of which went to the Jones lawyers, and no apology or admission of wrongdoing on Clinton's part. Jones v. Clinton had lasted for nearly four full years.*

✦

*Over the span of two days, **December 11 and 12, 1998**, the House Judiciary Committee voted to approve and present to the full House four articles of impeachment against President Clinton. House Republican leaders immediately appeared on national television and urged the president to resign before he was thrown out of office. Meanwhile, on **December 16, 1998**, a large room in the Gerald Ford House Office Building was loaded with boxes of grand jury testimony, FBI reports, and interview transcripts with hundreds of witnesses. It was later reported that much of the material consisted of uncertified and uncorroborated material that were unrelated to the articles of impeachment. House Republican leaders insisted that every Republican member of Congress visit this "Evidence Room," and organized trips there for private presentations.*

*One week before Christmas, on **December 19, 1998**, the full House of Representatives impeached President Clinton by approving two of the four articles presented by the Judiciary Committee. Articles II and IV (perjury in the Jones deposition and abuse of power) failed by votes of 229–205 and 285–148, respectively. Article I (perjury in the grand jury) passed by a vote of 228–206, and Article III (obstruction of justice) was approved 229–205. The case was then remanded to the United States Senate for trial.*

❧

In the week before the impeachment trial began in the Senate, the Drudge Report regurgitated an old story with a new twist, entitled: "World Exclusive: White House Hit With New DNA Terror; Teen Tested for Clinton Paternity." Matt Drudge reported that the son of a black Arkansas prostitute who "looks just like" Bill Clinton, was going to have his DNA tested to see if it matched that of the president. On the successive days of **January 3, 4, 5, and 6, 1999**, *this story was mentioned in or by the* New York Post, Fox News, the Tonight Show, and The Washington Times, *respectively. At approximately the same time, NBC correspondent Lisa Myers interviewed Juanita Broaddrick (the woman who had formerly accused Bill Clinton of rape) for the prime time television news program* Dateline. *Network executives, however, refused to air the interview until after the impeachment trial had concluded. As Republicans railed against the decision, conservative members of the press, and at least one senator, started wearing protest buttons that read, "Free Lisa Myers."*

The impeachment trial of President Bill Clinton, presided over by Supreme Court Chief Justice William H. Rehnquist, began in the Senate on **January 7, 1999**, *and lasted five weeks. House Republicans presented their case, and lawyers for the president refuted it. Monica Lewinsky testified by videotape, and basically denied both of the charges against Clinton. With only fifty-five Republicans in the Senate, there was little doubt they would not be able to garner the sixty-seven votes (two-thirds majority) necessary to remove the president from office. And on* **February 12, 1999**, *the 190th anniversary of Abraham Lincoln's birth, the U. S. Senate acquitted President Clinton by votes of 55–45 on Article I (perjury), and 50–50 on Article II (obstruction of justice).*

"You know, I'm doing things that are hard, that are controversial. And anybody who doesn't want to assume responsibility can stand on the sidelines and criticize. I never expected that I could take on some of these interests without being attacked."

—Clinton, when asked at a news conference
why his approval ratings were so low
May 14, 1993

"These people say, 'What did you know and when did you know it?' I say, 'Who are these people and what planet am I on.'"

—Clinton, expressing frustration about
constant attacks involving Whitewater
March 1994

CHAPTER SIXTEEN

COURAGE

When President Clinton held his first prime time news conference in mid-June 1993, both CBS and ABC refused to broadcast it, while NBC carried only the first half hour and then cut to other programming. All three commercial networks opted to carry summer reruns instead. This was the first time that an American president had been denied network air time. The networks' reasoning, however, was obvious for anyone who was plugged in to the national media: The reruns were getting higher ratings than the President.

Just the week before, several major magazines had run cover stories that reflected the nation's growing sense that there was a problem in the White House. Under the headline, "A Question of Competence," *U.S. News & World Report* described the president as "preoccupied with an astonishing series of mistakes and bungles." *Newsweek's* cover featured a picture of a contemplative Bill Clinton with the large headline: "What's

Wrong?" And *Time's* cover was even more condemning, with a two-inch-high Bill Clinton looking up at the large headline: "The Incredible Shrinking President." The accompanying article noted that Clinton's time in office had been "beset since its inception by miscalculations and self-inflicted wounds."

The *Time* cover story also pointed out the findings of a recent TIME/CNN poll that revealed Clinton's meager 36 percent approval rating as the lowest ever for a "postwar President four months into his term." Here is how Clinton fared against previous presidents at the same time in their first terms:

Truman	92 percent
Johnson	78 percent
Eisenhower	74 percent
Kennedy	74 percent
Carter	64 percent
Nixon	62 percent
Bush	62 percent
Reagan	59 percent
Ford	42 percent
Clinton	36 percent

ENDLESS CRITICISM

One year after *Time* ran its "Incredible Shrinking President" issue, the magazine published a list (compiled by *Talkers* magazine) of the "ten most vilified personalities on talk radio since June 1990." Bill and Hillary Clinton were rated one and two, respectively, followed by Saddam Hussein, Iraq's murderous dictator. "There is no question Bill Clinton is the most criticized individual in the history of the medium," stated Michael Harrison, editor of *Talkers*.

Of interest was the fact that the survey included persons only since 1990, right about the time that the national media began speculating that the governor of Arkansas might run for president. Clinton officially declared his candidacy in October 1991, and by early 1992, Clinton critics were in a frenzy that he might actually be elected president. Religious fundamentalist groups, for example, brandished signs that read: "To Vote for Bill Clinton is to Sin Against God."

After the election, vilification and name-calling intensified. He was accused of arranging murders and of being hooked on cocaine. He was labeled a man without a core, a draft-dodger, an underachiever, an over-achiever, Bumblin' Bill, the Libido-in-Chief, a Richard Nixon without perspiration, inappropriate for the office, undependable, a flop, an abject failure, one who desires to be loved by all sides. An entertainer mocked him by singing "Pander Bear" to the tune of Elvis Presley's "Teddy Bear," and a cartoonist caricatured him as a waffle. And early in his first term nearly every element of the mass media speculated as to who would be the Republican Party's nominee in 1996, since that person was sure to become the next president.

Two notable charges that dogged Bill Clinton during nearly his entire two terms in office were the issues surrounding his investment in an Arkansas land deal called Whitewater Development Company, and a sexual harassment suit filed by former Arkansas state employee Paula Jones. Both of these pseudo-scandals were purported to have happened while Clinton was governor of Arkansas, and were only brought to the forefront of national media exposure after he was elected president. In the Whitewater case, Clinton finally bowed to increasing political pressure from Congress and asked Attorney General Janet Reno to appoint a special counsel to investigate the matter. But that did not satisfy Senate Republican Leader Bob Dole, who immediately began demanding congressional hearings as well. Representative Jim Leach (Rep. Iowa) echoed Dole's demand in the House: "The reason that [such] hearings may well be appropriate," said Leach, "is that what we're dealing with here are issues, really, of public trust more than criminality, and public trust is more the realm of Congress."

Republicans also utilized terminology that created subtle allusions to Richard Nixon and the Watergate scandal. Dole suggested that a "cover up" was under way. Senator Alfonse D'Amato was more blatant when he claimed that Democrats were "stonewalling and creating their own Whitewatergate." There were insinuations of tax fraud and graft associated with Whitewater, which prompted Republicans to mockingly ask: "Can a President credibly advance an ethic of national service if his own model is one of self-service?"

In addition to politically motivated attacks on his character and personal behavior, Bill Clinton had to endure the same policy-related attacks to which all presidents are subjected. Regardless of which position he took on any issue, he was sure to be criticized, sometimes by both sides. Such disparagement began right after he took the oath of office and never really let up. After Clinton froze Haitian assets in 1993 and instituted a trade embargo against the Caribbean nation in an effort to return ousted president Jean-Bertrand Aristide to power, both foreign and U.S. leaders criticized the president for not acting in a more authoritative manner. A few months later, when Clinton warned Haiti that force might be used to return Aristide to power, he received immediate protests from Canada, Mexico, Cuba, and members of the Organization of American States, including Brazil, Ecuador, Peru, and Uruguay.

In September 1994, after he decided to invade Haiti, Republicans and conservative radio talk show hosts blasted him for placing American soldiers at risk. A majority of Congress would not support his actions. And opinion polls reported that more than 70 percent of the public disapproved of invading the tiny Caribbean island. That criticism, however, was mild compared to what he heard form Americans on other issues. In October 1993, Republican senator Alfonse M. D'Amato referred to Clinton's policy in Somalia as "sick," "namby-pamby," and "claptrap." The president's tough stance on Japanese trade policy was criticized as "gratuitous brinkmanship" by a member of his own party, Senator Bill Bradley. The day after lifting the U.S. trade embargo against Vietnam, Clinton was verbally assaulted by two men as he jogged past the Vietnam Veterans War Memorial. One man carried a sign that read: "Clinton betrays POWs" while the other yelled that he was a "back-stabber."

In addition to foreign policy, criticism for Clinton's domestic agenda ran long and harsh. The issue of health care reform is a good example of resistance experienced by the new president. Many business leaders argued that Clinton's plan provided too much care and was too costly. At the same time, women's groups and retired person's groups refused to endorse it, because they said it fell short on care for women and the elderly. On one hand, the National Association of Manufacturers, the Business Roundtable, the United States Chamber of Commerce, the American Medical Association, drug companies, and insurance companies voted resoundingly to oppose all of Clinton's health care proposals. However, when he tried to compromise on key elements of the plan, members of organized labor and liberal Democrats blasted him for making too many concessions.

Early heavy criticism of Bill Clinton was due, in part, to the fact that the Republican Party, for the first time in a dozen years, was both out of the White House *and* in a minority in both houses of Congress. In the April 11, 1994, issue of *Time*, historian Alan Brinkley noted that Bill Clinton "is the first President who has generated this kind of right wing hatred." In part, such extreme loathing was a result of the fact that Clinton was very young. But Clinton's being a Democrat made things even worse for him. "Liberals tend to value tolerance highly, so there's a greater reluctance to destroy enemies than among the right," said Brinkley. "Democrats are historically more likely to cooperate with Republican administrations than Republicans with Democratic administrations."

The media onslaught was especially difficult in Clinton's first half year in office. Because Clinton was so different from former Presidents Reagan and Bush, the media continually picked apart his leadership style. It was unconventional. It was news. Added to this unique situation was the expansion of TV talk shows, so-called journalistic "tabloid television," elimination of the fairness doctrine, and the increased audience for hundreds of talk radio programs, all of which created extraordinarily fierce competition for news stories. And at that time, the most controversial newsmaker of all was Bill Clinton. In June 1993, the Center for Media and Public Affairs released statistics showing that, during the first four months in office, 64 percent of all references to President Clinton were negative. That compared to a similar study in 1989 that garnered George H. W. Bush only forty-one percent negative comments.

THE ROLLER COASTER OF PUBLIC OPINION

During Bill Clinton's tenure in office, the ups and downs of his presidential approval ratings (with both extreme peaks and valleys) were unprecedented in American poll-taking history. Driving his approval ratings down, in part, was the Republican Party strategy to criticize the new president at every turn in hopes that the mounting onslaught would drop his popularity so low that he would, in effect, be unable to govern. They were also hoping to sway public opinion to the point of taking back control of Congress in the 1994 midterm election. If that wasn't a tough enough thing to deal with, matters were made worse when President Clinton, himself, gave the wolves plenty to gnaw on. As a matter of fact, during his first year in office, he almost self-destructed.

Clinton's initial nominee for attorney general, Zoe Baird, was forced to withdraw because she admitted during Senate confirmation hearings that she had knowingly failed to pay taxes for people employed to care for her children. When New York Judge Kimba Wood was subsequently dropped from consideration for the same reason, the press labeled the entire series of events "NannyGate." Later, the dismissals and subsequent reinstatement of seven members of the White House travel staff garnered the nickname, "TravelGate." When Clinton was accused of holding up flights at L.A. International Airport by taking time to get a haircut from Beverly Hills hairdresser Christophe, the press labeled the incident Hair Force One.

At virtually the same time, Clinton had allowed the issue of gays serving in the armed forces to dominate national headlines for months. Unrelenting criticism from the military reached a crescendo in June 1993 when Air Force Major General Harold N. Campbell publicly called President

Clinton a "pot-smoking," "womanizing," "draft-dodging," commander in chief. Moreover, Clinton had suffered the defeat of a Jobs Stimulus Bill, his first major legislative proposal, at the hands of a Senate filibuster by Republicans. He also abruptly withdrew the nomination of his choice to head the Justice Department's Civil Rights Division, Lani Guinier, after conservatives criticized him for nominating a "Quota Queen." When he dropped Guinier in June 1993, Clinton was at rock bottom in the polls with only a 36 percent approval rating, a point at which, according to experts, he could statistically sink no lower.

Gradually, Clinton clawed out of the deep hole he had dug for himself. He traveled to Japan for the G–7 Summit, where he received kudos from the press for his interaction with foreign leaders. He bombed Baghdad for Iraq's complicity in a thwarted attempt on the life of former president George H. W. Bush. He appointed Ruth Bader Ginsburg to the Supreme Court and began to mend his strained relationship with the American military by endorsing a "Don't Ask, Don't Tell, Don't Pursue" policy toward gays in the military. And he worked to secure passage of a deficit-reduction bill in Congress.

By September, when he shepherded Yitzhak Rabin and Yassir Arafat together for the signing of the Israel-PLO peace accord on the White House lawn, Clinton's poll ratings had climbed dramatically. And when his health care address to a joint session of Congress came on the heels of the administration's Reinventing Government initiative, he had pulled himself out of the hole altogether. Immediately after the health care speech, some polls showed his approval ratings at 60 percent, right where they had been when he took office.

A major crisis in the United States involvement in Somalia caused a brief dip in the polls, but Clinton again pulled himself back up by securing passage of NAFTA and the Brady Bill. By late December 1993, he was hovering around 60 percent in approval ratings, and government numbers proved that the economy was on the rebound. "Look at the direction we're going in," reported the president. "We have unemployment down, investment up, no inflation, and low interest rates. We are moving in the right direction." Clinton was immediately rebutted, however, by more conservative economists who claimed that the president should get no credit for the recovery and that it was part of a "natural corrective process." *The New York Times* quoted Republican leader Jack Kemp as saying that "the strong economy now resulted almost entirely from years of inflation-fighting by the Federal Reserve Board."

The polls during Bill Clinton's second year in office were eerily similar to those of his first year. As a matter of fact, his approval ratings had experienced such an uninterrupted downslide that, by the first week of

June 1994, they were again hovering in the low-40s. In 1993, Clinton's decline was due largely to his own mistakes and miscues, but this time the slide was engineered mostly by conservative Republicans.

Appointment of a special prosecutor to investigate Whitewater was announced on January 20, one year to the day of Clinton taking the presidential oath of office. In February, conservative activists organized a press conference in Washington where Paula Jones and former Arkansas state troopers levied fresh charges of sexual harassment against the president. In March, Hillary Clinton was accused of illegal commodities trading in the 1980s (called "bribery" by one columnist). By the time summer rolled around, not only had religious organizations released a damaging series of anti-Clinton videos, but formal Whitewater hearings were being held by both the House and Senate Banking Committees.

Reacting to the sensationalism of such a high-profile scandal, the media joined the fray. For example, when Clinton held a joint press conference with Eduard A. Shevardnadze, president of Georgia, the two men fielded questions alternately from members of the Georgian press and members of the American press. The Georgian journalists posed a variety of questions on foreign affairs; the Americans asked only about Whitewater. And so it went, back and forth, for the entire news conference.

In addition to members of the media, it seemed as though every conservative or Republican jumped on the anti-Clinton bandwagon. Columnist James J. Kilpatrick denounced Clinton's choice of Ruth Bader Ginsburg for the Supreme Court as part of his "vows before the Gods of diversity." Peggy Noonan, former Reagan and Bush speechwriter, asserted that "four years from now Clinton will have done no good, and he'll be carted out on a gurney." Kentucky Republican congressman Jim Bunning labeled Bill Clinton "the most corrupt, the most amoral, the most despicable person I've ever seen in the presidency."

Several polls conducted in 1994 indicated that a majority of Americans saw the Republican assertions as nothing more than political character assassination. But Clinton still suffered considerably in the polls. "When I read someplace that there have been three times as much coverage of Whitewater as there had been of health care," said Clinton of his downslide, "I'm amazed that there hasn't been more change in the polls."

The ongoing negative criticism had such a detrimental effect that, by the time mid-term election campaigns began in the fall of 1994, congressional and gubernatorial candidates from the Democratic Party were being advised to keep an arm's length from the president. And after

Oklahoma Congressman Mike Synar, a twelve-year incumbent and unabashed Clinton supporter, was defeated in a primary runoff, many other candidates pointedly asked the president to stay out of their districts.

Paradoxically, though, from the time Congress adjourned in September until the November elections, Clinton's overall approval ratings improved considerably. In part, the increase was buoyed by accomplishments in foreign affairs, such as the U.S. occupation of Haiti, a forceful response to Iraqi troop buildups, a nuclear arms agreement with North Korea, and a peace accord between Israel and Jordan.

During Clinton's first two years in office, there was a clear correspondence between in his approval ratings and whether or not Congress was meeting. When Congress was *in* session, Clinton's favorable ratings went down. When Congress was *out* of session, they went up. This may have been due, in part, to the fact that when members of Congress were in town, Republicans continually hammered at him, and the press tended to focus on that negative criticism as news. However, when senators and congressmen were out of town, press coverage of the president was reduced to a trickle.

By the 1994 midterm elections, the cumulative impact of all the negative criticism against Clinton and the Democrats had taken its toll. And when combined with Newt Gingrich's catchy "Contract With America" and a well-organized political machine, the Republican Party dramatically captured both houses of Congress. With Republicans then in control of congressional committees, Whitewater hearings in the House and Senate were intensified. Independent Counsel Kenneth Starr also increased the pressure by indicting a number of Clinton associates in the scandal. The national media continued with its sustained coverage of every damaging accusation. And a plethora of anti-Clinton books were published over the next two years. Negative criticism against Clinton rose to a fever pitch just before the 1996 presidential election with charges of Democratic campaign finance abuses and White House "auctioning" sleepovers in the Lincoln Bedroom to the highest bidder.

When the Republicans took over Congress, it appeared that Bill Clinton's influence was going to be neutralized, and that he had little chance of gaining a second term as president. But over the two intervening years, a resilient Bill Clinton again managed to claw his way out of the hole of negative public opinion. He revised his strategy in working with Congress, learned from past mistakes, and fought back against unfounded accusations. And much to the Republican Party's chagrin, from November 1994 to November 1996, the president's approval ratings rose steadily from the low 40s to the upper 50s and low 60s. That rise in popularity resulted in Clinton's easy reelection over Republican candidate Bob Dole.

During the entire four years of President Clinton's second term, his approval ratings stayed high and fluctuated between the upper 50s and lower 60s. Never again did he get anywhere near his lowest recorded poll number of 36 in June 1993. Rather, on five different occasions, Clinton's approval rating reached a personal high of 73 percent. Two of those instances occurred on the day he was impeached in the House of Representatives (December 19, 1998) and the day he was acquitted in the Senate (February 12, 1999).

The American people knew the score. And on January 20, 2001, when Bill Clinton left office, they rewarded him with a 67 percent approval rating—the highest ever recorded for an outgoing President of the United States.

Job Performance Approval Ratings for President Bill Clinton, 1993–2001

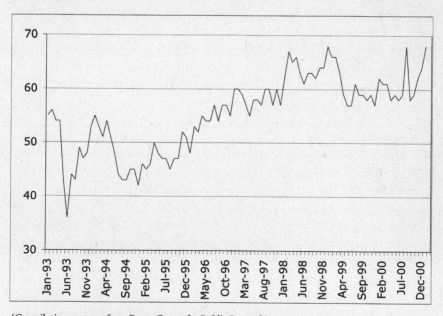

(Compilation averages from Roper Center for Public Research)

STRATEGIES FOR DEALING WITH CRITICISM

On June 14, 1993, at a news conference announcing Ruth Bader Ginsburg's nomination to the Supreme Court, Brit Hume of ABC News posed a question to President Clinton, and received a response for which no one was prepared. "The withdrawal of the Guinier nomination, sir," said Hume, "and your apparent focus on Judge [Stephen] Breyer and your turn, late, it seems, to Judge Ginsburg may have created an impression, perhaps unfair, of a certain zigzag quality in the decision-making process here. I wonder, sir, if you could kind of walk us through it and perhaps disabuse us of any notion we might have along those lines. Thank you."

Because the question came immediately after Judge Ginsburg's passionate remarks had moved him to tears, Clinton reacted emotionally and shot back a scolding reply to Hume: "I have long since given up the thought that I could disabuse some of you turning any substantive decision into anything but political process," he responded. "How you could ask a question like that after the statement she just made is beyond me. Goodbye!" With that, the president abruptly cut off questions and ended the news conference.

It's interesting to note that Brit Hume's question came at the very moment President Clinton's approval ratings were at rock bottom in the polls, and shortly after *Time* magazine's "Incredible Shrinking President" issue hit newsstands. Clearly, his frustration and emotion had been building up like a volcano waiting to erupt.

Despite a few similar displays of temper, Bill Clinton's public responses to the criticism hurled his way were, by and large, professional, courteous, and most often, free of ill will and bitterness. Because he was always in the spotlight, Clinton had to control the damage with one hand while managing the nation with the other. And he was pretty effective at doing so—tending to handle each situation differently depending on the nature of the attack. The following seven strategies were clearly discernable in Bill Clinton's leadership style over an extended period of time:

1. Ignore the insignificant. Counter the consequential.

As a rule, President Clinton largely ignored the daily drumbeat of negative news, preferring, rather, to focus on his long-term goals and strategies. "If I worried about every poll," he said in May 1993, "I'd never get any work done." There was so much criticism that Clinton realistically did not have time to answer every single charge. Some allegations he felt were so insignificant that he did whatever he could to get them off the front pages even if it meant that he would somehow have to swallow his pride.

For instance, Clinton apologized for the "Hair Force One" fiasco at the Los Angeles airport, which was remarkable when you consider that *Newsday* later gathered FAA records and found that there had been "no circling planes, no backed up runways, and only one two-minute delay." This was quite a contrast to original news reports that mentioned several ten-minute delays, and two twenty-minute delays. Even though the incident had been blown out of proportion by the press, Clinton had no qualms about apologizing and getting on with "the business of running the country."

On the other hand, Clinton would fight back against harsh criticism, especially if he deemed it consequential to his long-term goals. During the first week in January 1994, he called his top aides into the Oval Office, pushed a newspaper across his desk, and demanded to know why nobody is defending him on the Whitewater story? He slammed his fist on the desk and vowed that he would not be a punching bag for the news media. Immediately afterward, members of the administration hit the road in defense of the president. George Stephanopoulos appeared on ABC's *This Week*, David Gergen was on ABC's *Nightline*, and Mack McLarty was on CNN. Vice President Al Gore also jumped in to help Clinton by appearing on CBS's *Face The Nation* and NBC's *Meet The Press*. And Clinton, himself, held a prime time news conference to answer reporters' questions on Whitewater.

Later in 1994, the president fought back against criticism from conservatives by calling a live radio talk show from Air Force One while flying into St. Louis. He charged that members of the religious right were cynical and intolerant. "They say that anybody that doesn't agree with them is Godless," railed Clinton. "Anyone who doesn't agree with them is fair game for any wild charge. I don't suppose that there's any public figure that's been subject to more violent personal attacks [in modern times] than I have. That's fine. I deal with them. But I don't believe it's the work of God!"

2. Take your story directly to the people.

In mid-May 1993, after all the negative focus on his first 100 days in office, Clinton hit the road, venturing to Cleveland, Chicago, and New York. He did the same thing in March 1994, when the Whitewater heat was hottest—traveling to Michigan, Massachusetts, and Florida—and also making a special appearance in New Hampshire, where he had made a major comeback in the primary of 1992.

At each stop, Clinton held the equivalent of a town meeting, answering any and all questions openly and directly. In what might have been Clinton's most effective strategy in handling criticism, he went directly to the people with his story, just as he had done during the presidential campaign when he was accused of infidelity and draft-dodging.

Clinton garnered hundreds of hours of personal exposure with private citizens, and each event was televised, either locally or nationally. In essence, the president fought back with the single best weapon in his arsenal—himself.

He took criticism from the military head-on by going directly to servicemen. In the summer of 1993, Clinton journeyed to South Korea to visit the troops at Camp Casey serving on the border with communist North Korea. While there, he spent time mingling with the soldiers, shaking hands, telling stories, and chatting.

Clinton seemed to enjoy all the trips he took, whether foreign or domestic. They breathed new life into him. "I'm doing the best I can, believe me," Clinton told people. "You may think I'm wrong, and maybe time will prove me wrong, but I'm trying to make the best decision I can to create jobs and incomes for the American people so that we come out ahead on this deal, not behind."

Usually the people with whom he met had a positive reaction. They appreciated his openness and courage. They enjoyed the opportunity to see a different side of the President of the United States, the human side. This, of course, was part of Clinton's overall strategy: to let people get to know him personally, and to see that he was not what his detractors were making him out to be.

3. Keep on working. Propose new initiatives.

When faced with mounting criticism and unfounded accusations, many leaders choose to immerse themselves in their work. In part, that's exactly what Clinton did. In mid-December 1998, one day before the House of Representatives was to consider four articles of impeachment against him, the president ordered a four-day bomb attack on Iraq. It was, said the president, in retaliation for continued failure to cooperate with U.N. weapons inspectors. House Republicans carped about the timing and renewed calls for Clinton to resign from office. But the president had planned to make the strike as soon as weapons inspectors issued their findings, and he had already secured the agreement of British prime minister Tony Blair. While Clinton made a good case in explaining the timing of the attack, it also had the effect of refocusing the nation's attention and delaying impeachment hearings.

Years earlier, in 1993 and 1994, when his approval ratings were in downward slides, Clinton introduced new initiative after new initiative in order to grab the headlines back and create fresh exposure on national television. The proposals of a national service plan and campaign finance reform served to create an image reminiscent of John F.

Kennedy's youthful idealism and vigor. Campaign finance reform reminded Americans of the excesses of the Congress during the Reagan-Bush years, and also brought back the sentiment that Clinton was trying to make things right again. Clinton also pressed the United Nations to impose sanctions against North Korea. He conferred with Yitzhak Rabin at the White House to determine new ways that Syria could be brought into the Mideast peace process.

Clinton also proposed welfare reform, a national apprenticeship program for young people not going to college, and a crime-fighting program that would place more than 100,000 additional police officers on the streets. All these new initiatives changed the focus of negative criticism away from him and toward discussion of the issues. More important, however, the people observed their president trying to solve the problems of the nation. And that's what Clinton wanted them to believe. "I just get up in the morning and go to work," he would say. "That's what I got hired to do."

4. Keep your sense of humor.

Clinton frequently turned to humor to help relieve the strain of his office, to give him a momentary respite, and to ease tension during a difficult situation. After exploding at Brit Hume and calling off questions at Ruth Bader Ginsburg's introduction ceremony, for instance, Clinton sought to make amends and diffuse the situation. At a news conference the very next day, he made a brief opening statement, then turned to Brit Hume and suggested that he should get a follow-up to his earlier question. While that comment stirred laughter from the news people, tensions were totally alleviated when the president further quipped: "You know what I'm really upset about?" he asked Hume, who had recently been married. "You got a honeymoon and I didn't."

During the opening remarks of his commencement address to 1993's graduating class at West Point, Clinton joked about the "Hair Force One" incident. "You have met high standards for discipline, for physical fitness, for academics," he told the cadets. "And I must say, I am impressed by your haircuts." That remark had its desired effect on the audience. One cadet, who was interviewed by a reporter from *The New York Times*, agreed: "It's kind of neat for him to make a joke about the haircut thing," said the cadet. "He said, 'Hey, I make mistakes.' For me to see him do that makes him likable to me over all. It was kind of tense before he came, people were really wondering about him."

And in January 1995, Clinton employed humor to diffuse a tense situation after CBS television reporter Connie Chung aired an interview with House Speaker Newt Gingrich's mother "whispering in her ear" that her son thought Hillary Clinton was "a bitch." In his next meeting with Gingrich, Clinton responded to a reporter's question with, "Mr. Gingrich will whisper in your right ear and I will whisper into your left." In private, the president reassured the Speaker: "God knows what she [Chung] could've gotten my mother to say."

5. Turn a Negative into a Positive

As a politician, Bill Clinton repeatedly turned negatives into positives. This was a refined skill firmly grounded in reality, one developed largely from political necessity to ensure survival. It was as if, with each negative situation, Clinton asked himself the question, "All right, this issue is not going away. How can we turn it around and make it work for us?"

Perhaps the most striking example of this talent was Clinton's relationship with the American armed forces. He took office on very shaky footing by being the first President of the United States since World War II not to have served in the military. And he immediately made the situation worse by proposing to allow gays to serve in the armed forces. Clinton never did completely turn around all the hostility that some service people felt toward him. However, he managed to win over many officers and enlisted men by showing respect for them, by honoring them, and by simply mingling with them. Clinton displayed great courage by speaking at the Vietnam Veterans War Memorial on Memorial Day in 1993, even though some veterans in the crowd booed him. The very next Memorial Day, in 1994, he was present for ceremonies at Arlington National Cemetery and spoke eloquently of remembrance and sacrifice, even though he was again momentarily interrupted by a heckler who called him a "traitor" and a "draft-dodger."

However, it was at the fiftieth anniversary of the D-Day invasion of Europe, on June 6, 1994, that Clinton seemed best to have turned the situation around. In both public speeches and private conversations, he praised veterans who had fought in World War II. He listened to their stories, wiped away genuine tears at their heroism and sacrifice, and told each of them that it was an honor for him to meet them. But most importantly, Clinton managed to keep all the attention centered around the veterans of D-Day. He did not try to take credit for the ceremonies and he kept refocusing concentration on the people who had fought on the coast of Normandy on June 6, 1944.

"When they were young, these men saved the world," said Clinton. "We're the children of your sacrifice," he told the veterans. The president's message was clear: His generation owed their generation a great deal, and it was his personal mission to convince people his age and those even younger of that fact.

As a result, many military personnel gradually began to perceive Bill Clinton as a man who had matured, and who clearly understood and appreciated the sacrifice that all veterans had made for their country. At the very least all veterans could see him as sincere in his tribute to them. And perhaps, that's the best that Clinton could have done given the situation with which he started. "The darkness of every storm provides a new chance for renewal," said Clinton in September 1994.

6. Find ways to unwind. Avoid tension and bitterness.

In addition to humor, Clinton found many ways to unwind and escape the stress of the presidency. He watched movies, took guests on tours of the Oval Office, and read several books a week. In October 1994, he commented to a group of Baptist publishers and editors that he often read the Bible and other religious books. "It's made a huge difference in enduring [the] isolation of this job," he said.

In addition, Clinton played cards, whether a game of hearts with his aides or Hungarian rummy with his daughter, Chelsea. And he'd relieve stress physically by jogging or taking in a quick round of golf. Clinton also made frequent excursions out of town that were designed to get away from it all. During a brief vacation back to Arkansas in January 1995 (which included duck hunting and visiting old friends), he casually mentioned to reporters that he'd "worked like a dog" during his first two years as president. "I worked every weekend; I worked at night," he said. "I'm glad we got done what we did, but I also think it's important to keep your batteries charged, your roots watered."

Bill Clinton combined many methods of relieving stress to remain relatively free of bitterness and ill will toward those who leveled criticism at him. Remarkably, he did not seem to let it affect his overall mission as president. In March 1994, when announcing the appointment of Lloyd Cutler as Special Counsel to the President in the wake of Bernard Nusssbaum's forced resignation, Clinton was asked by a reporter if he was bitter about the entire episode.

"No," he responded. "Because I think as you grow older, bitterness is something you have to learn to put aside. As you strive to be more mature, one of the things you have to give up in life is your bitterness about everything. You have to work through that. That's part of my personal mission in life. I think you can't be a very good President if you're consumed with bitterness. If I wake up every day all agitated about this, then I can't deal with the problems of the people. If I'm thinking about me, I can't be thinking about them. The American people hired me."

On February 12, 1999, after votes in the United States Senate impeachment trial failed by wide margins to remove him from office, President Clinton made a brief statement and took one question from a reporter.

"In your heart, sir, can you forgive and forget?" he was asked.

Clinton paused a moment, looked the reporter straight in the eye, and replied, "I believe any person who asks for forgiveness has to be prepared to give it."

7. Accept criticism as a fact of life and keep faith in the people.

As head of state, Bill Clinton understood the nature of the job. At a news conference held near the 100 day mark of his presidency, he remarked: "On one day people say he's trying to do too much, he's pushing too hard, he wants too much change; and then, on the other day, [they say] well, he's really not pushing very hard."

On the first anniversary of his inauguration, the president fielded a question from Larry King about why the criticism had been so harsh against him: "Look around the Western world and at the recent history of the United States," answered Clinton. "If you sign on for a political career in the latter half of the 20th century, you just have to expect a level of [criticism] that didn't exist before."

To a large extent, all leaders must trust the people to ferret out the truth surrounding unfounded accusations and slander. There is simply not enough time to address everything that is charged. Establishing relationships with people, and having faith in their common decency, play a strong part both in a leader's eventual repudiation and in the vindication of false charges. "The American people [will] be able to see through it," Clinton once told Larry King. "When they see the politics of personal destruction, they will see it for what it is."

PERSEVERANCE, OPTIMISM, AND A LEADER'S COURAGE

Just prior to the 1992 New Hampshire primary, national allegations of draft-dodging and extramarital affairs dropped Bill Clinton from the favorite to win the primary, to a seemingly hopeless also-ran. But Clinton immediately responded by appearing on CBS's *60 Minutes* and ABC's *Nightline*—and then he barnstormed the state to speak personally with voters. In the end, Clinton finished a strong second to New England-born Paul Tsongas. After that, he was tagged with a new nickname: "The Comeback Kid."

"He didn't respond like most candidates do when the campaign hits the ropes," noted *Time* magazine. "If Gary Hart was a sulker, Paul Tsongas a whiner, and Jerry Brown an out-of-body existentialist, Clinton was the sunny optimist, emerging on the coldest, darkest days of New Hampshire to pump hands at a VFW hall as if he were twenty points ahead in the polls."

In addition to a "sunny optimism," Bill Clinton possessed an unusual self-confidence when faced with political adversity that helped him persevere through virtually any storm. "It's a legacy my grandparents left to me," Clinton explained. "If you get beat down, just get up again. Find something to be grateful for every day."

Because leaders are agents of change, they always encounter resistance. They get knocked down, knocked back, and often experience abject failure. Bill Clinton understood this basic leadership fact of life, and was philosophical about it. "I'm grateful for the opportunity to serve," he said. "The bad days are part of it. I didn't run to have a pleasant time. I ran to have a chance to change the country. And if the bad days come with it, that's part of life. It's humbling and educational. It keeps you in your place."

The truth is that the only leaders people remember are those who keep going, who remain steadfast despite difficulty or delay, who never give up, who persevere. The others are forgotten because they fail in the long run.

In a leader's struggle to persevere, there is no more important weapon than personal courage, which can be defined simply as strength in the face of adversity. All good leaders eventually come to points in their careers where they have to stand up to threats, where they have to say no, where they have to face down the bully. And as anybody who has ever held an executive leadership position knows, *that* is not an easy thing to do.

Ernest Hemingway once defined courage as "grace under pressure." As President of the United States, Bill Clinton was under tremendous pressure *all the time.* In fact, he experienced as much, if not more, pressure than any person who has ever occupied the office. He not only had to deal with the inherent stress brought by the job, but he also had to contend with eight years of unyielding political attacks on his personal character.

During his two terms as president, Bill Clinton stood up to his detractors with a certain grace and style. He stood tall when members of his own party blamed him for the Democratic defeat in the 1994 midterm elections. Responding respectfully, Clinton reminded them that their responsibility as leaders was not to lay blame, but to "join me in the arena and fight, and roll up your sleeves, and be willing to make a mistake now and then, be willing to put your shoulder to the wheel, be willing to engage, be willing to struggle, and be willing to debate."

And President Clinton certainly stood tall against the Republicans once they took control of Congress. A great example of Clinton's political courage occurred in late 1995 and early 1996 during a showdown over the budget. In November, the federal government was being funded by a continuing resolution (CR) and a bill that extended the debt ceiling. But the new Republican-controlled Congress sent President Clinton an ultimatum. If he wanted to keep the government running, he would have to sign their revised versions of the CR and the debt limit extension, which included provisions to increase Medicare premiums by 25 percent, weaken environmental laws, and cut federal funding for public education. The overall Republican plan was to make large tax cuts and increase the federal deficit. But President Clinton not only wanted to prevent the proposed cuts, he wanted to work toward balancing the budget.

During a tense meeting, one of the Republican leaders stated that if the president didn't give in to their demands, they would shut down the government and his presidency would be over. "Never!" Clinton shot back. "Not even if I drop to five percent in the polls!"

After the president vetoed both the continuing resolution and the debt ceiling bill, large portions of the government were, indeed, shut down, and 800,000 federal workers sent home. People weren't getting paid, veterans lost their benefits, and any important government services were simply unavailable. The public outcry was deafening.

When congressional leadership blamed Clinton, the White House went into campaign mode and hit the airwaves to tell their side of the story. Both sides tried procedural counter maneuvers to win the showdown. Clinton signed several appropriations orders that kept parts of the government running. Congress sent more budget-related bills to the White House, but Clinton vetoed them. Finally, after the Christmas holidays, the political pressure became so great that Republicans were forced to reopen the government on the president's terms. Clinton signed the new CR and debt ceiling bill, and then sent Congress his seven-year plan for a balanced budget.

In one of the conciliatory budget meetings, Speaker of the House Newt Gingrich told the president that he really believed the threat of a government shutdown would work. "We made a mistake," Gingrich admitted. "We thought you would cave."

Bill Clinton didn't cave.

"Yes, it is painful. Yes, it is difficult. But it is progress. It is change. It will make a difference. And it is focused on the long run interests of the people of this country. We have come this far. This is not time to turn back. We have been bold. This is no time to be timid. We have faced this crisis squarely. This is no time to blink."

—Clinton, urging wavering Democrats in Congress to stand with the budget deficit reduction bill.
July 20, 1993

"I have no intention of resigning. It never crossed my mind."

—Clinton, when asked if he would resign after impeachment
December 13, 1998

*Over the last two years of his presidency, Bill Clinton continued to be hounded by the conservative right, albeit less obsessively. In **February 1999**, the supermarket tabloid* Globe, *reran the old story that Clinton had engaged in orgies with three black hookers at his mother's house when he was governor of Arkansas. In **April 1999**, Republicans engineered a 213–213 vote, which effectively blocked a nonbinding resolution to approve the president's decision to implement air strikes in the Balkans. House Whip Tom DeLay called the vote "Act Two of Impeachment." DeLay and his colleagues had their eyes on a future prize, however. As he commented later, "When the sun rises following the election of 2000, I think we [Republicans] will control both ends of Pennsylvania Avenue."*

As Bill Clinton became more and more of a lame duck president, conservatives began shifting their targeted attacks toward Hillary Clinton. A book by Barbara Olson entitled, Hell To Pay: The Unfolding Story of Hillary Rodham Clinton, *was published in **November 1999**. And in **January 2000**,* The Hillary Trap: Looking for Power in All the Wrong Places, *by Laura Ingraham was released to the public.*

⁓

*In the **November 2000** national elections, George W. Bush defeated Vice President Al Gore in the race for President of the United States, and Hillary Clinton was elected to the United States Senate representing New York (the seat formerly held by Alfonse D'Amato).*

⁓

During Bill Clinton's final months as President of the United States, Kenneth Starr's successor, Robert Ray, issued the following statement on the Whitewater investigation: "This office has determined that the evidence was insufficient . . . that either President or Mrs. Clinton knowingly participated in any criminal conduct . . . or knew of such conduct." This was the exact same conclusion announced by Robert B. Fiske more than six years earlier, on June 30, 1994.

"All I can do is show up for work every day and do the very best I can. That's what I did today, and that's what I intend to do tomorrow."

—Bill Clinton
News conference
April 30, 1998

EPILOGUE

D
uring the 1995–1996 showdown over the budget, Republican congressional leaders planned to implement large tax cuts and increase the federal budget deficit. This strategy was, in part, a continuation of "trickle-down" economics, most often associated with the policies of Ronald Reagan. But Bill Clinton had a different idea. While running for president in 1992, he asserted that "'trickle down' has failed," and that "the Republicans in Washington have compiled the worst economic record in fifty years: the slowest economic growth, slowest job growth, and slowest income growth since the Great Depression." The way to reverse course and create a good economy, said Clinton, was not to introduce large tax cuts but, rather, to "strive to close the budget deficit" as part of a larger national economic strategy.

By implementing that policy, and then sticking to his guns during the budget showdown, Bill Clinton engineered the longest sustained economic boom in United States history. During the eight years of his presidency, the national gross domestic product rose from $6.6 trillion to over $10 trillion—an expansion of nearly 50 percent. Economic growth averaged 4 percent per year, and grew for a record 116 consecutive months. The unemployment rate dropped to 4 percent (the lowest in thirty years), 22.5 million new jobs were created, and the core inflation rate went from 4.7 percent to 2.5 percent. Perhaps more remarkable is the fact that, during Clinton's tenure, a record federal deficit was eliminated, the yearly federal budget was balanced, and a record surplus of $237 billion (year 2000) was created. As Clinton left office, the Office of Management and Budget projected a surplus of $5 trillion over the coming ten years— enough to fund Social Security and Medicare for decades and pay off the entire federal debt (by 2009). The vibrant economy resulted in further impressive statistics, including the smallest Welfare roles in twenty-seven years, the lowest poverty rate in twenty years, and the highest home ownership in United States history. In addition, crime rates dropped to record lows, family incomes rose, and the size of the federal government became the smallest since the administration of John F. Kennedy.

A big part of Clinton's success was his commitment to expanding America's role in the international economy. "Because every $1 billion of increased American exports will create 20,000 to 30,000 new jobs," stated Clinton in 1992, "we will move aggressively to open foreign markets to quality American goods and services." And that's exactly what he did. As president, Bill Clinton traveled farther and wider than any of his predecessors. He also welcomed hundreds of world leaders to the White House in a never-ending effort to build relationships and create new alliances. Through his support of NAFTA, GATT, ASEAN, CAFTA, and other world trade agreements, Clinton paved the way for America's leadership role in a vibrant global economy. Moreover, Clinton not only increased trade investment between the United States and the nations of Africa (through the Africa Growth and Opportunity Act of 2000), he also established permanent normal trade relations with China, the most populous nation in the world. In addition to all his economic successes, Clinton secured passage of a remarkable amount of new legislation, made enormous strides in preserving the environment, revamped entrenched entitlement systems, kept global terrorism in check, and presided over eight years of sustained peace and prosperity.

Bill Clinton led America to all these tremendous achievements during extraordinarily changing times, with Congress controlled by the opposition party for six of his eight years as president, and amid constant, never-ending attacks on his personal character. When asked at a 1998 news conference about the divergence between his high job approval ratings and the public's perception of him personally, Clinton commented about the ongoing negative campaign against him:

> It's obvious to the American people that this has been a hard, well-financed, vigorous effort over a long period of time by people who could not contest the ideas that I brought to the table, couldn't even contest the values behind the ideas that I brought to the table, and certainly can't quarrel with the consequences and the results of my service. And therefore, personal attack seems legitimate.

Clinton went on to call the personal attacks "distracting," but also said, "I do not think the right thing for me to do is to respond in kind. . . . I have never done that in my public life. I don't believe in it, and I'm not going to participate in it." To do so, he said, "would be more of a reflection on my character than on their [his antagonists'] reputation." Rather, Clinton said he chose to "worry about the American people" and focus on his job. "All I can do is show up for work every day and do the very best I can," he said. "That's what I did today, and that's what I intend to do tomorrow."

With time, it has become apparent that Bill Clinton worked hard and, as he said, did not respond in kind to all the personal attacks leveled against him. But one question still remains largely unanswered: How did Clinton achieve so much in the face of such formidable adversity?

Some people suggest the answer lies in Clinton's "rock star" status, or the fact that he became a "larger than life" president. They attribute his success to being a result of "The Clinton Charisma"—referring to some sort of magical, personal magnetism that simply cannot be resisted. In fact, the word "charisma" is derived from the Greek word *charis,* which means "grace." Remember Ernest Hemingway's definition of courage—"grace under pressure."

In the modern arena, when somebody mentions a leader's charisma, they are usually alluding to a number of personal qualities and abilities that enable an individual to influence, persuade, and motivate others. These might include superb oratorical skills, a dynamic positive energy, and unusual calmness, confidence, and assertiveness in any given situation. Mostly, though, charisma refers to a leader's undeniable ability to bring out the best in people by connecting with them—physically, intellectually, and emotionally.

Leadership, itself, is also about bringing out the best in people. It's about bringing people together, organizing them, and then achieving results. In that context, then, charisma is really about being an exceptional leader. And Bill Clinton's charisma, in particular, referred to his exceptional people skills. Many people who met him commented that Clinton exuded remarkable personal presence in a crowd. When he shook a person's hand, he leaned slightly forward, looked that person in the eye, and made that individual feel like he or she was the only person in the room, and that they were the complete focus of his attention. And this wasn't an act. Clinton enjoyed people, cared about them, loved interacting with them. It's one reason he entered politics in the first place. And he was astute enough to understand that his natural people skills helped his overall leadership effectiveness. In fact, one of Clinton's key leadership principles was to inspire more people to take action. That way, he could achieve more results. "If you want to bring out the best in a country," he said, "you have to try to bring out the best in people. You have to try to elevate them, to make them believe that things are possible."

Overall, there are many lessons modern leaders can learn from Bill Clinton's leadership style. Upon close inspection, Clinton provided vision, was decisive, set goals, built relationships and alliances, displayed enormous stamina and courage, employed effective communications, was innovative, and learned while on the job.

Moreover, Clinton combined these traditionally recognized principles of leadership with the standards of a modern, rapidly changing society. He valued diversity, implemented teamwork, utilized new technology, and interacted in a more casual and informal manner consistent with the times. He strategically employed compromise and fashioned consensus, upon which the basic precepts of leadership (and the Constitution) are based. Clinton also moved persuasion, inspiration, and involvement to the forefront—so lost in the realm of "command and control" hierarchies. And he employed constant communications and an ongoing campaign mode, both of which are critical in connecting with a large and diverse populace.

With his morning runs and frequent forays out of the White House, Clinton strategically sought out daily contact with the people he represented, which helped him understand their wants and needs, their hopes and dreams, and the values of the people he represented. And in the end, that may be the most important thing a leader can do.

"I believe that it's very important for the President to be able to stand up for the values of the American people," said Bill Clinton. "I think this administration has a good record, and I believe I have a good record of standing up for the things that will help us to raise our children stronger and keep our families stronger and make our country stronger.

"At least I have done my best."

BIBLIOGRAPHY

Aldrich, Gary. *Unlimited Access: An FBI Agent Inside the Clinton White House.* 1996. Regnery Publishing, Washington, D.C.

Allen, Charles F. and Jonathan Portis. *The Comeback Kid: The Life and Career of Bill Clinton.* 1992. Birch Lane Press, Secaucus, N. J.

Bennett, William. *The Death of Outrage: Bill Clinton and the Assault on American Ideals.* 1998. The Free Press, New York.

Bentley, P. F. *Clinton: Portrait of Victory.* 1993. Warner Books, New York.

Blumenthal, Sidney. *The Clinton Wars.* 2003. Plume, Penguin Group, New York.

Brock, David. *Blinded By the Right: The Conscience of an Ex-Conservative.* 2002. Three Rivers Press, New York.

Clinton, Bill. *My Life.* 2004. Alfred A. Knopf, New York.

Clinton, Bill. *Between Hope and History: Meeting America's Challenges for the 21st Century.* 1996. Times Books, Random House, New York.

Clinton, Bill and Al Gore. *Putting People First.* 1992. Times Books, New York.

Conason, Joe and Gene Lyons. *The Hunting of the President: The Ten-Year Campaign to Destroy Bill and Hillary Clinton.* 2000. Thomas Dunne Books, St. Martin's Griffin, New York.

Coulter, Ann. *High Crimes and Misdemeanors: The Case Against Bill Clinton.* 1998. Regnery Publishing, Washington, D.C.

Dumas, Earnest, editor. *The Clintons of Arkansas.* 1993. The University of Arkansas Press, Fayetteville.

Flowers, Gennifer. *Passion and Betrayal.* 1995. Random House, New York.

Gallen, David. *Bill Clinton as They Know Him: An Oral Biography.* 1994. Gallen Publishing Group, New York.

Harris, John F. *The Survivor: Bill Clinton in the White House.* 2005. Random House, New York.

Ingraham, Laura. *The Hillary Trap: Looking for Power in All the Wrong Places.* 2000. Hyperion, New York.

Jones, Charles O. *Clinton & Congress: 1993–1996, Risk, Restoration, and Reelection.* 1999. University of Oklahoma Press, Norman.

Kelley, Virginia with James Morgan. *Leading With My Heart.* 1994. Simon & Schuster, New York.

Levin, Robert E. *Bill Clinton: The Inside Story.* 1992. SPI Books, New York.

Levy, Peter B. *Encyclopedia of the Clinton Presidency.* 2002. Greenwood Press, Westport, CT.

Mariniss, David. *First in his Class: A Biography of Bill Clinton.* 1995. Simon & Schuster, New York.

Moore, Jim with Rick Ihde. *Clinton: Young Man in a Hurry.* 1992. The Summit Group, Fort Worth, TX.

Oakley, Meredith L. *On the Make: The Rise of Bill Clinton.* 1994. Regnery Publishing, Washington, D.C.

Olson, Barbara. *Hell To Pay: The Unfolding Story of Hillary Rodham Clinton.* 1999. Regnery Publishing, Washington, D.C.

Smith, Stephen A., editor. *Bill Clinton on Stump, State, and Stage: the Rhetorical Road to the White House.* 1994. University of Arkansas Press, Fayetteville, AR.

Stewart, James B., *Blood Sport: The President and His Adversaries.* 1996. Simon & Schuster, New York.

Tannen, Deborah. *You Just Don't Understand: Women and Men in Conversation.* 1990. Ballantine Books, New York.

Toobin, Jeffrey. *A Vast Conspiracy: The Real Story of the Sex Scandal that Nearly Brought Down a President.* 1999. Touchstone, Simon & Schuster, New York.

Tyrrell, R. Emmett, *Boy Clinton: A Political Biography.* 1996. Regnery Publishing, Washington, D.C.

Tyrrell, R. Emmett and Anonymous, *The Impeachment of William Jefferson Clinton.* 1997. Regnery Publishing, Washington, D.C.

Weekly Compilation of Presidential Documents. (WCPD) 1993–2001. Government Printing Office, Washington, D.C.

Woodward, Bob. *The Agenda.* 1994. Simon & Schuster. New York.

NOTES

INTRODUCTION

"This is *our* time," WCPD, 1–20–93; "We simply cannot say," WCPD, 8–10–93; "It is becoming clear," *The New York Times*, 7–31–94; *Star*, 1–28–92; *Star*, 2–11–92; Nichols reportedly received, from Conason and Lyons, p. 22; *Star* reportedly paid Flowers, from Conason and Lyons, p. 22; *The Wall Street Journal*, 2–8–92; *The Globe*, 2–18–92

I
DIVERSITY

"I try to bring people together," WCPD, 1–26–95; "I will give you an administration," 5–11–92; "Unless we can find," WCPD, 8–30–93; Demographic statistics from, *The Washington Post, National Weekly Edition*, 1–21–94/2–6–94; "Every time I have consulted," WCPD, 5–14–93; "best and most creative advice," WCPD, 1–14–93; "leaders from humble backgrounds," WCPD, 1–24–94; "believed in the cause of equal opportunity," from Dumas, p. xvi; fifteen percent African-Americans, from Dumas, p. xvi; "the most unprejudiced person," from Dumas, p. 50; "wanted to be involved with people," from Dumas, p. 12; "Panetta had a bad day," WCPD, 4–25–94; Reich quote from *The Washington Post*, 5–9–93; "a strength and not a weakness," WCPD, 5–14–93; "Diversity is not an end," WCPD, 5–16–94; "faces in this crowd," WCPD, 11–21–93; *The New York Times*, 3–8–92; "no facts can be identified," from Clinton, *My Life*, p. 671; Dole quote, "illegitimate," from Brock, p. 147; "a repudiation of our forefathers," from Brock, p. 147; "deserves the hatred of God," from Brock, p. 147; Gingrich quote, "left wing Democrats," from Brock, pp. 66–67; funded by wealthy donors, from Brock, pp. 86–87.

2
CONSENSUS THROUGH TEAMWORK

"Back east where I work," WCPD, 8–16–93; "teamwork and free flow of ideas," WCPD, 1–14–93; Gore quote, "another Great Lake," from *The New York Times*, 7–18–93; "ensure that they work together as a team," WCPD, 7–8–93; *Newsweek*, 1–17–94; Safire's question and response from *The New York Times*, 9–16–93; *Time*, 1–24–94; Clinton's reasons for economic task force, WCPD, 12–14–92; "We reached out to hundreds of people," WCPD, 71–93; Pressler's comment from *The New York Times*, 10–16–94; Cheney's comment on CNN, 10–14–93; *The New York Times*, 9–24–93; Clinton quote on health care task force, WCPD, 9–22–93; "We're going to have an honest and open debate," WCPD, 8–2–93; "more than sixty percent supported it," from *The Wall Street Journal/NBC News* poll, 3/10/94; Tannen, p. 167; Clinton APEC quote, WCPD, 11–19–93; "Nobody knows what kind of future," WCPD, 8–13–94; "Teamwork is the order of the day," WCPD, 7–8–93; *The Wall Street Journal,* 6–17–93; *NBC Nightly News,* 11–11–93; "Nussbaum spirited away," *The Washington Times,* from Conason and Lyons, p. 97.

3
RELATIONSHIPS AND ALLIANCES

"the challenge of all advanced nations," WCPD, 7–5–94; "worked year-in and year-out," WCPD, 6–29–93; Clinton visiting Republicans from *The New York Times,* 3–5–93; Lieberman and Paster quotes from *The New York Times,* 3–6–93; *The New York Times,* 3–5–93; Clinton quote, "Come back with your colleagues," 1–28–94; *Business Week,* 3–14–94; *The Wall Street Journal,* 11–19–93; Michael Walsh quote, WCPD, 7–28–93; Stephanopoulos quote about Greenspan, from *USA Today,* 6–7–94; *The New York Times,* 4–8–94; Jeffords comment, *The New York Times,* p. 3–5–93; *The Washington Post, National Weekly Edition,* 4–12–93/4–18–93; Clinton quote on Summit of the Americas, WCPD, 3–11–94; Clinton's APEC remarks, 11–20–93; Press Conference with Miyazawa, 7–6–93; Clinton quote on "Partnership for Peace," 1–13–94; Clinton to G–7 ministers, 3–15–94; Rostenkowski quote from *The New York Times,* 5–14–93; APEC Report, 11–15–94; "No public enterprise can flourish," WCPD, 9–13–93; "future for you to write," WCPD, 1–13–94; "got better as it went along," WCPD; 11–20–93; "reportedly subsidized by Scaife," from Brock, pp. 210–211; *American Spectator,* 12–18–92; Clinton calls charges "outrageous," from Brock, p. 171

4
COMPASSION AND CARING

"I want the services," WCPD, 7–8–93; "develop a genuine interest," WCPD, 1–14–94; "we need help," from *Newsweek,* 7–26–93; Cox remarks and "eye-dabbing scene," from *The New York Times,* 8–4–94; "a big red cross on my car," WCPD, 1–17–94; Rafsky question and "I feel your pain," 4–2–92; from actupny.org; *Newsweek,* 1–24–94; Clinton's remark to Andrea Mitchell from *The Washington Post, National Weekly Edition,* 1–24–94/1–30–94; *Newsweek,* 5–3–93; Clinton quote, "Remember that we're all people," 7–21–93; Clinton quote, "The knives didn't stick," from *The New York Times,* 7–24–93; *Time,* 5–2–94; Clinton speech in Memphis, WCPD, 11–13–93; Clinton remarks at sight of LA earthquake, WCPD, 1–19–94; "not leave out in the cold," WCPD, 3–12–93; Clinton's NAFTA remarks, WCPD, 11–9–93; Clinton's remarks in Charleston, WV, WCPD, 8–9–93; Clinton quoting James Agee, 4–20–94; "look into the eyes of our children," WCPD, 12–25–93; Aleksandr Fyodorov, WCPD, 1–14–94; "try to develop," WCPD, 1–14–94; Tannen, pp. 68, 291; Clinton remark, "it sort of came naturally," from *Time* 9–27–93; "we're going to deliver," WCPD, 12–6–94; "compassion is part of my philosophy," WCPD, 4–8–94; "a speedy and credible resolution," WCPD, 1–2–94; "suing over a stupid lie," from Blumenthal, p. 87

5
RUNNING WITH THE PEOPLE

"You have to communicate," from *Time,* 11–16–92; "worked out accommodations," WCPD, 7–20–93; "I walked the crowds today, WCPD, 1–18–94; "shake awake,"

Newsweek, 7–12–93; *The New York Times,* 7–26–93; "met a lot of interesting people on those runs," Clinton, *My Life,* p. 516; Clinton remark on *Meet the Press,* 11–7–93; "I get very homesick," WCPD, 7–23–94; *The New York Times,* 7–3–94; Wright remarks, from Dumas, p. 29; "my duty to try," from Dumas, p. 115; Roberts remarks, from Dumas, p. 125; Clinton remarks at Camp Casey, WCPD, 7–11–93; Clinton on WHO Radio in Des Moines, WCPD, 7–14–93; "really looks like America," WCPD, 10–20–94; "place buzzing like a beehive," from *The New York Times,* 9–22–93; "go out and find facts yourself," from *Time,* 11–16–92; "dozens of children rushed out to greet me," WCPD, 4–16–94; "I traveled across our country," WCPD, 4–9–94; "don't want to be in the way," WCPD, 1–17–94; Rep. McKinney's remarks, from *The New York Times,* 7–26–93; Portenski's comments, from *Baltimore Sun,* 5–5–93; "been in the hills," WCPD, 12–21–94; *The Washington Times,* 2–9–94; *The New York Times,* 3–4–94; Leach speech, *Congressional Record,* March 24, 1994; *Time,* "Deep Water," 4–4–94; *700 Club,* 4–18–94

6
LISTENING AND PUBLIC SPEAKING

Newman and Woodward dinner, from *The Washington Post,* 3–17–93; Nicklaus's remarks, from *Rocky Mountain News,* 8–18–93; Clinton, "They're killing me out there," from Dumas, p. 90; Bassett remarks from Dumas, p. 71; Clinton, "The Great Listener," *Time,* June 7, 1993; *The New York Times,* 12–10–93; Comments about Clinton's speech at the 1988 Democratic national Convention, from Allen and Portis, p. 127–129; *The Tonight Show Starring Johnny Carson,* 7–28–88; Clinton's remarks to Louisiana media, 8–4–93; *Time,* 12–26–94; Safire's comment, "best speech of his life," from *The New York Times,* 9–16–93; *Newsweek,* 1–17–94; Clinton's Memphis speech, WCPD, 11–13–93; "Government is broken," WCPD, 3–3–93; "health care system is badly broken," WCPD, 11–22–93; Cisneros remark from *The New York Times,* 7–8–93; Clinton remarks, "linking initiatives," 9–5–93; Clinton remark, "greatest figures of American judiciary," 6–14–93; 1992 Democratic convention, WCPD, 7–17–92; "to listen, to learn," WCPD, 12–3–93; *The Washington Post,* 5–4–94; Evans-Pritchard remarks, from Conason and Lyons, p. 124; Report of the Independent Counsel, 6–30–94; Washingtonpost.com; Safire comment, from Conason and Lyons, p. 132

7
CONVERSATION AND STORYTELLING

"I was beginning to tell a story," WCPD, 5–9–94; "bring this level of intensity," WCPD, 10–8–93; congressmen avoiding Clinton, from *The New York Times,* 5–29–93; Roberts remarks, from Dumas, p. 128; Bumpers' remarks, from *The New York Times,* 3–5–93; Whillock's remarks, from Dumas, p. 81; Congressmen's comment, "not talked to president," *Fort Worth Star-Telegram,* 5–28–93; Rep. Mann's remarks, "artificial socket for my arm," *The New York Times,* 11–9–93; "make three calls," WCPD, 11–2–93; "sumo wrestling," from *The New York Times,* 1–11–94; "nervous as a cat in a tree," WCPD, 10–23–93; "jot and tiddle," WCPD, 10–4–93; "tree full of owls," WCPD, 5–10–94; Clinton to Safire, "don't speak in a language," from *The New York Times,* 10–10–93; Coleman's remark, "gift of a true storyteller," from Dumas, p. 54; Anderson's remarks, from Dumas, p. 134; "I once had a hearing," WCPD, 1–25–94; "elderly couple who broke down and cried," WCPD, 1–22–93; "not just bad policy," WCPD, 1–22–93; "was in tears and shaking," WCPD, 10–5–93; Clinton's State of the Union Address, WCPD, 1–25–94;

Clinton's remarks about James Darby, WCPD, 7–16–94; Clinton's remarks at Future Diner, WCPD, 9–26–93; Story's ending to Democrats, WCPD, 10–8–93; at Yale, WCPD, 10–9–93; to Congress, WCPD, 1–25–94; Clinton's remarks, "consistently explain," *Newsweek,* 12–13–93; "Vernon, you're beautiful," from *Wall Street Journal,* 12–22–93; *The Washington Times, 10–19–94;* Brown paid by Arkansas Project, from Conason and Lyons, p. 165; *Passion and Betrayal* by Gennifer Flowers, 5–96; *American Spectator,* 7–9

8
VISION AND HOPE

"Our obligation and our power," WCPD, 9–9–94; "chief mechanic," *Time,* 9–27–93; "I know the present is difficult," WCPD, 1–14–94; Clinton remarks to Boys nation, 7–29–94; "a very clear idea," *USA Today,* WCPD, 8–6–93; "thinking about tomorrow," WCPD, 8–6–94; "takes a carpenter to build one," WCPD, 9–24–94; Shalala's comments, from *Wall Street Journal,* 9–22–93; "security tied to economics," WCPD, 11–19–93; Clinton speech at UN, WCPD, 9–27–93; "I have a vision," WCPD, 6–21–94; "I have sought to ensure," WCPD, 1–10–94; Member of Japanese delegation, "no one expected," from *The New York Times,* 11–21–93; *The New York Times,* 11–16–94; "go into the 21st century," WCPD, 12–8–94; "Every day I try," WCPD, 5–14–93; "give our children a future," WCPD, 1–25–94; "work hard and play by the rules," WCPD, 12–3–93; "keep people thinking positively," WCPD, 7–17–93; "restored a sense of hope and optimism," WCPD, 1–14–94; "only lose tomorrow," WCPD, 10–12–94; "I still believe in a place called Hope," Democratic National Convention, 7–16–92; *The Washington Times,* 9–6–95; *The New York Times,* 12–19–95

9
CHANGE AND RISK-TAKING

"It is not enough," WCPD, 6–7–93; "When you live in a time of change," WCPD, 9–15–93; Have quote, "modern age over," World Economic Forum, Davos, Switzerland, 2–1–94; "Maybe it's partly a function of the times," WCPD, 8–3–94; *The Wall Street Journal,* 8–3–93; Presidential debate, PBS.org, 10–11–92; "country needs vital center," WCPD, 8–16–93; *Time,* 6–6–94; Clinton remark, "people can't imagine," from Bentley, p. 47; *The New York Times,* 9–11–93; *USA Today,* 9–22–94; *Newsweek,* 11–22–93; Clinton remarks on Truman, WCPD, 6–21–94; "saddest people he knew," from Dumas, p. 136; "I like fighting these fights," from WCPD, 5–31–94; "people adversely affected by change," WCPD, 6–22–94; Clinton at University of North Carolina, WCPD, 10–12–93; Clinton at the UN, WCPD, 9–27–93; Inaugural address, WCPD, 1–20–93; Safire, *The New York Times,* 1–8–96; Liddy's comments, from Brock, p. 272; *The Washington Post,* 3–28–96; *The New York Post,* 7–15–96; "unindicted co-conspirator" by BBC, from Conason and Lyons, p. 229; Safire, *The New York Times,* 6–6–96

10
DRIVING TO ACHIEVE

"We can do better," WCPD, 4–25–93; "I know they are tired," WCPD, 8–14–93; *The New York Times,* 7–19–93; Bentsen quote, "an incredible grind," from *The Wall Street Journal,* 8–20–93; Blair quote, "Clinton's down time less" from *USA Today,* 7–14–93; "I normally work pretty late," WCPD, 7–20–93; "don't rest," WCPD, 12–8–93; "afraid I'd fall over in public," from *USA Today*, 1–11–94; Staff members citing "a new standard of intensity," from *The New York Times*, 11–24–93; "formidable energy," *Time*, 2–7–94; "elected to end gridlock," WCPD, 7–20–93; Clinton remark on Franklin Roosevelt, WCPD, 7–27–93; *Time*, 11–16–93; "criticized for doing more than one thing at once," WCPD, 5–10–93; "Our ability to recreate ourselves," *Time*, 2–7–94; "the President will," WCPD, 9–7–93; *Time*, 6–28–93; *Wall Street Journal*, 8–26–94; Clinton remark on Theodore Roosevelt, WCPD, 3–19–94; *Wall Street Journal*, 8–15–94; *Newsweek*, 1–17–94; Clinton on *Meet the Press*, 11–7–93; Clinton remark on Martin Luther King, Jr., WCPD, 1–17–94; Clinton at University of North Carolina, WCPD, 10–12–93; Polk story, from Dumas, p. 26; Clinton remark on Franklin Roosevelt, 5–19–94; Clinton remark, "They're never going to stop us," from Woodward, p. 334; "show up every day," WCPD, 11–7–93; "we cannot be tired today," 6–24–94; *Blood Sport: The President and His Adversaries*, 3–96; *Unlimited Access: An FBI Agent Inside the Clinton White House*, 7–96; *Boy Clinton: A Political Biography*, 9–96; *The Washington Post*, 2–13–97; Rehnquist remark, from Blumenthal, p. 192; Safire, *The New York Times*, 1–20–97

11
DECISIVENESS

"Focus like a laser beam," *ABC News*, 11–4–92; "sorry the polls are," WCPD, 9–14–94; Barbour quote from *Newsweek*, 12–26–94; *Newsweek*, 7–12–93; Schroeder remark, from *Time*, 8–23–93; "leave now or we will force you from power," WCPD, 9–15–94; *The New York Times*, 5–11–94; "everything we can to protect," WCPD, 10–4–93; Clinton remark, "think more about the alternatives," from *The New York Times*, 10–4–93; Letter from Republicans, from *USA Today*, 10–7–93; Clinton remarks on Somalia, WCPD, 10–7–93; Interview with Safire, *The New York Times*, 9–19–93; Tannen, p. 27, p. 21; Clinton's letter to Congress' leaders, WCPD, 10–18–93; Clinton "apparently believes protecting" from *The New York Times*, 5–8–93; "I like to get everybody together," WCPD, 5,6–94; "don't have to win them all," 7–25–93; Jones reportedly received $100,000, from Conason and Lyons, p. 321; settlement agreement reported from Toobin, P. 121; Coulter remark, from Conason and Lyons, p. 302; Trooper quote, from Conason and Lyons, p. 275; Amount spent on investigators spent, from Conason and Lyons, p. 266; *Drudge Report*, 7–28–97

12
KEEPING THE CAMPAIGN GOING

"One of the reasons," WCPD, 6–7–93; "Every single piece of evidence," WCPD, 7–20–93; Clinton's six-word message regarding health care, WCPD, 9–22–93; Clinton's health care speech, WCPD, 9–22–93; Letterman remark, "Good luck with this government thing," *Late Night with David Letterman*, 9–8–93; "I really believed," WCPD, 10–28–93; *Meet The Press*, 11–7–93; "like flies on a June bug," WCPD, 11–1–93; Clinton's radio addresses on NAFTA, WCPD, 9–18–93; 10–16–93; 11–6–93; 11–13–93; "ear hurt from talking on phone," from *The New York Times*, 11–8–93; "tonight's vote is a defining moment," WCPD, 11–17–94; *The New York Times*, "political equivalent of lighting victory cigar," 11–18–93; *The New York Times*, "a Herculean display," 11–18–93; Foley's remarks, from *USA Today*, 11–18–93; Dumas' remarks, from Dumas, p. xvi; Dole's remark, "acted as if campaign still in progress," from *Wall Street Journal*, 8–10–93; Powell's remark, "wave of the future," from *The New York Times*, 11–6–93; "we must speak to the millions," Democratic National Convention, cnn.com, 7–18–88; "there is still a continuing job to do,"

WCPD, 8–3–93; Dannemeyer newsletter comments, from Conason and Lyons, p. 308; Barr letter to Hyde, nationalcenter.org, 3–11–97; Dannemeyer telephone message, from Conason and Lyons, p. 308; *The Impeachment of William Jefferson Clinton*, 10–97; *The Wall Street Journal*, 10–10–97; Clinton deposition transcript, January 17, 1998, from TheWashingtonPost.com

13
CONTINUAL LEARNING

"A legacy my grandparents left to me," PBS, 7–7–92; "the test of leadership," WCPD, 5–25–94; "a system of lifetime learning," 7–29–94; *The New York Times*, 9–23–93; Clinton remark, "I have to learn," in interview with *The Washington Post*, 5–14–93; "going over to Bill's house to watch him read," Dumas, p. 38; roommate's remarks from Dumas, p. 57; "I came from a family," WCPD, 1–14–94; "even with a staff of bright people, from Dumas, p. 132; "didn't have much else to do," from *The New York Times*, 12–10–93; Clinton remark, "improve our ability to communicate," 5–29–93; *The New York Times*, 11–17–93; *Time*, 1–17–94; Remark from Russian college student, from *The New York Times*, 1–15–94; "God, I'm learning a lot," from *The New York Times*," 5–26–93; poll from *The New York Times*, 6–6–93; "That's what good leaders do," from *Time*, 11–16–92; Clinton remark about "Yanus," from *Asian Wall Street Journal*, 8–31–93; "If USA doesn't do a better job educating," WCPD, 2–22–94; "in order to visualize the future," WCPD, 5–18–94; "could absorb facts," from Dumas, p. 59; *The New York Times*, 5–30–93; Clinton remark about Sub S corporations, WCPD, 7–26–93; Clinton remark about California, WCPD, 7–27–93; "I was impressed," from *The New York Times*, 2–20–93; Remark by Koppel, WCPD, 9–22–93; Clinton's seven-point agenda, WCPD, 2–22–94; Clinton's remark about deducting college tuition, WCPD, 12–15–94; "I have made many mistakes," WCPD, 1–26–95; "got a lot to learn from each other," 7–5–94; *The Drudge Report*, 1–18–98; ABC's *This Week*, 1–18–98; Clinton's denial, WCPD, 1–26–98; NBC's *The Today Show*, 1–27–98; Novak column, 2–15–98, from Blumenthal, p. 407; Hubbel's comment, from Blumenthal, p. 443; Safire, *The New York Times*, 6–4–98; NBC's *The Today Show*, 7–16–98; *High Crimes and Misdemeanors: The Case Against Bill Clinton*, 8–98; *The Death of Outrage: Bill Clinton and the Assault on American Ideals*, 9–98

14
COMPROMISE

"I understand and appreciate," WCPD, 7–20–93; "reason we had to compromise," WCPD, 10–3–93; Clinton remarks to Wisconsin reporter, from *Newsweek*, WCPD, 8–9–93; "compromise not weakness if making progress," WCPD, 7–20–93; Roberts remarks from Dumas, p. 123, 124; Smith's remarks from Dumas, p. 14; Dumas remarks from *San Diego Union Tribune*, 7–26–93; Wright's remarks from *San Diego Union Tribune*, 7–26–93; Powell, "an honorable compromise," 7–19–93; *The New York Times*, 6–2–93; "never expected to get 100 percent," WCPD, 8–10–93; "God, I love this," from *Wall Street Journal*, 11–18–93; "If you send me legislation that does not," WCPD, 9–22–93; "no pride of authorship," WCPD, 10–27–93; "keep open, keep flexible," WCPD, 5–25–94; "When I put ideas out," WCPD, 6–15–94; "not right at 100%," WCPD, 7–19–94; "agreed to change plan," WCPD, 7–23–94; Foley's remarks from *San Diego Union Tribune*, 7–26–93; J.F.K.'s quote, "Compromise need not mean cowardice," from *Profiles in Courage*, p. 20; Watson's advice, WCPD, 12–4–93; "The process we begin today," WCPD, 4–2–93; "not the tooth fairy," WCPD, 9–21–93; Clinton's deposition, 8–17–98, TheWashingtonPost.com; Clinton's confession, WCPD, 8–17–98; Starr Report, 9–9–98; Statement of constitutional law professors, 11–6–98; from Blumenthal, pp. 501–502

15
INFORMALITY AND OPENNESS

"We agreed to make next year's," WCPD, 7–8–93; "a remarkably open presidency," WCPD, 1–20–94; "L. L. Bean diplomatic dress code," *The New York Times,* 11–21–93; "just what the President had in mind," from *The New York Times,* 11–21–93; "In this post–Cold War era," WCPD; 11–29–93; "We have agreed," APEC Conference statement, CNN.com, 11–29–93; "next year's session even more informal," from *USA Today,* 7–9–93; "shed all pretense of formality," *The New York Times,* 1–15–94; Trudeau story from *The New York Times,* 6–13–93; Paula Zahn, CBS, 5–25–93; *The Agenda,* 1994; Clinton on Freedom of Information Act, WCPD, 10–4–94; "If we're going to have a shoot-out," WCPD, 8–5–94; "If you seek advice, you will have leaks," WCPD, 5–16–94; "could have disguised differences," WCPD, 2–11–94; Ted Koppel interview, ABC's *Nightline,* 2–12–92; *60 Minutes* interview; 1–26–92; Clinton's denial, WCPD, 1–26–98; "will uphold the highest possible ethical standards," WCPD, 1–21–93; Clinton in support of Ron Brown, WCPD, 10–1–93; Clinton on Espy, WCPD, 10–3–94; "good ethics as basis of good government," WCPD, 10–6–93; *Time,* 9–27–93; "informed of plan," WCPD, 4–20–93; "telling truth for a change," WCPD, 6–19–93; Clinton at ML King Middle School, from *USA Today,* 5–18–94; "central tenet is trust," WCPD, 9–8–93; "I hated to do it," from Clinton, *My Life,* p. 830; "evidence room" information, from Blumenthal, p. 540; *The Drudge Report,* 1–1–99

16
COURAGE

"I'm doing things that are hard," WCPD, 5–14–93; "what planet am I on," WCPD, 3–28–94; *U.S. News & World Report,* 6–7–93; *Newsweek,* 6–7–93; *Time,* 6–7–93; Harrison remark from *The Washington Post, National Weekly Edition,* 5–30–94/6–5–94; Rep. Leach's remark from *The New York Times,* 12–17–94; Senators Dole and D'Amato remarks from *The New York Times,* 3–4–94; comment, "Can a President credibly advance," from *Time,* 3–21–94; Senator D'Amato's remarks from *The New York Times,* 10–16–93; Senator Bradley's remarks from *USA Today,* 2–23–94; Protesters at Vietnam Memorial from *The New York Times,* 2–5–94; "first president who has generated this kind of right wing hatred," *Time,* 4–11–94; Gen. Campbell's remarks from *The New York Times,* 6–9–93; Clinton remarks on economy, 12–19–93; Kemp's remarks from *The New York Times,* 12–20–93; Kilpatrick remark from *The New York Times,* 4–14–94; Noonan remark from *Forbes,* 4–25–94; Bunning remark, *The Washington Post,* 9–26–93; "when I read someplace," WCPD, 3–24–94; Britt Hume story, WCPD, 6–14–93; "if I worried about every poll," WCPD, 5–14–93; *Newsday,* 6–30–93; "not the work of God," WCPD, 6–24–94; "doing the best I can," WCPD, 7–4–93; "just get up in the morning," WCPD, 9–13–93; "You got a honeymoon," WCPD, 6–15–93; West Point Commencement, 5–29–93; Cadet remark from *The New York Times,* 5–30–93; Clinton to Gingrich quoted in *USA Today,* 1–6–95; "they saved the world," WCPD, 6–6–94; "darkness of every storm," WCPD, 9–9–94; "a huge difference," WCPD, 10–13–94; "keep your batteries charged," *Arkansas Democrat-Gazette,* 1–4–95; Clinton remark on bitterness, WCPD, 3–8–94; "any person who asks for forgiveness," WCPD, 2–12–99; "on one day," WCPD, 5–14–93; Remarks on CNN's *Larry King Live,* 1–20–94; "American people will be able to see through it," WCPD, WCPD, 1–20–94; *Time,* 1–17–94; "legacy my grandparents left to me," interview with Bill Moyers, PBS, 7–7–92; "The bad days are part of it," WCPD, 1–20–94; "join me in the arena," WCPD, 12–7–94; "Not even if I drop to five percent," from Clinton, *My Life,* p. 682; "We thought you would cave," from Clinton, *My Life,* p. 694; "Yes, it is painful," WCPD, 7–20–93; "no intention of resigning," WCPD, 12–13–98; "Act Two of Impeachment," from Blumenthal, p. 645; "When the sun rises," from *The New Yorker,* 5–24–99; *Hell to Pay: The Unfolding Story of Hillary Rodham Clinton,* 12–99; *The Hillary Trap: Looking for Power in All the Wrong Places,* 1–2000; Robert Ray's conclusions, CNN.com, 9–20–2000

EPILOGUE

"All I can do is show up," WCPD, 4–30–98; "trickle down has failed," Clinton, *Putting People First,* p. 5; "because every $1 billion," Clinton, *Putting People First,* p. 13; "It's obvious to the American people," WCPD, 4–30–98; "If you want to bring out the best in a country," 1–14–94; "at least I have done my best," WCPD, 4–30–98.

INDEX

economy, 3, 26–7, 35, 37–9, 42–3, 46, 52,
54, 64, 75, 93–4, 100–1, 103–6,
111–13,= 119, 125, 135, 173, 194, 212,
227–8; *See* budget; federal deficit;
globalization; job creation
education, 13, 70, 100, 114, 117, 173, 175,
181
the "elves," 85, 146, 163, 177
entitlement programs, 102, 111, 116,
228
environmental reform, 54, 100, 127, 188
Espy, Mike, 10, 53, 57, 150, 200
Europe, 43, 51, 68, 90, 103–4, 126, 154,
158, 171

Faircloth, Lauch, 59, 86, 107
Family and Medical Leave Act, 40, 53, 94,
127
Federal Bureau of Investigation (FBI), 15,
18–19, 33–4, 107, 119, 122, 132, 137,
139, 162, 164, 190, 204, 212
federal deficit, 3, 26–7, 38, 56, 111, 114,
128, 149–50, 183–4, 202, 212, 224–5,
227–8
Federal Emergency Management Agency
(FEMA), 53
Fiske, Robert B. 59, 85–6, 226
Flowers, Gennifer, 5–6, 98, 146
Foley, Thomas B., 112, 160, 186, 187
Ford, Gerald, 11–12, 39, 71, 155, 157
foreign policy, 24, 41–6, 52, 57, 102–3,
114–15, 138, 142, 155, 184, 210, 213,
214; *See* alliances; Bosnia; China;
Haiti; North Korea; Somalia
Foster, Vince, 33–4, 47, 51–2, 72–3, 85–6,
97–8, 107, 121, 163
France, 16, 42, 138
Freedom of Information Act, 196–7
Frenzel, William, 12, 154
fundamentalist Christians; *See* Christian
fundamentalists

G-7 Summit, 21, 35, 43–4, 125, 137, 176,
193–4, 212
Georgetown University, 13, 50, 138, 169
Gergen, David, 11–12, 170, 217
Germany, 42, 90, 172–3
Gingrich, Newt, 19, 31, 97, 204, 214, 220,
224

Ginsberg, Ruth Bader, 11, 83, 136, 212–13,
215–16, 219
Global Agreement on Tariffs and Trade
(GATT), 1, 41, 46, 103, 125, 228
globalization, 1, 4, 15, 31, 42–3, 55, 103–5,
112–13, 119, 174
Gore, Al, 2, 14, 21, 22, 23, 26, 27, 28, 39,
69, 89, 93, 100, 119, 151, 153, 155–8,
162, 170, 217, 226
Great Britain, 16, 42, 138
Great Depression, 114, 126–7, 157, 199,
227
Greenspan, Alan, 38–9
Guinier, Lani, 198, 212, 215–16
Gulf War, 2, 54
gun control, 117, 127

Haiti, 12, 24, 25, 45, 52, 57, 79, 115, 135,
138–9, 143–4, 172, 184, 198, 201,
209–10, 214
Hale, David, 33–4, 97, 107–8, 122
heath care reform, 14, 25, 27–9, 35–7,
39–40, 49–50, 52, 54, 55–7, 78, 82, 89,
92–3, 97, 100–2, 113, 116, 117, 119,
127, 128, 129, 152–3, 173, 184, 185–7,
189, 201, 210, 212–13
The Heritage Foundation, 19
homelessness, 24, 54
Hosokawa, Morihiro, 43, 194, 198
Hume, Brit, 215–16, 219
Hurricane Andrew, 53, 67
Hussein, Saddam, 172, 208

impeachment, 162–4, 190–1, 204–5, 218,
221, 225, 226
Iraq, 25, 45, 57, 137, 144, 172, 201, 208,
212, 214, 218
Isikoff, Michael, 85, 146–7
Israel-PLO Peace Accord, 42, 58, 81, 201,
212

Jackson, Cliff, 5–6, 34, 47–8, 59, 85
Japan, 21, 42–3, 66, 104–5, 115, 125, 137,
154, 158, 159, 194, 210, 212
Jefferson, Thomas, 127–8, 160
job creation, 3, 24, 38, 42–3, 54, 93, 105,
182, 227
jogging (with others), 37, 63–5, 69, 71, 89,
94, 158, 230